A JOURNEY THROUGH EPHESUS

David Gwartney

CONTENTS

INTRODUCTION

Several years ago, as I was studying for an upcoming message series on the New Testament book of Ephesians, I ran across a description of the Temple of Artemis. I was intrigued with the ancient structure and soon came to realize that the Temple of Artemis was one of the *Seven Wonders of the Ancient World*. It was the first time that I had associated one of the wonders of the world with the city of Ephesus - the very city in which Paul spent a great deal of time during his missionary journeys. Growing up in church, I had never heard that Ephesus was home to this ancient wonder. It was never explained that Paul would have spent his time in Ephesus working in the shadow of this temple, one of the largest in the Roman Empire. A landmark of this importance would have undoubtedly influenced Paul's ministry in Ephesus, yet I rarely heard it referenced. What other contextual tidbits had I missed and how might those details influence the way I read scripture?

That insight, along with the opportunity to travel to places such as Israel, Egypt, Greece, and Turkey, sparked my passion for digging into the context of the Bible in order to bring about greater understanding, or perhaps an entirely different way of reading the Bible. Paul's letters offer a unique opportunity to dig into the context of scripture. Paul was writing to churches in specific cities and regions that were part of the Roman Empire in the first century. Places like Corinth, Ephesus, Philippi, and Thessalonica were cities where Paul had preached and established church communities. He walked the city streets, met the local residents, and got a taste of the unique culture of each place. He would have done business with local merchants, eaten the favorite dishes of the region, and listened to the stories that shaped each community. These simple realities can sometimes get lost when names like *Corinthians* or *Philippians* represent nothing more than peculiar names for books in the Bible.

In this book, it is my intention to delve into the contextual background behind Paul's letter to the Ephesians. Yet it is also my hope to keep the story of Paul and Ephesus in the foreground – not to wander so far into the contextual thicket that the story can no longer be followed. I have referred to this approach as a *narrative commentary* – the balancing act between the story and the context behind a passage of scripture.

It has been my experience that most biblical commentaries take one of two approaches. The first approach skims the surface of the story, quickly moving to the question, "what does this mean for me?" Little or no details are provided about the actual context. As a result, the application of a passage of scripture may have little correspondence with what was actually intended. With this approach, the Bible is little more than a collection of maxims, platitudes, and self-help advice, and the reader ultimately determines the interpretation.

The second approach deep-dives below the surface, exploring outlines, sentence structures, and examining the original language. While this level of analysis can be helpful and even necessary, if the exploration does not resurface and connect back to the narrative, then the primary storyline can be disjointed or completely lost. Often, these types of commentaries are inaccessible to everyone but the scholar or academic.

To put it another way, sometimes people of faith are wary of straying off the pages of Holy Scripture in order to fill in the gaps, just as academics can be equally wary of wandering onto those same pages for fear of introducing religious biases into their study.

From the outset of this endeavor, let me make three assumptions that may defuse some inevitable objections. I realize that not everyone will agree with this approach or some of my conclusions, but by clarifying these up front, perhaps some potentially nagging questions can be alleviated from the outset.

My first assumption is this: Paul actually wrote Ephesians and intended – at least to some degree – that the letter would be sent to Ephesus. While this may not seem like a bold assumption to some, the authorship and the recipients of Ephesians have both been disputed. On the authorship of this letter, there have been some recent calls for Ephesians to be firmly included in the Pauline corpus, so authorship is becoming less of an issue. However, Paul's intended audience is more problematic, due to the fact that the phrase "in Ephesus" in the opening verses is actually a later addition to the text. On the surface, nothing else in the letter seems to confirm the church in Ephesus as the intended recipients. While saving the in-depth discussion for later, my contention is that at the very least, Ephesus was one of the destinations for this letter from Paul. Moreover, the city of Ephesus represented the whole of the Roman province of Asia. So Paul would have intuitively directed many of his comments to an Ephesian audience, even if the letter circulated to other cities.

The second assumption is in some ways less contentious, yet is often minimized or neglected in studies of the New Testament. Much of the Greco-Roman, or pagan, culture was transmitted through mythological stories. Most of the Roman Empire held some level of belief in the myths and the pantheon of Roman gods and their Greek counterparts. Mythology permeated the structures and public spaces of Greco-Roman cities, residents had house shrines to local deities, and the myths comprised much of the narrative of Greco-Roman life. Consequently, there are many references that may seem innocuous to modern ears that would have carried strong allusions to the ancients. While I will often elaborate on many of these references, it is not my assertion that Paul was alluding to the myths in each and every instance. I only wish to suggest that much of what Paul wrote may have contained an implicit critique of pagan mythology and culture. And as we will examine next, Gentile converts would have understood much of what Paul wrote in this way.

The third assumption relates to the second in that Paul was well aware of the pervasiveness of myth in Greco-Roman culture, and as a Roman citizen growing up in a Greek city, he would have been familiar with these myths in a way that a Jew in Israel may not have been. In correspondence such as the epistles of Paul, there are two layers (at least!) of meaning happening concurrently. The obvious layer of meaning is what Paul intended to say. Thus, the most immediate interpretation of the words of Ephesians is based on what we know of Paul, what we would expect Paul to say, and what he said elsewhere in his other correspondence.

The secondary, and less obvious, layer of meaning is how the recipients would have understood the words of Paul. We can all recollect an incident where a person said one thing, but the hearer interpreted something completely different. The same words were used, but they took on a different meaning based on the experience and background of each person. With this in mind, I am going to assume that Paul was in a unique position to not only explain the gospel in light of his Jewish upbringing, but to also explain it in such a way that Gentiles would understand the gospel in light of their pagan culture. Paul was smart enough and a skilled enough communicator to navigate conveying a Jewish gospel to a pagan culture. Much more could be said on this assumption but simply put, Paul not only wrote what he meant to write, but he understood how the recipients would hear it. And he was uniquely qualified to pull it off.

Finally, I can think of no better way to begin our journey through Ephesus than to repeat the words of the Apostle Paul himself: "I [pray] that the God of our Lord Jesus Christ, the glorious Father, may give you the Spirit of wisdom and revelation, so that you may know him better."

1 A BRIEF INTRODUCTION TO EPHESUS

The founders of Ephesus…sent to the oracle of the god and asked where they should build their city. And he declared to them that they should build a city "wheresoever a fish shall show them and a wild boar shall lead the way."

It is said, accordingly, that some fishermen were eating their noonday meal in the place where are the spring today called Hypelaeus and the Sacred Harbour. One of the fish popped out with a live coal and fell into some straw, and a thicket in which a wild boar happened to be was set on fire by the fish. The boar, frightened by the fire, ran up a great distance on the mountain which is called Tracheia, and when brought down by a javelin, fell where today stands the temple of Athena.

So the Ephesians crossed over from the island after living there 20 years, and settled Tracheia and the areas of the slopes of Coressus.

- Athenaeus, *The Learned Banquet*

It was an overcast March day when the taxi dropped my brother and me off at the site of Ephesus. From the street, it was rather unimpressive. We located a small structure that served as the place to purchase tickets and enter the site. The overcast conditions would soon turn to a light drizzle, but this would not dampen our spirits.

The first thing that becomes apparent upon entering the archaeological site of Ephesus today is the scale of the site. From the upper entrance, you walk through a marketplace, past small temples, archways, and the Odeon, only to realize you have not yet reached the main thoroughfare. The site sits between two hillsides, nowadays covered with thick grass. But you soon realize that the grass only conceals what must have been block upon block of residential streets and neighborhoods. The scope of the city that has been excavated is impressive, but almost equally as impressive has to be the portion of the city that still lies beneath the grassy hillsides and surrounding marshes.

I had the pleasure of living in Chicago for almost thirteen years. Though warm weather people may consider living in Chicago as something other than a pleasure, I counted it as such and was proud to identify myself as a Chicagoan. Part of the pride of being a Chicagoan is the strong connection one feels to the history and images – the myths - connected to the city. These myths are captured in the many names by which Chicago is known: the Windy City, the Second City, the City by the Lake, or the City of Broad Shoulders. Tales such as those surrounding Mrs. O'Leary's cow and the Great Chicago Fire or the Curse of the Billy Goat help build a strong cultural identity. Throw in the successes (and frequent failures) of the city's sports franchises, wonderful restaurants and world-class museums, and its numerous ethnic neighborhoods, and you have the essence of a great city.

The same could be said for the great cities of antiquity. Great cities have great stories. Romulus and Remus, born of a romantic encounter between the god Mars and a vestal virgin, are cast out of an ancient kingdom, suckled by a she-wolf to help them survive, and grow up to found settlements on two of the hills that would eventually become Rome. Another hill in the Levant becomes the setting for a man named Abraham to build an altar in order to sacrifice his son Isaac, only to be stopped by an angel before the ultimate sacrifice takes place. That hilltop site would later give significance to the construction of a temple that would become the focal point of Jerusalem. Alexander the Great stood on an empty beach in Egypt and began to pour lines of barley flour on the sand, outlining his vision for a magnificent city that would become Alexandria.

Every great city needed a compelling myth behind its foundation to elevate its status in the world. Now keep in mind, *myth* does not necessarily denote that a story is fictitious. In the classical sense, myths are stories that articulate and maintain a worldview. They also cast light on actual events by interpreting what was thought to be transpiring in the corresponding spiritual realm. Thus, mythological stories are *mythological*, not because they describe events that never happened, but because they show that historical events should not be separated from their larger historical significance within a worldview.[1] In other words, a myth develops because a particular event takes on tremendous significance, and stories are told that help transmit not only the event, but its significance as well. Myths are usually a mixture of cultural

2

interpretations and explanations that evolved from a significant happening. Even if the actual event has long been lost, the myth gives meaning and significance to a culture.

THE BEGINNINGS

Like many great ancient cities of importance, the foundation of Ephesus is rooted in compelling myth, giving it social, economic, and religious influence. Thus, the story above told by Athenaeus of the founding of Ephesus conveys much about the worldview of the Ephesians. The original settlers probably scouted the area for some time before concluding that the area was worth a significant financial investment to develop. The late professor Jerome Murphy-O'Connor, who chronicled much of what ancient writers wrote about Ephesus, concludes, "This made it all the more important to have the approval of the god by his designation of a site for the future city."[2] The city, as well as the temple, was a product of Athenian settlers doing extensive surveying of the area, a significant financial investment in the area, and perhaps most important, a divine endorsement. Whether or not a fish actually fell into the coals, causing a brush fire, should not detract from the importance of the story.

But this is not the only myth surrounding the beginnings of Ephesus. Some sources trace the origins of Ephesus back to the Amazons, the mythical (there is that word again!) race of women warriors. The ancient writer Diodorus Siculus listed several cities along the coastline of Asia Minor as having been settled by the Amazons, "a society governed by women who went to war and allocated only domestic tasks to men."[3] Ephesus was not, however, on this list. It would be the first century BC geographer Strabo that would add Ephesus to the list of Amazon cities, when he wrote, "At any rate the founding of cities and the giving of names to them are ascribed to the Amazons, as, for instance, Ephesus and Smyrna and Cyme and Myrine."[4] Strabo personally found the stories of the Amazons to be "beyond belief." Yet writers who came after Strabo followed his writings and maintained the link between the founding of Ephesus and the Amazons.

Regardless of whether the connection between Ephesus and the Amazons was real, the supposed connection clearly became entrenched as part of its myth. Pliny the Elder recorded that statues of Amazons were part of the décor of the Temple of Artemis as far back as the fifth century BC. Traditionally the Amazons had been linked to many cities of that region. But the connection with Ephesus, in particular, may have been especially captivating given that Artemis was a female deity (Artemis is also identified with the Roman goddess Diana). Thus, the emergence of this female deity's influence may have been strengthened if the founding of her temple could be traced back to a race of legendary females. It could be said that one of the storylines written into the beginnings of Ephesus was that of *girl power*.

THE IONIAN PERIOD

The settlers in Athenaeus' account of the fish and the boar have historically been identified as Ionian settlers. The term *Ionian* refers to a common ethnicity - people originating from Peloponnesus and then coming under Athenian power - as well as a common dialect. Looking to settle new territories, the Ionians left Athens and settled the islands of the Aegean Sea and the western shore of Asia Minor, founding such towns as Miletus and Smyrna. Thus, most histories of Ephesus credit the formation of the town from scattered settlements in the area to Androclus, who led these Ionian settlers to the region in the eleventh century BC, and whose father was king of Athens. Antipater of Sidon, who gave the earliest account of the *Seven Wonders of the World*, referred to Ephesus as "the city of Androclus."

Some historians, both ancient and modern, have questioned the validity of these accounts that trace the founding of Ephesus back to the eleventh century BC. Just as Rome recreated much of its early history, tracing it back to the traditional date of 753 BC and filling in the blanks along the way, similarly, some see these early accounts of Ephesus as "Athenian imperial fiction of the fifth century BC."[5] Like mythology or ancient history, it can often prove difficult to separate hard facts from good stories or pure propaganda.

We are not on solid historical ground until around the sixth century BC. By this time, the Ionian league was a loose affiliation of twelve of these settlements, including Ephesus, sharing some ethnic and religious commonalities. Ephesus began to flourish, but would also change hands numerous times over the next several centuries.

It was during this mid-sixth century that Croesus, king of Lydia, encroached upon these Ionian cities and gained control of Ephesus. According to the historian Herodotus, it was during a siege of Ephesus by Croesus that the saving power of Artemis was made manifest. Herodotus claimed that the presence of the Temple of Artemis, along with some clever strategy by its citizens, convinced Croesus to withdraw his army and spare the city. Croesus was soon after defeated in 546 BC by Cyrus the Great of biblical renown, and Ephesus became part of the Persian Empire.

The presence of the Temple of Artemis in the mid-sixth century also gives evidence of when the great temple was first constructed. Again, Herodotus wrote that this same Croesus provided funding for a greater part of the columns for the magnificent temple. So while the presence of this temple may have saved Ephesus from destruction at the hands of Croesus, it was apparently at that time still under construction, and Croesus himself contributed to its completion in the form of offerings. This has led many to date the original temple to around 550 BC. Pliny informs us that the construction of the original temple spanned a period of 120 years. Some sources indicate that there may have been a smaller shrine to Artemis on the site even before this original temple was constructed. This would not be surprising since the cult of Artemis predates the temple in Ephesus by several centuries. The temple itself would undergo at least two destructions and subsequent reconstructions over the centuries to come (see *The Destruction and Rebirth of the Artemision* below).

III

THE DESTRUCTION AND REBIRTH OF THE ARTEMISION

The Temple of Artemis, or the Artemision, as it is sometimes referred to, endured at least three major devastations, prompting a new temple to be reconstructed in its place each time.

The archaic temple was constructed around 550 BC, took about 120 years to finish, and stood for around 200 years until a fire consumed it in 356 BC. The dating of this fire is well documented as it coincided with the birth of Alexander of Macedon, who history would remember as Alexander the Great. Plutarch records that "it was no wonder that the temple of Artemis was burned down, since the goddess was busy bringing Alexander into the world."[6] The clear implication was that, had the protection of Artemis been present, the temple certainly would not have been destroyed.

The link between Alexander the Great and the Artemision was strengthened when Alexander visited Ephesus in 330 BC. Sources indicate that the rebuilding was well underway upon Alexander's arrival and when he saw the magnificent temple, even partially constructed, he offered to become its benefactor. The town surprisingly turned down Alexander's offer to fund its completion. It would be this version of the temple that would become one of the *Seven Wonders of the World* and stood until 263 AD, long after the Apostle Paul spent his time in Ephesus.

In 263 AD, the Scythians invaded Asia, carving a path of destruction along the way. This destruction not only claimed the Temple of Artemis, but also decimated the economy of Ephesus along with it. By the fifth century AD the remains of the temple were recycled for use in Christian churches throughout the region as far away as Constantinople. Today, a lone reassembled pillar stands on the site of the temple.

The fact that the Temple of Artemis maintained a presence in Ephesus for nearly a thousand years reveals its significance. As one guidebook on Ephesus notes, "The fact that Artemesius was restored each time after the many disasters it suffered shows just how widely followed the cult of Artemis was in Ephesus."[7] For my part, I am surprised how many times I encounter a biblical commentary on Ephesians that makes no mention of the Temple of Artemis.

III

For the next 200 years, Ephesus tried to avoid getting caught in the crossfire between Greece and Persia. For a brief time, Ephesus came under the rule of Athens and then Sparta. But for the most part, it would remain part of the Persian Empire until Alexander the Great passed through Ephesus in 330 BC, freeing them from Persian rule and bringing most of the known world under his dominion. Alexander was so impressed by the city and its re-emerging temple that he offered to cover all past construction expenses. But the town, perhaps wary of relinquishing control of both city and temple to Alexander, shrewdly responded, "that it was inappropriate for a god to dedicate offerings to gods."[8]

Upon the death of Alexander and the ensuing land grab by his generals, Ephesus ended up in the hands of one of Alexander's officers, Lysimachus, in 294 BC. Once Lysimachus had subdued the city, he refortified it by moving its residents to a more defensible position between two prominent hills and then built a wall around the city. The former site was slowly becoming a marsh, which was having both negative economic and public health implications. He also brought in new settlers to Ephesus and changed the way in which it was governed. Though most of these changes were forced upon the residents, they also served to improve the city and laid the foundation for the thoroughly Hellenistic city of Ephesus to emerge.

The kingdoms of Alexander the Great continued to war with each other and Ephesus eventually came under Seleucid control and their king, Antiochus III. Antiochus III ruled the Seleucid Empire for over fifty years and ambitiously looked to expand his empire. But that ambition eventually led him to challenge Rome, and when he was defeated at the battle of Magnesia in 190 BC, Ephesus changed hands once again. Rome was content to let the Attalids of Pergamum rule the region for much of the century.

When Attalus, the last in a line of rulers of Pergamum, died childless in 133 BC, he left his domain directly to Rome. Not everyone was happy with this arrangement and when a usurper tried to stir a revolt, the cities of the region, led by Ephesus, held him off until Rome arrived and put an end to the uprising. The region was reorganized as the Roman province of Asia, and Ephesus became its capital city.

THE ROMAN PERIOD

Ephesus would thrive during this period under the *pax romana*. One of the reasons Rome was so successful in expanding the empire was that as it took over new territories, it would leave the native culture largely intact. Rome learned this, in part, from the conquests of Alexander the Great. Many cultural practices were allowed to continue undisturbed. And when it came to religion, Rome would usually permit worship of the local gods to continue. This period of relative stability in Ephesus allowed the city to grow, along with its infrastructure and the road system surrounding the city. Being part of the Roman Empire brought increased commerce and wealth to Ephesus. When it came to being conquered by Rome, a good rule of thumb to follow was to pay your taxes, be loyal to Rome, and in return, Rome would leave you alone. Yet Ephesus was hardly a quiet bystander as the Roman Empire grew in power. Many of the significant figures of this period found themselves passing through Ephesus, and thus Ephesus found herself circuitously influencing Roman history.

The most serious threat to Roman rule in Ephesus occurred around 89 BC when King Mithridates of Pontus led his army into Asia Minor in an attempt to wrest the region from Rome. Seeing an opportunity to break free of Roman taxation, Ephesus threw its support behind Mithridates, even following his order to kill all Romans and Italians seeking refuge in their temples. It would be an ill-fated decision. The Roman general Sulla eventually defeated Mithridates, and imposed heavy fines on those cities that had supported him. When Sulla came through Ephesus on his way to Rome, his soldiers harassed the citizens, requiring them to give food, supplies, and lodging to the army. Sulla would prove to be a *Caesaresque* figure even before Gaius Julius became the original Caesar. Sulla became Rome's first sole dictator, setting the precedent for Roman generals and politicians to come.

This event proved to establish a pattern for Ephesus. As Murphy-O'Connor well observed (quoting the *Oxford Classical Dictionary*), "Not only did Ephesus pick the wrong side in the war between Mithridates and Rome, but it opted for Pompey against Caesar, for the assassins of Caesar against Mark Antony, and for the latter against Octavian."[9] If the Ephesians were attempting to align themselves with the political victors of these various power struggles, they picked the wrong side almost every time.

Mithridates would continue to pester Rome, however, until the general Pompey decisively defeated him in the mid-60s BC. Incidentally, it was during this same campaign by Pompey that Judea would officially come under Roman control, when he marched on Jerusalem in 63 BC. On his trek back through Asia to Rome, where he was awarded a triumph through the streets of the city, he used Ephesus as his launching point, transporting his soldiers via ship to the coast of Italy.

Julius Caesar thrust himself onto the scene when he marched down from Gaul into Italy in 49 BC. Pompey fled Rome and, along with Scipio, would contest Caesar's audacious move, beginning a civil war. It was during this conflict that, in Julius Caesar's own words, "On two occasions Caesar saved the Ephesian funds." Stationed in Asia, Scipio was apparently growing desperate to fund the campaign against Caesar and ordered that the large funds deposited in the Temple of Artemis be turned over to him (temples also functioned as banks; see feature, *Temples As Banks*). But when Caesar marched against Pompey in Greece, Pompey sent an urgent message to Scipio to come to his aid in Thessaly, and the withdrawal of funds never took place. Caesar defeated Pompey and Scipio at Pharsalus in 48 BC. This was the first instance that Caesar took credit for saving the Ephesian funds.

On the second occasion, Caesar chased Pompey to Egypt, only to find that Pompey had been murdered. It was here in Alexandria that Caesar met Cleopatra, of great renown. Caesar would return to Rome through Asia the following year. When he arrived in Ephesus, he discovered that a supporter of Pompey, Amplius, was attempting to remove a large sum of money from the temple. Upon Caesar's arrival, Amplius fled the city and the funds were once again protected.

Julius Caesar was assassinated in 44 BC, prompting his adopted heir Octavian (Caesar Augustus) and his general Mark Antony to hunt down the perpetrators, Brutus and Cassius, and the armies loyal to them. They were defeated at Philippi in 42 BC. Octavian then returned to govern Italy from Rome, while Antony governed the eastern provinces.

The ambitions of both Antony and Octavian assured that the power sharing arrangement would not be a peaceful one for long. Antony and Cleopatra engaged in their famous love affair, and in the eyes of Rome he began acting more like an Eastern monarch rather than a Roman consul.

In 41 BC Mark Antony found himself traveling through the city of Ephesus. The historian Appian wrote, "when Antony arrived at Ephesus he offered a splendid sacrifice to the city's goddess, and pardoned all those who, after the disaster to Brutus and Cassius, had fled to the temple as suppliants."[10] He immediately saw Ephesus and the province of Asia as a source of great wealth. Cassius and Brutus had apparently demanded ten years' worth of taxes from the province over only a two-year period. Antony proved to be only marginally less demanding, allowing a two-year period of time to collect nine years' worth of taxes.

It was also in this same year that Ephesus would be dragged into Antony and Cleopatra's love affair when Cleopatra's sister, Arsinoe, was living under asylum in the Temple of Artemis. Cleopatra had previously lost the throne of Egypt to her younger brother before Julius Caesar arrived in Alexandria and threw his support behind her. Caesar sent Arsinoe to Rome for his triumph, but then spared her life, granting her asylum in Ephesus at the temple (see *The Temple as a Place of Asylum*). Cleopatra, however, did not want another potential rival to the throne. She was also said to have great persuasion over Antony. So when she wanted Arsinoe eliminated, not even the inviolability of Artemis prevented Antony from entering the temple and killing her. Josephus explained, "she got her sister Arsinoe to be killed, by the means of Antony, when she was a supplicant at Diana's temple at Ephesus; for if there were but any hopes of getting money, she would violate both temple and sepulchers."[11] Experts have recently identified the remains of the body of a young woman in an octagonal tomb in Ephesus as those of Arsinoe.

When it was discovered that Antony's will made provisions for his children with Cleopatra to assume power upon his death, it was the scandal Octavian needed to convince the senate to declare war. And it was at Ephesus that Antony chose to assemble his fleet in preparation for war. Joining Antony in Ephesus, Cleopatra contributed 200 ships, as well as supplies for the army. But Octavian defeated Antony at the battle of Actium in 31 BC, ushering in the age of the Roman emperors. Facing the inevitable outcome and humiliation, Antony and Cleopatra chose to take their own lives in one of the most recognizable and recounted stories in history. Cleopatra was the last of the Egyptian Pharaohs.

III

THE TEMPLE AS A PLACE OF ASYLUM

According to Jerome Murphy-O'Connor, "In antiquity Greek temples were considered automatically inviolable because of their sanctity."[12] Thus, individuals could take refuge in temple complexes when they feared for their safety. The right of asylum was not absolute, however. Each case was examined to determine whether there were valid reasons for seeking asylum. Often, runaway slaves sought the protection of the temple, but they would need to demonstrate that there was just reason for fleeing. Political figures also sought the protection offered by temples, much like embassies of today. If granted, individuals could remain on temple grounds until their case was resolved, the danger had passed, or in some cases, they simply lived the remainder of their lives in the temple complex. It would have been considered a sacrilege if that protection was violated, as in the case of Mithridates ordering the slaughter of Romans and Italians in the Artemision, or in the case of Arsinoe.

III

Josephus also informs us that Herod the Great passed through Ephesus when meeting with Marcus Agrippa. Herod was meeting with Agrippa in order to secure the rights of Jews in Asia to practice their own laws and customs and to bring a halt to any violence that might have been perpetrated against them. Agrippa was agreeable and Josephus concludes that the Jews were able to carry on their way of life in the province of Asia under this legal protection.

These are the stories and myths that contributed to the renown of Ephesus. It is this Ephesus - this thoroughly Hellenized city, this financially wealthy city, the capital of the Roman province of Asia, whose history is inextricably tied to the Temple of Artemis – that the Apostle Paul would arrive at around 52 AD. Another guidebook on Ephesus frames it in these terms: "Almost all religious, cultural and civic buildings, the remains of which are on the picture postcards you see today, belong to this [Roman] period."[13] Ephesus held a storied history well before Paul entered the city. It is Paul's arrival in Ephesus to which we will now turn.

2 THE APOSTLE PAUL'S BRIEF VISIT TO EPHESUS

The city has both an arsenal and a harbor. The mouth of the harbor was made narrower by the engineers. ... But the result was the opposite, for the silt, thus hemmed in, made the whole of the harbor as far as the mouth more shallow. ... Such then is the harbor. And the city, because of its advantageous situation in other respects, grows daily more prosperous, and is the largest emporium in Asia this side of the Taurus.

- Strabo, *Geography*

A long colonnaded street takes you from the Great Theater past the commercial agora to what would have been the harbor. Except now, where at one time ocean would have carried ships into the port, marshy waters cover grassy fields during the rainy season. Nowadays, the shoreline is about 5 miles away and cruise ships sail into the nearby port city of Kusadasi. The silt mentioned by Strabo has turned the inlet into farmland. Priene is another ancient city not too far away from Ephesus that ultimately gave way to a similar fate. Silt deposited from rivers eventually filled in the bay, turning commercial harbors into uninhabitable marshes. When the harbor was gone, the city lost much of its commercial traffic. Marshlands became breeding grounds for mosquitos. Malaria ultimately forced the residents to relocate or abandon the site altogether.

The city that the Apostle Paul sailed into would have borne little resemblance to the skeletal remains of today's archaeological site. By all accounts, Ephesus was a vast, thriving, cosmopolitan city with many of the amenities of the great cities of today. Ephesus was, by some estimates, the third largest city in the Roman Empire. Only Rome itself and the Egyptian city of Alexandria boasted larger populations. Ephesus would have been similar in size to other major cities of the Roman Empire, such as Thessalonica and Antioch. Though estimating these urban populations of the Roman world can be a daunting task, many place the population of Ephesus between 180,000 to 225,000. We can compare this to Diodorus' assertion that Alexandria's population at this same time was approximately 300,000. Estimates for the population of the city of Rome begin at around a half-million and continue upwards to a million inhabitants.[1]

Sometimes facts like these are only appreciated by historians and archaeologists. More often than not, I have read similar facts touting size and population figures without letting the reality sink in, so some comparisons might help. By comparison, Paul would have been walking into the ancient equivalent of the city of Chicago, with only New York City and Los Angeles offering larger populations and cultural experiences. The New York City of the day – Rome - would have been unrivaled in its public buildings, monuments, and dense urban population. The Los Angeles of the Roman Empire, Alexandria, would have offered a much different cultural experience – more Egyptian than Roman, although heavily Greek as well – amidst the same vast urban sprawl. And in between the two, at least geographically, lay the Chicago of the ancient world – more New York than L.A., but on a smaller, less-frenzied scale. (We might be tempted to press the analogy further, but we will stop at the comparisons of relative size of the metropolitan areas.) Ephesus was less than half the size of Rome, but would have dwarfed most other cities in the Roman Empire. It held out all the cultural offerings of Rome and Alexandria, with its own unique Greek flavor. Ephesus was the seat of Roman power in Asia Minor. Indeed, even for a world traveler such as Paul, Ephesus was the big city, with all its wonders and trappings.

In fact, when Paul sailed into the harbor at Ephesus, it would have been perhaps the largest city he had encountered at the time, although Antioch may have been comparable.[2] We can, for a moment, peek over Paul's shoulder as his vessel passes the island of Samos toward the Asian coast. Navigating their way to the Ephesian harbor, the crew finally arrives at the large harbor bustling with ships, along with merchants loading and unloading their wares. Paul would have seen homes and shops as far as the eye could see. The city's gymnasium, one of the centers of Roman social life, faced the harbor. But towering above all the activity was the great amphitheater of Ephesus. This theater would be the site for a real-life drama that would play out during Paul's extended stay in Ephesus. Out of sight, but no doubt in the forefront of his curiosity would have been the Temple of Artemis, already deemed one of the wonders of the ancient world.

It was probably early in the year 52 AD when Paul sailed into the harbor and beheld the magnificent city. It was the last leg of a long journey spreading the good news, what is more commonly referred to as *Paul's Second Missionary Journey*. Whether Paul would have labeled it as such is another question; it is more likely that it was simply another slice of his life's calling. However, for our purposes, this second missionary journey had begun a couple of years earlier in Jerusalem, with the leaders of the young Christian church there sending Paul and Barnabas to Antioch along with a letter clearing up some confusion that had arisen around the issue of what was to be required of Gentile converts. Would they need to take on all the rites and rituals distinctive to the Jewish people? Or would this new expression of faith in Yahweh be distinctly un-Jewish? After much debate, the council concluded that "it seemed good to the Holy Spirit and to us not to burden you with anything beyond the following requirements: You are to abstain from food sacrificed to idols, from blood, from the meat of strangled animals and from sexual immorality" (Acts 15:28-29).

After spending some time in Antioch preaching and teaching, Paul had the desire to revisit the churches he had established on his initial missionary journey. But Paul and Barnabas would have a falling out over the young John Mark: Barnabas wanted to give him a second chance after he had earlier deserted them, while Paul did not want the baggage of a repeat incident. So Paul chose Silas to accompany him the rest of the way. A young disciple, Timothy, would be added to the team in Lystra. They would travel through Asia Minor and set sail from Troas to Philippi in the province of Macedonia. It would not have been a missionary journey without some time in prison, this time in Philippi. But that rarely slowed Paul down. Paul had to be slipped out of Thessalonica under the cover of night, and after debating the philosophers of Athens, he arrived in Corinth. Paul would settle in Corinth for almost two years before setting off for Jerusalem in time for the Passover celebration.

And it is on this voyage back to Jerusalem for the Passover celebration that we rejoin Paul on the ship's deck surveying the activity in the harbor of Ephesus. It did not take Paul long to figure out that Ephesus would be a city to which he must return. If he could make it here, he could make it anywhere. But for now, a brief visit would have to suffice. He was already anticipating the atmosphere that could only be found in Jerusalem during one of the great annual religious festivals. And he wanted to update the Jerusalem council in person regarding the previous couple of years. The Gentiles were truly embracing this faith in a Jewish messiah!

I WILL COME BACK IF IT IS GOD'S WILL

At this point we also catch up with Luke's narrative of this journey that would bring Paul to Ephesus. Luke was a traveling companion of Paul and the author of Luke and Acts. Acts chapter 18 quickly moves us through Ephesus, perhaps reflecting Paul's own urgency to arrive back in Jerusalem for Passover, and sets the stage for Paul's return to this cosmopolitan city. Luke also gives us background details for a few events that took place there in Paul's absence.

They arrived at Ephesus, where Paul left Priscilla and Aquila. He himself went into the synagogue and reasoned with the Jews. When they asked him to spend more time with them, he declined. But as he left, he promised, "I will come back if it is God's will." Then he set sail from Ephesus. (Acts 18:19-21)

Before Paul hurries off to Jerusalem, we are given a couple details of his initial visit to Ephesus. First, Priscilla and Aquila accompany Paul from Corinth and begin to lay the foundation for a church in Paul's absence. Paul had met Priscilla and Aquila in Corinth over their shared trade of tent-making. Perhaps over swapping trade secrets, they formed a close bond and by all accounts worked well together in spreading the gospel. Being uprooted from Rome because of the expulsion of Jews (and possibly Christians) under the emperor Claudius, they would travel with Paul and settle for some length of time in Ephesus. Indeed, their house in Ephesus would later become the primary meeting place for the church there. More will be said about this couple to follow, but while Paul finished his return trip to Jerusalem, he could have every confidence that the foundation being laid was structurally sound.

Next, and not surprisingly, Paul does manage to squeeze in a visit to the local synagogue where he "reasoned with the Jews." This should not be surprising as in nearly every city on these first two missionary journeys, from Salamis on the island of Cyprus to Corinth, Paul's first stop was the local synagogue. Luke himself states, "As his custom was..." (Acts 17:2) when noting, almost redundantly, Paul's practice of entering a city and heading straightway for its local synagogue. The essence of Paul's gospel centered on a Jewish Messiah, the long-anticipated hope of Israel's turbulent history. As theologian N.T. Wright observes, "All early Christianity was Jewish Christianity."[3] We can almost track with Paul's thought process: If every major city throughout the Roman Empire likely housed a Jewish synagogue, and if Jesus was the long-awaited Messiah – the fulfillment of Jewish hope and now the incarnation of hope for all creation - then one simply would need to reason this hope to every synagogue and the people who were a part of it. After all, the moment when Paul, who was himself a Pharisee, understood this hope (with a little convincing from the Almighty directly), it would give new direction to his religious zeal.

Yet it was only earlier in this same chapter of Acts, back in Corinth, that Paul would throw his arms in the air exasperated from his many battles in these very synagogues. "Enough of this!" Paul would exclaim, "From now on I'll go directly to the Gentiles." Apparently, Paul reasoned that the pagans would be an easier lot to deal with than the firmly entrenched.

Unfortunately, similar battles can take place within the Christian church today. From worship wars to generational gaps, what can seem like a natural transition from the traditions of the past to the hopes of the future ends up being a parting of ways. I personally have worked with a number of older congregations in urban settings, who are facing gentrification and suburban flight, and asking the question, "How are we to survive and carry on the work?" The obvious answer in many situations, amidst an influx of younger urban dwellers and growing cultural scenes, is to share resources with church planters and younger congregations, who often find meeting space and resources at a premium. Both groups stand to benefit. Yet I have witnessed many of these same congregations make the choice to close their doors and liquidate the resources rather than embrace a hope for the future. I too have thought at times, "Enough of this! Bring on the pagans."

Despite Paul's previous assertion, Ephesus would be no exception to this custom. Old habits were hard to break. And, at least initially, there was reason to think things might be different here. He was invited to spend more time reasoning at the synagogue, but perhaps knowing all-too-well how this would end, he resisted the temptation and stayed resolute to his timeline of reaching Jerusalem for Passover. Leaving the door open, he did part with these words, "I will come back if it is God's will." Several manuscripts of this text even add the explanation, "I must be at the festival that is taking place in Jerusalem."

Finally – and it has already been stated, but needs to be explained explicitly – Paul's first time in Ephesus was brief because he was anxious to arrive in Jerusalem for Passover. This is not obvious from an initial reading of the text. But there does seem to be urgency in Luke's words describing this first visit to Ephesus. Why else would Paul not walk through a door standing open to him at the Ephesian synagogue? As noted above, some manuscripts do, in fact, state that Paul was in a hurry to get to Jerusalem. Similar language is used only two chapters later in Acts, when Luke, referring to the end of the third missionary journey, writes, "Paul had decided to sail past Ephesus to avoid spending time in the province of Asia, for he was in a hurry to reach Jerusalem, if possible, by the day of Pentecost" (Acts 20:16). While occurring only a few pages later in the text, a full three years had expired and Paul had this same desire to be back in Jerusalem for one of the major feasts.

Returning to Acts 18, many versions of this text go on to state that upon his arrival in Caesarea, Paul "went up and greeted the church and then went down to Antioch," further shrouding this goal of Jerusalem. But we can be sure that the church he went *up* to greet was not the church in Caesarea, nor can one go *down* to Antioch from Caesarea.[4] One always *went up* to Jerusalem; it was a way of giving Jerusalem honor and respect, as well as accurately reflecting the topography of the region.

This brief visit was enough, however, to whet his appetite and he would grow as equally anxious for his return to Ephesus. Leaving the harbor, Paul now looked back on a city large enough and central enough to hold his God-given vision to reach the Gentile world with the hope of a new kind of kingdom. He would return!

A word needs to be said regarding the vow that Paul had taken, and the subsequent shaving of his head at the end of his time in Corinth. Most commentators link this vow to a vision in Corinth, where God promised Paul, "Do not be afraid; keep on speaking, do not be silent. For I am with you, and no one is going to attack and harm you, because I have many people in this city" (Acts 18:9-10). If it is not referring to this vision, then Luke did not think it important to give us the alternative account. Regardless, there is little doubt that this vow was a temporary Nazarite vow, which Paul took from time to time. Among the stipulations of a Nazarite vow listed in the Hebrew Scriptures was that, while under the vow, a person was not to drink wine, nor were they to cut their hair (see Numbers 6). When the period of completion was over, the person was to shave their head. If this vow was related to the vision, it was a way of offering thanks to God for God's promised protection while in Corinth.

Paul did make it to Jerusalem in time for Passover (Luke does not indicate otherwise) and then spent some time in Antioch. But his anticipation of returning to Ephesus would not permit him to stay in Antioch long. Paul would set out through Asia Minor revisiting the churches in the region of Galatia, before making his way back to Ephesus. If he left Ephesus earlier that year before Passover, probably in early spring of 52, then he must have arrived back later that fall. Incidentally, for those keeping score, his arrival in Jerusalem in this passage of scripture marked the end of his second missionary journey while his departure from Antioch signaled the beginning of his third such journey. The majority of this next road trip would be spent in the city of Ephesus.

MEANWHILE, BACK IN EPHESUS...

During these six or so months while Paul traveled from Jerusalem to Antioch, then throughout the region of Galatia, Luke informs us that plenty was going on back in Ephesus. Quite independently of the missions' work being furthered by Priscilla and Aquila, a Jew named Apollos had arrived in Ephesus. For Apollos, the move from Alexandria to Ephesus was more of a lateral move, rather than that of being a greenhorn entering the big city of Ephesus.

Meanwhile a Jew named Apollos, a native of Alexandria, came to Ephesus. He was a learned man, with a thorough knowledge of the Scriptures. He had been instructed in the way of the Lord, and he spoke with great fervor and taught about Jesus accurately, though he knew only the baptism of John. He began to speak boldly in the synagogue. When Priscilla and Aquila heard him, they invited him to their home and explained to him the way of God more adequately. (Acts 18:24-26)

We are given several details about Apollos, all of which stress his intellect and his eloquence. In fact, in Luke's description of Apollos, some take the Greek word *logios*, to not simply mean "learned" or "eloquent", but to identify him specifically as a *Sophist*. The Sophists' school of rhetoric began in Athens in the fifth century BC, but was still popular in the second century AD. As a form of rhetoric, it stressed the imitation of well-known literature and other speeches, as well as the memorization of certain rhetorical formulaic devices.[5] Opponents criticized it for its reliance on show over substance. Additionally, it was known to have been popular in Alexandria at this time, an indication that Apollos would have been exposed to Sophist rhetoric while living there. At any rate, by adding to the work another sharp mind, cultured world traveler, and fellow Jew passionate about Jesus, Apollos was a welcome addition to the team!

Luke is also very careful to stress that while in Alexandria, he had been taught accurately about Jesus. Being an intellectual Jew, he applied his thorough knowledge of the scriptures to this new revelation of Jesus as the promised Messiah and used his passion and eloquence to engage others in this good news. Yet Luke also adds one more detail, that "he knew only the baptism of John." This is another way of saying that Apollos had no knowledge of the promised Holy Spirit, which was associated with being baptized as a follower of Jesus: "Go and make disciples of all nations, baptizing them in the name of the Father and of the Son and of the Holy Spirit" (Matthew 28:19). This was not simply the water baptism of John that would express repentance and anticipation of the one to come, but this baptism was a full recognition that the One *had* come, accompanied with the very real presence of God's Spirit in the life of the disciple.

It is easy to jump directly from the platform of Matthew 28 into the pool of our Christian doctrine today and forget that the early spread of the gospel from Jerusalem to Judea and Samaria to the ends of the earth was broadcast with varying levels of clarity in the early days. Luke recounts other such occurrences on Paul's journeys, including a similar situation Paul would encounter upon his return to Ephesus. It appears that Apollos was taught about Jesus from other Jews who had made the pilgrimage to Jerusalem for that most eventful of Passovers and may have witnessed the death and resurrection of this Jesus firsthand. It is easy to imagine these pilgrims returning to Alexandria after that Passover, yet before the events of Pentecost fifty days later, where the Holy Spirit came upon the believers in Jerusalem. Consequently, these pilgrims and their converts would become followers of Jesus, but the only baptism they knew about was the baptism of John. The Holy Spirit was a foreign concept to them. So we are introduced to Apollos, who understood Jesus *accurately*, yet did not understand what it meant to be baptized "in the name of the Father and of the Son and of the Holy Spirit."

This is the Apollos that Priscilla and Aquila would encounter in Ephesus. Apollos, like Paul, began reasoning in the synagogue and it did not take long for Pricilla and Aquila to catch wind of this fellow Jesus-follower and his powerful, though incomplete, teaching. They invited Apollos into their home and equipped him with the full story, including Pentecost! This event speaks to the effective work of Pricilla and Aquila during Paul's absence, as well as their own thorough knowledge of the scriptures. Professor Murray Harris writes, "It is a tribute to the tactfulness of Pricilla and Aquila and the humility of Apollos that this distinguished Jewish scholar was willing to learn from a humble Christian couple."

During their times together, along with the other believers who met in their home at Ephesus, it must have come up that Priscilla and Aquila, along with Paul, had spent some time in Corinth, for next we read of Apollos' desire to go to Corinth. We can imagine that Priscilla and Aquila thought Apollos might utilize his unique gifts to follow up with the work they were involved with in Corinth and they sent Apollos off with their full recommendation. And, at least initially, he was quite the help. He stepped right into his role of refuting the opposition and greatly strengthening the church at Corinth.

Much could be said about the work of Apollos in Corinth and more will be said about Apollos below.[6] For our purposes, however, there are times where it is helpful to ask the question, "Why did Luke include this particular detail?" (Why any of them, for that matter?) Details like this are certainly helpful if you are researching the events of Ephesus during the time of Paul, but that seems far removed from the intention behind the book of Acts. There are many views on Luke's purpose for writing Luke/Acts, but it appears that, at some level, Luke was preparing a legal defense for Paul's trial in Rome. Luke, more so than any of the other gospel writers, included very detailed information – dates, places, names of rulers, governors, and other Roman officials – that could easily be checked and verified if so desired. Whatever other reasons Luke may have had - certainly among them was to leave a record that would encourage believers everywhere - it appears that Luke was writing with an eye to legitimize the work of Paul, and to a larger extent, to legitimize the spread of Christianity throughout the Roman Empire.

III

THE PURPOSE OF LUKE/ACTS

There are several opinions regarding Luke's purpose for writing his gospel along with the book of Acts, as well as the identity of the individual *Theophilus*, who is mentioned both in Luke 1:3 and in Acts 1:1. Among them:

1. *A historical account of the origins of Christianity.* Like the other gospel writers, Luke simply wanted an account of the life of Jesus and the church.

2. *An apologetic of Christianity for the church.* This view purports that Luke's primary aim was to equip believers with a defense of their faith against growing opposition.

3. *An encouragement to Theophilus to make his faith public.* According to this view, Theophilus was a high-ranking official who had secretly become a believer. Luke was encouraging him to make his decision public and to strengthen the church.

4. *A legal defense for Paul.* Paul was on trial in Rome before Nero and needed a defense of his missionary work, as well as Christianity needing a defense of its legitimacy in the Roman Empire.

III

With this in mind, the work of Apollos is not mentioned again in the book of Acts. It is only noted that he was in Corinth when Paul arrived at Ephesus. But Luke may have had in mind a couple of reasons for documenting these particular details. First, by showing the partnership of Jews like Aquila and Apollos (Priscilla probably was not Jewish), Luke is demonstrating that, despite the frequent opposition from Jewish leaders, Christianity was not at that time, a rival religion, but represented a sect within the Jewish religion. Stated quite simply, if Christianity was a new religion, it was illegal within the Roman Empire; if it was a sect within Judaism, then it had legal standing. By extension, if Christianity was illegal, then Paul was engaged in illegal activity. The legitimacy of Christianity is a theme throughout Luke's writings. Specifically, when it comes to Apollos, it has been suggested that Apollos may have been on the "witness list" for Paul's trial. As such, it would have been good to give some background on him, as well as present a bit of his *curriculum vitae*.

TEAM EPHESUS

Throughout this journey, it will be helpful to become familiar with others who will make appearances in the story of Paul and Ephesus. It might be easy to picture Paul working in solitary conditions; perhaps a faithful companion was around to provide him with some company. Yet when we compile this list, an entirely different picture emerges: Paul had entire teams working alongside him, working in his absence, delivering letters around the region, and being trained to carry on the work when he moved on to the next city. Some names are barely given a mention in the New Testament, yet they obviously made enormous contributions to support the church and the work of Paul.

What follows is a snapshot of what is known about the people surrounding Paul and who contributed to his work in Ephesus.

Achaicus. Achaicus was a Christian from Corinth. He is only mentioned once in scripture, traveling with two others, as having journeyed from Corinth to Ephesus during Paul's extended stay there. In Paul's first extant letter to the church in Corinth, Paul mentions these three from Corinth as supplying him with "what was lacking from you" (1 Corinthians 16:17). With all the bad news coming out of the Corinthian church, these three apparently embodied what Paul had hoped for the entire church community there in Corinth. He was now holding them up before the Corinthian community as examples to follow.

Achaicus and the other two probably delivered the first letter *from* Corinth - mentioned in 1 Corinthians 7:1: "Now for the matters you wrote about..." - and Paul was now preparing a response to send back to Corinth, via this same envoy. It is possible that Sosthenes may have also been with this group if we accept that he visited Paul in Ephesus as well (see below). Little else is known about Achaicus, besides speculation regarding the origin of his name. It is little doubt a reference to the province of Achaia, where Corinth was located.

Apollos. As mentioned previously, Apollos was a Jewish teacher from Alexandria (Acts 18:24). He may have been part of a school of rhetoric known as the Sophists. Apollos arrived at Ephesus after Paul's brief visit on his second missionary journey, where he met Pricilla and Aquila. He left Ephesus before Paul's return and ministered to the church in Corinth (Acts 19:1). Apollos used his rhetorical skills and knowledge of the scriptures to teach extensively in Corinth.

Paul's first letter to the church at Corinth mentions Apollos several times, almost always in relation to the divisions that had arisen in that church (1 Corinthians 1:12). What is debated is whether Apollos was part of the problem behind the divisions or whether the divisions simply emerged out of the immaturity of the believers there. It is not difficult to imagine that possessing an eloquent and charismatic personality, some were simply drawn to the person and not to the message. We can observe such cases in today's church! In both extant letters to the church at Corinth Paul repeatedly defends the message of the gospel above the eloquence in which it is delivered, even defending his own lack of eloquence (1 Corinthians 1:17). The divisiveness seems to have weighed on Apollos, causing him to leave Corinth; but Paul encouraged him to return (1 Corinthians 16:12). Nevertheless, sometime later Paul writes in his letter to Titus that he is to help Apollos in his work and see that he has everything he needs (Titus 3:12).

The caricature of Apollos from the New Testament as one rarely being associated with positive contributions to the early church, may go beyond the text. Some have even suggested that Apollos is the author behind the book of Hebrews, citing his knowledge of the Hebrew Scriptures and mastery of the Greek language and rhetoric. Again, this is a possibility, but goes beyond the scope of current evidence.

Aristarchus. Aristarchus was from Thessalonica (Acts 20:4). Although he is not mentioned specifically in Paul's visit to Thessalonica on his second missionary journey, he is counted among his traveling companions in Ephesus, so he probably joined up with Paul sometime after Paul and Silas were driven from his hometown. Perhaps most notably, Aristarchus was one of the two men, along with Gaius, seized by the crowd during the riot in Ephesus and dragged into the amphitheater (Acts 19:29). He accompanied Paul throughout the rest of his third missionary journey and even accompanied Paul and Luke to Rome for Paul's trial (Acts 27:2). This has led some to speculate the precise role of Aristarchus in Paul's ministry, observing that while under arrest, not just anyone would be able to accompany Paul on the vessel bound for Rome.[7]

Aristarchus is referred to as Paul's "fellow prisoner" when Paul writes to the church at Colosse (Colossians 4:10). This imprisonment may have been voluntary on Aristarchus' part. The church in Colosse would have been familiar with Aristarchus from his time with Paul in Ephesus. This same scripture reference seems to imply that Aristarchus was Jewish. During this confinement, Aristarchus is also mentioned as Paul's "fellow worker" in his letter to Philemon (Philemon 24). Church traditional actually holds that Aristarchus was martyred alongside Paul.

Aristarchus is a minor figure that does not receive much press. Yet the picture painted of him is one of a faithful traveling companion of Paul, as well as a constant source of encouragement to Paul. The press he does get is truly admirable!

Erastus. The mention of Erastus at Ephesus is brief, enough to let us know he was there before being sent ahead with Timothy to the churches in Macedonia (Acts 18:22). His identification as a public figure is more intriguing. He was from Corinth and probably became a believer during

Paul's stay there. He would then join Paul in Ephesus. When Paul catches up with Timothy and Erastus back in Corinth, he mentions that Erastus holds the position of the city's director of public works when writing Romans (Romans 16:23).

A large inscription was uncovered in Corinth, and is still visible to visitors today, that reads, "Erastus in return for his aedileship laid [the pavement] at his own expense." This title of *aedileship* is similar enough to that of the director of public works that many take this to refer to the Erastus of the New Testament.

Finally, Paul mentions that Erastus was back in Corinth in a letter to Timothy, whom he had sent to oversee the church in Ephesus (2 Timothy 4:12). Little else is known about Erastus and his contribution to the work in Ephesus, but he gives us insight into the kind of people Paul was working with. According to tradition, he was suffered martyrdom later in Philippi.

Fortunatus. Like Achaicus, Fortunatus was a Christian from Corinth. He also is only mentioned once in scripture in this same reference to the traveling party coming from Corinth to Ephesus: "I was glad when Stephanas, Fortunatus and Achaicus arrived, because they have supplied what was lacking from you" (1 Corinthians 16:17). With all the bad news coming out of the Corinthian church, Fortunatus was listed among the three, whom Paul was holding up as examples for the Corinthian church to follow.

As previously mentioned, he and the other two probably delivered the first letter mentioned in 1 Corinthians 7:1 and Paul was now preparing a response to send back to Corinth via this same envoy. Little else is known about Fortunatus, beyond speculation regarding the origin of his name, whether he might have been a slave or freedman, even belonging to one of the prominent households of Chloe or Stephanas referenced by Paul in his letters to Corinth.

Gaius. Gaius' role at Ephesus reads much like that of Aristarchus. He is mentioned most notably as one of the two men dragged into the amphitheater by the crowd during the riot (Acts 19:29). He is also listed as a traveling companion who accompanied Paul throughout the rest of his third missionary journey (Acts 20:4). This same reference reveals that he was from Derbe, though this is problematic as the previous reference identifies him as Macedonian. It could be that the reference to Gaius being "Derbean" is referring to someplace other than Derbe in Galatia or that this reference actually should be attached to Timothy's name in this same list.

The fact that Gaius was a common name means that other references to this name in the New Testament makes the link to the Gaius from Paul's time in Ephesus dubious. Paul mentions that he baptized a person named Gaius in Corinth (1 Corinthians 1:14) and that he enjoyed his hospitality while staying in Corinth (Romans 16:23). John also addresses his third letter to a church leader named Gaius (3 John 1). It is theoretically possible that each of these references is identifying the same person, while it is also possible that each is a reference unrelated to the Gaius mentioned alongside Paul in Ephesus.

Onesiphorus. Onesiphorus was probably from Ephesus, but is not mentioned in the account of Paul's ministry there. Yet Paul mentions him twice in his letters to Timothy, whom Paul sent to Ephesus to oversee the church that had been established there.

And the review is a glowing one! When many had abandoned Paul because of his trial in Rome, Onesiphorus made a point to go to Rome, track Paul down, and encourage him. Paul heaps blessings and mercy on Onesiphorus for his faithfulness and devotion, making special mention of the "many ways he helped me in Ephesus" (2 Timothy 1:16-18). No doubt, he was now helping Timothy in many similar ways. At the close of this same letter, Paul sends his greeting to him, along with Priscilla and Aquila (2 Timothy 4:19). Onesiphorus is another example of a faithful servant of the gospel who is barely given a mention in scripture, yet no doubt we ourselves would be refreshed if we knew a more extensive account of his involvement in Ephesus.

Paul. The apostle himself is included on this list in order to present a brief biographical sketch of his life. Luke first mentions Paul, or Saul as he was referred to early on, as a young man watching the clothes of those stoning Stephen (Acts 7:58). Saul was a member of the Pharisees whose early résumé boasted the right pedigree, education, and connections. Paul's own words summarize his career path: "For you have heard of my previous way of life in Judaism, how intensely I persecuted the church of God and tried to destroy it. I was advancing in Judaism beyond many of my own age and was extremely zealous for the traditions of my fathers" (Galatians 1:13-14).

That would all change on a business trip to Damascus. Luke records the event in Acts 9, describing how, while on the road to Damascus, "a light from heaven flashed around him," leaving him blind. Saul heard the voice of Jesus asking, "Saul, Saul, why do you persecute me?" Saul was led to Damascus, where he recovered and encountered a disciple named Ananias. He was baptized and began teaching in the synagogues that "Jesus is the Son of God."

His transformed zeal turned his mission from that of persecuting the church to that of advancing the church throughout the Roman and Gentile world. He would take three major missionary journeys throughout the Roman world, planting churches and strengthening the believers, before being arrested over the issue of the legitimacy of Christianity as a legal religion in the Roman Empire. He would be released from his first imprisonment in Rome and tradition holds that he went as far as Spain on another missionary journey before being imprisoned again in Rome and finally executed sometime around 68 AD.

Paul labored tirelessly for the spread of the gospel. Again, borrowing his own words summarizing his zeal,

I have worked much harder, been in prison more frequently, been flogged more severely, and been exposed to death again and again. Five times I received from the Jews the forty lashes minus one. Three times I was beaten with rods, once I was pelted with stones, three times I was shipwrecked, I spent a night and a day in the open sea, I have been constantly on the move. I have been in danger from rivers, in danger from bandits, in danger from my own people, in danger from Gentiles; in danger in the city, in danger in the country, in danger at sea; and in danger from false believers. I have labored and toiled and have often gone without sleep; I have known hunger and thirst and have often gone without food; I have been cold and naked. Besides everything else, I face daily the pressure of my concern for all the churches. (2 Corinthians 11:23-28)

This résumé from the second half of his life reads much different from his earlier one! His writings constitute much of the New Testament. Truly, volumes have been written about his life, but this will serve to catch us up to speed on the events of his life before and after Ephesus.

Priscilla and Aquila. We have already been briefly introduced to this couple, who ministered alongside Paul in Corinth and Ephesus. Aquila was a Jew from Pontus and together the couple was in the tent-making business, as was Paul (Acts 18:2). They resided in Rome for a time until they were expelled under the edict of the emperor Claudius. They met Paul in Corinth and then accompanied him to Ephesus, where Paul left the foundational work of the church there in their able hands. They would form a close bond with Paul. As previously mentioned, it was Priscilla and Aquila who would encounter Apollos at the synagogue in Ephesus and provide him with clearer instruction on the baptism of the Holy Spirit. They would recommend Apollos to the church back in Corinth.

The dates associated with Paul's correspondence aid in piecing together the ongoing work of Priscilla and Aquila. During Paul's extended stay at Ephesus, he writes to the church at Corinth, sending along greetings from Priscilla and Aquila (1 Corinthians 16:19). Here he also specifically indicates that their house served as a meeting place for the church in Ephesus. However, when Paul writes to Rome a couple of years later, he sends his greetings to Priscilla and Aquila there in Rome (Romans 16:3). This may indicate that the couple went back to Rome for a time after the situation had relaxed, following the death of Claudius. Here Paul states that "they risked their lives for me" while in Ephesus, perhaps referring the riot and their close association with Paul. Yet later, in his letter to Timothy in Ephesus, Paul indicates that Priscilla and Aquila are back in Ephesus working alongside young Timothy (2 Timothy 4:19).

A final word could be said about Priscilla and Aquila that has caused some speculation. It has to do with the order their names appear in scripture. Of the seven times they are mentioned in the New Testament, five times Priscilla is listed first. In a culture (almost any culture of that day) where women were under the authority of their husbands, it is rightly curious that Priscilla is usually mentioned first. In the Roman Empire, a male citizen not under the authority of another household was known as the *paterfamilias*. He was given complete authority over his household; those within his household, including wife, children, and slaves, technically did not own anything. The *paterfamilias* owned and held jurisdiction over all of it.[8] So the most common explanation is that Priscilla came from a prominent Roman family and was therefore of higher rank or social status than her husband. Professor Ramsay, the noted British archaeologist and New Testament scholar, suggests as well that Aquila was probably a freedman - that is, a former slave who had gained his freedom.[9] Much has been made of the origins of their names and other clues, but whether she was of higher social status, or whether it was simply a conversational convention, we are not told outright. So along with always being mentioned as a couple – one name always goes with the other – we will keep to the same naming convention that they are given in scripture.

Sosthenes. Sosthenes was from Corinth; in fact, he was the synagogue ruler in Corinth during Paul's time there on his second missionary journey. The few references we have to Sosthenes are somewhat obscure. Sosthenes was present, as the standing synagogue ruler, when Paul was summoned before the proconsul Gallio because of charges the Jews were bringing against him. Luke writes that when Gallio dismissed the charges, Sosthenes was beat at the hands of those present (Acts 18:17). Most likely these were Greeks taking the opportunity to vent anti-Jewish sentiment, though some hold that he was beat by other Jews upset that he failed to present a compelling case. Either way, it seems that at this point during Paul's time in Corinth, he and Sosthenes were adversaries.

So it is surprising when we read the opening of Paul's first letter to the church in Corinth, greetings from Paul *and* Sosthenes (1 Corinthians 1:1). This would indicate that later during Paul's time in Corinth, Sosthenes had become a believer. This was not without precedence as another (or previous) synagogue ruler in Corinth, Crispus, also "believed in the Lord" and was baptized by Paul.

So why do we include him in our list of *Team Ephesus*? Since Paul wrote 1 Corinthians from Ephesus and the letter is introduced as being from Paul and "our brother Sosthenes" it is possible that Sosthenes spent some time in Ephesus as well. There are three explanations for his inclusion as being a contributor to this letter. First, having become a believer, Sosthenes went to Ephesus and updated Paul on some of the issues that the Corinthian church was dealing with. If this is the case, he may have even returned to Corinth with the letter in hand. Another explanation could be that Sosthenes had become a prominent leader in the church in Corinth and Paul was including him as a contributor as a way of supporting his leadership. Perhaps Sosthenes had even corresponded with Paul regarding church matters. In this case, Sosthenes did not necessarily spend any time at Ephesus. Finally, it is possible that this was a different person named Sosthenes, though it is not a common name and the link with Corinth seems convincing.

Stephanas. Stephanas was the third person of the envoy from Corinth mentioned by Paul, along with Achaicus and Fortunatus, as having visited him in Ephesus (1 Corinthians 16:17). Of the three, Stephanas seems to have held the prominent status, as he and his household are mentioned a couple of times in Paul's first letter to the Corinthians. But it is this initial reference where he, too, is upheld as an exemplary figure in the Corinthian church.

Stephanas and his household were singled out by Paul as "the first converts in Achaia" (1 Corinthians 16:15). This has led some to presume that Stephanas was from Athens, as Paul visited Athens before arriving at Corinth on his second missionary journey. This need not be the case, but regardless, he was held out as a prominent member of the Corinthian church. Paul wrote concerning Stephanas and his household: "They have devoted themselves to the service of the Lord's people. I urge you, brothers and sisters to submit to such as these…" (1 Corinthians 16:15-16).

Stephanas also had the distinction of being one of the few who was personally baptized by Paul in Corinth (1 Corinthians 1:16), though this was a distinction that Paul attempted to downplay, given the factions that arose in that church. The two references to Stephanas, where he is mentioned along with *his household*, indicate that he served as a further example of a *paterfamilias*. His household probably consisted of more than simply a wife and kids, but also perhaps other relatives, as well as slaves. His entire household was evidently involved in the support of Paul and their service to the saints.

Timothy. Luke gives us plenty of background on Timothy. During Paul's second journey, he arrived at Lystra where he met Timothy. Timothy's mother was a Jew and a follower of Jesus, but we are simply told his father was Greek, an indication that he was probably not a follower of Jesus (Acts 16:1). Since he was introduced to the reader by means of his parents, Timothy was probably young, still a part of his parents' household. Timothy must have been an impressive young man, for we are also told that the believers in Lystra, as well as the next town over, Iconium, spoke well of him. Paul also picked up on this and wanted to take Timothy along for the rest of the journey.

Timothy is mentioned alongside Paul and Silas throughout the rest of the journey. When they arrived in Berea, Paul had to leave town quickly because of opponents who were stirring up trouble for him back in Thessalonica.

Timothy and Silas stayed behind in Berea, but later joined Paul in Corinth, where they set up shop for a while (Acts 17:14-15). Concerned for the believers in Thessalonica, Paul sent Timothy back to them to encourage them (1 Thessalonians 3:2). Timothy brought word back to Paul regarding Thessalonica (1 Thessalonians 3:6) and subsequently Paul wrote his second letter to the believers there, following up on Timothy's report.

He may have stayed in Thessalonica for a time, or returned to Corinth (or home for a while), but Timothy next rejoins Paul in Ephesus on his third journey. It was Timothy, along with Erastus, that Paul sent ahead to the Macedonian churches to inform them of Paul's arrival (Acts 19:22), and then on to Corinth (1 Corinthians 4:17). At the conclusion of his third journey, Timothy is among those listed as accompanying him to Jerusalem (Acts 20:4).

After Jerusalem Paul was taken into custody and imprisoned, first in Caesarea then Rome. From Paul's letters he wrote while in prison, we know that Timothy was close at hand. The letters of Philippians, Colossians, and Philemon all include Timothy, along with Paul, as the senders of these letters. Timothy had gained enough credibility with Paul that, after being released from prison, Paul apparently visited Ephesus again and left Timothy behind to oversee and protect the church there (1 Timothy 1:3). Timothy remained in Ephesus until summoned by Paul to Rome when Paul was again imprisoned (2 Timothy 4:9); Tychicus was possibly sent to Ephesus to replace Timothy in his absence.

That Timothy was seemingly only a teenager when he became a permanent fixture in Paul's work is remarkable, given the amount of responsibility soon handed over to him. Six of Paul's letters include Timothy as one of the senders and two more of his letters are personal letters to Timothy. His youth may account for some apparent lack of confidence and some fears that Paul addresses in his letters to him, as well as to other churches regarding Timothy (1 Corinthians 16:10). Yet Paul can also be heard referring to Timothy as his "true son in the faith" (1 Timothy 1:2) and stating that Timothy had "proved himself" (Philippians 2:22) regarding all that was handed over to his care.

One other reference is of interest. In the letter to the Hebrews, the author (unknown, possibly Paul) mentions that Timothy has been released from prison (Hebrews 13:23) and that when he arrives, he and the author will come see them (the unknown recipients). Why Timothy was in prison we do not know. We do know that from his youth, Timothy served faithfully and tirelessly, even sharing some of Paul's sufferings for the spread of the gospel.

Trophimus. Trophimus is mentioned as being among the people who accompanied Paul to Jerusalem at the end of his third missionary journey (Acts 20:4). He is mentioned alongside of Tychicus (see below) and both are identified as being from the province of Asia. The next chapter of the book of Acts mentions Trophimus again and this time he is identified specifically as "Trophimus the Ephesian" (Acts 21:29). He is further identified as being Greek, a non-Jew.

It is with this identification that Trophimus would find himself in the middle of a major controversy while in Jerusalem. He is pointed out specifically as being a Gentile, because it would be Trophimus who would be pegged by some Jews from the province of Asia as illegally accompanying Paul past the Court of the Gentiles, thus defiling the temple. The charges were trumped up, as it is soon revealed that they had seen Paul and Trophimus together the previous day and had simply assumed that he must have accompanied Paul into the inner courts of the temple. Besides, Trophimus would have been the one in trouble and there is no mention of him being apprehended or questioned. Yet these accusations, along with some other inflammatory charges, were enough to take Paul into custody and would lead to his trial and eventual extradition to Rome.

Trophimus is finally mentioned briefly in Paul's closing remarks in his second letter to Timothy (2 Timothy 4:20). Yet this brief mention reveals the level of dedication Trophimus must have had toward Paul's work. Trophimus was apparently still accompanying Paul on some of his travels, because Paul writes that he left Trophimus sick in Miletus. Timothy was at this time overseeing the church in Ephesus, so it would make sense that Paul would have given him an update on the whereabouts of this Ephesian team member. It is believed that Trophimus ultimately was executed by the emperor Nero sometime after Paul's death.

Tychicus. Tychicus is another person recorded as having accompanied Paul to Jerusalem at the end of his third missionary journey (Acts 20:4). Furthermore, he is mentioned as being from the province of Asia and some would hold more specifically, from Ephesus. If the letters to Ephesus and Colosse are any indication, Tychicus functioned as Paul's representative, delivering those letters in person. In both cases (Ephesians 6:21 and Colossians 4:7) Paul indicates that Tychicus would update the church on the latest happenings in Paul's life. In both instances, Paul uses almost identical language, presenting Tychicus as a "dear brother and faithful servant in the Lord." He also assures the church that Tychicus will be an encouragement to them. If Tychicus was from Ephesus, then no doubt he worked closely with the churches in Ephesus and Colosse.

Later, while Timothy was working with the church in Ephesus, Paul writes that he is sending Tychicus to Ephesus (2 Timothy 4:12), possibly inferring that Tychicus was to be Timothy's replacement there. In that letter, Paul is requesting that Timothy come to him in Rome. Earlier, between his Roman confinements, Paul writes to his associate Titus, who is overseeing the church at Crete, indicating that he is considering Tychicus as a replacement. This would free Titus up to come visit Paul in Nicopolis (Titus

3:12). In each of these circumstances, Paul reveals that he has utmost confidence in the person of Tychicus.

III

While other New Testament figures may have been at Ephesus, they are not mentioned alongside the work of Paul. For example, tradition holds that the Apostle John spent considerable time in Ephesus later in his life, and may have even brought Mary, the mother of Jesus, with him since she was entrusted into his care.[10] Titus was also linked closely to Paul's work in Corinth and Macedonia, but he is never definitively placed in Ephesus.

A specific word should be said about the author of Acts. While Luke records the events of Paul in Ephesus, there is no indication that Luke was with Paul in Ephesus. Precisely because Luke did accompany Paul to certain places and then records the events firsthand, Luke uses the first-person, *we*, where he was with Paul. He then switches to the third-person, *he*, when he was apparently not with Paul. The events of Ephesus recorded in Acts are written in the third-person, indicating that Luke stayed behind in Philippi on Paul's second missionary journey. Luke switched back to the first person when Paul met up with other traveling companions in Macedonia and then accompanied Paul to Jerusalem at the conclusion of his third missionary journey. On the way to Jerusalem, Paul (and Luke) greets the Ephesian elders, but does not go to Ephesus.

3 PAUL'S EXTENDED STAY IN EPHESUS

Since there is a kind of common highway constantly used by all who travel from Ephesus towards the east, Artemidorus traverses this too. From Ephesus to Carura, a boundary of Caria toward Phyrgia, through Magnesia, Tralles, Nyssa, and Antioch on the Maeander is a journey of 740 stadia.

- Strabo, *Geography*

O ftentimes, one of the first landmarks designated on a map of the archaeological site of Ephesus is the Magnesian Gate. Traveling from the east, this would have been the main gate into the city. Only nowadays, you will not find it within the archaeological site proper. Looking like a lost tourist, I had my map open trying to orient myself to the site and searching in vain for the Magnesian Gate. I could locate it on the map, but had no luck in identifying the actual structure. It was only after exiting the site and heading down the paved road back to town on foot, that I happened upon the remains of a large structure, overgrown with weeds. Pausing for a moment and once again pulling out my map, I realized that I had found the elusive gate!

The beginning of Acts 19 hurries Paul from Antioch on the Orontes through Asia Minor and returns him to Ephesus: "While Apollos was at

Corinth, Paul took the road through the interior and arrived at Ephesus" (Acts 19:1). During Paul's absence, Priscilla and Aquila were laying the groundwork from their house in Ephesus, while Apollos had been commissioned to help strengthen the church in Corinth. Luke seems as eager as Paul to return the reader to the city of Ephesus.

In reality, Paul would have spent several months making the journey from Antioch back to Ephesus. Luke has already indicated that during this time Paul "traveled from place to place throughout the region of Galatia and Phrygia, strengthening all the disciples" (Acts 18:23). The route that Paul took was the interior road through the region - what Strabo referred to as the *common highway* - as opposed to the trade routes that followed the coastline. The common highway was no mere footpath; the Romans had paved this busy road back in 129 BC and it extended as far east as India.[1] This road would have followed the path of Paul's second journey, revisiting the churches in Derbe, Lystra, Iconium, and Pisidian Antioch.

Paul himself gives us some insight into some of his agenda while making his way back to Ephesus. In his letter to Corinth (remember 1 Corinthians was written from Ephesus) Paul writes, "Now about the collection for God's people: Do what I told the Galatian churches to do" (1 Corinthians 16:1). The Galatian churches are these very churches mentioned above Paul would visit on his way back to Ephesus. The collection would be a major point of emphasis on this third missionary journey. Whether it was a request by the church in Jerusalem or an idea of Paul's to strengthen relations between the Jerusalem church and the Gentile churches, Paul was urging these Gentile churches to set aside sums of money on a regular basis that Paul would eventually deliver to the Jerusalem church to distribute to those in need. Believers belonging to the church in Jerusalem may have found it especially difficult to make ends meet living in the shadow of the Temple cult. Paul could think of nothing better in promoting unity than to have the Gentile brothers and sisters supporting Jewish believers during their hardships in Jerusalem.

So having traveled through the interior of Asia Minor, visiting the churches and promoting the collection, Paul arrived back in Ephesus in the late fall of 52 AD. This date is actually our best guess, but attempting to construct a timeline helps in framing the context of Paul's extended stay in Ephesus. A good place to begin is the fixed points of history – those dates that have been well established and frame a window of time through which we can peer (see *The Fixed Points* below). One fixed point that helps in establishing this timeline is the aforementioned expulsion of the Jews from Rome under the emperor Claudius. This allows us to "fix a point" from scripture to a historically attestable date. Historical references to Gallio's proconsulship in Achaia and Festus replacing Felix as governor of Judea also help in establishing a timeline.

III

THE FIXED POINTS

These are the important events that allow us to date events from Acts with reasonable accuracy:

1. *The expulsion of Jews from Rome – 49/50 AD.* The Roman biographer Suetonius confirms what Luke reported in Acts 18: Claudius expelled Jews from Rome, "since Jews constantly made disturbances at the instigation of Chrestus."[2] Who this Chrestus was and whether this could be a reference to Christ is debated.

2. *Gallio's proconsulship – 51/52 AD.* Acts 18:12 states that while Paul was in Corinth, Gallio was proconsul of Achaia. Inscriptions discovered indicate that Gallio was proconsul of Achaia in 51-52.

3. *Felix is recalled to Rome, replaced by Festus.* Felix was governor of Judea and was replaced by Festus in 59/60. Acts 24:27 states that Paul had been in prison in Caesarea for two years when Festus replaced Felix as governor.

III

So putting these points together, along with time frames given in Acts, we can construct a fairly accurate timeline of Paul's travels. Professor William Ramsay provides an excellent discussion on how he arrived at the dates of the events of Acts, (though the inscription referencing Gallio's proconsulship was not yet discovered, so Ramsay's dates would need some adjustment) so his work provides a rough outline.

The first fixed point is Claudius' expulsion of the Jews from Rome in 49/50. When Paul met up with Priscilla and Aquila in Corinth, it was following this expulsion. So Paul's stay in Corinth of a year and a half probably began sometime in the year 50. It was during this time in Corinth that Paul was brought before the proconsul Gallio. This would have had to have taken place in 51 or 52.

If we assume that Paul met Priscilla and Aquila in 50 and was brought before Gallio in 51, then Paul would have left Corinth early in 52. Referring to the longer reading of Acts 18:21 – that Paul wanted to get to Jerusalem, presumably for Passover – Paul would have arrived in Ephesus in March for his brief visit. In the year 52, Passover began on April 2nd. Allowing time for Paul to go to Antioch and then throughout Galatia, he would have returned back to Ephesus near the end of 52.

Paul stayed in Ephesus for three years and then traveled through Macedonia. He then stayed in Greece (probably Corinth) for three months, before making the return trip back to Jerusalem. He spent Passover in Philippi and wanted to be in Jerusalem for Pentecost. This Passover in Philippi was probably April 5, 57, putting him in Jerusalem for Pentecost on May 25, 57. It was during this return trip that he would meet the Ephesian elders at Miletus, bypassing Ephesus. And it was after this Pentecost feast in Jerusalem that Paul would go to Caesarea and be arrested and imprisoned. Acts 24:27 indicates that Paul was in prison for two years when Festus replaced Felix as governor of Judea. These two years would mean that Paul was in prison from late 57 to 59, which corresponds with the historical reference to Felix being recalled to Rome in 59 or 60.

This timeline seems to be consistent with the historical fixed points. However, with so many *probablys*, *presumablys*, and *roughlys*, reconstructing any timeline of this nature is merely an estimate. Luke describes the timing of some events with a great deal of certainty, while referring to other timeframes in vague chronological terms. In one reference we are told that Paul spoke in the synagogue of Ephesus for three months and then had daily discussions in a lecture hall for two years. In another reference, Paul tells the Ephesian elders that he was with them for three years. As a literary device, both are accurate enough; for a chronological timeline, we are left asking, "Which is it? Two years and three months, or three years?" All this explains why almost any of these dates will be contested by a selection of commentaries. Like Ramsay, a new discovery may show our timeline to be off by a year or so in certain areas, but until those discoveries, we will forge ahead with our timeline given here, proceeding with much humility!

A REOCCURRING ISSUE

Having arrived on foot, this time Paul would not have entered through the harbor, but through the Magnesian Gate on the east side of the walled city. Referring to the quote at the beginning of this chapter, it was called the Magnesian Gate because when leaving the city, the common highway led to Magnesia, the first major city beyond Ephesus. And he arrived to a familiar issue. Seemingly within Luke's narrative, Paul scarcely had time to set his bags down before he encountered some disciples who only had knowledge of John's baptism. They had not even heard that there was a Holy Spirit to be received.

Only a few verses earlier, Apollos had this same gap in knowledge, prompting Priscilla and Aquila to explain to him more adequately the baptism of the Holy Spirit at Pentecost. But Apollos had already moved on to Corinth. Paul is now the one who explains the difference between John's baptism and being baptized into the name of the Lord Jesus.

Paul said, "John's baptism was a baptism of repentance. He told the people to believe in the one coming after him, that is, in Jesus." On hearing this, they were baptized into the name of the Lord Jesus. When Paul placed his hands on them, the Holy Spirit came on them, and they spoke in tongues and prophesied. There were about twelve men in all."
(Acts 19:4-7)

This event is curious for a couple of reasons. As with Apollos, the event itself is an oddity as it presents us with believers who had fallen between the theological cracks as the message of Jesus and the indwelling of the Holy Spirit swept across the Roman world. Beyond this however, questions could be raised as to how these disciples remained in the cracks, given the presence of Priscilla and Aquila in Ephesus. Surely if the couple had known of these believers they would have taken the same care as with Apollos in teaching them more adequately about Jesus. It seems that this group of disciples had emerged quite autonomously of Priscilla and Aquila, and of Paul. Since the story is similar to that of Apollos, we might think that they could be believers brought to faith by Apollos before he himself understood more fully the role of the Holy Spirit. But we should suppose that upon leaving for Corinth, Apollos would have connected his converts with Priscilla and Aquila. Perhaps they represented a much larger and widely dispersed group than had previously been identified: believers that truly did follow only John the Baptist and his teachings because they knew of nothing else.

Furthermore, we must inquire again as to why Luke is choosing to include stories of these *incomplete* disciples of Jesus – these *crack-dwellers*. On the surface these stories do not seem to contribute to Luke's narrative to the extent that his other stories do. Professor Ramsay himself concluded, "This episode I must confess not to understand."[3] He does proceed to speculate that it may have something to do with Paul wanting to establish the importance of this type of disciple being re-baptized. We are not told that Apollos was re-baptized and perhaps Paul was setting the precedent, anticipating that this would not be the last time these incomplete disciples would be encountered.

But revisiting the purpose behind Luke/Acts, Luke may be demonstrating that the spread of this sect of Judaism was, in fact, happening quite autonomously of Paul. Certainly the apostle was actively spreading this gospel, but it may also be the case that this gospel was spreading on its own in advance of Paul. (Indeed, if we hold to the ongoing activity of the Holy Spirit, this should not be surprising.) In this scenario, Paul, and others like Priscilla and Aquila, were spreading the gospel, as well as educating disciples with the specifics of the gospel message. But Paul was not the *host carrier* - if we can employ that image – such that if you eliminated Paul, you would eliminate the spread of the gospel. And this may be part of Luke's message to the Roman authorities: The good news will travel with or without Paul and the Holy Spirit is quite capable of its transmission!

Nevertheless, upon being given this new information of the baptism of the Holy Spirit, these disciples were re-baptized into the name of the Lord Jesus by Paul. Paul then placed his hands on them, and "the Holy Spirit came on them, and they spoke in tongues and prophesied." This experience would be the exception to the rule of receiving the Holy Spirit directly upon becoming a follower of Jesus and being baptized. It served as a mini-Pentecost experience – the filling of the Holy Spirit, tongues, and prophesying - for those who possessed no knowledge of the event following the death and resurrection of Jesus. This mini-Pentecost also happened in front of Peter with the Gentile believers in Caesarea and served as a powerful demonstration that this gift of the Holy Spirit would know no ethnic boundaries.[4] And now it would happen also with Paul. Luke uses examples like these as a way to indicate that the spread of the gospel was breaking through barriers and continuing to advance. In this case, it was John the Baptist's disciples that were incorporated into the movement of Jesus-followers.

Being the exception to the rule, this mini-Pentecost experience unique to Acts should probably not be universalized. Theologian John Stott states that "there are no Samaritans or disciples of John the Baptist left in the world today"[5], so that we should expect the full and complete gift of salvation, including the gift of the Holy Spirit, upon faith in Jesus. It is no longer – nor was it normally in Paul's time - a multi-stage process.

AS WAS HIS CUSTOM

Just as a handful of disciples would form the foundation of Priscilla and Aquila's work in Ephesus in Paul's absence, these twelve disciples would be the firstfruits of Paul's extended stay in Ephesus. Similar to his first brief venture into Ephesus and true to his custom, Paul entered the synagogue and began dialoguing with the local Jewish leaders. No doubt Paul was hoping for the same open door that seemed to be left open from his previous visit, when we were told that the Jews "asked him to spend more time with them." His trip to Jerusalem had cut that opportunity short. But he was back and eager to share with them about the kingdom of God.

The gospel message – the good news – was this announcement of the kingdom of God. It was the announcement that the life, death, and resurrection of Jesus had ushered in God's kingdom. It was consistent with the message of Jesus: "From that time on Jesus began to preach, 'Repent, for the kingdom of heaven is near'" (Matthew 4:17). (Luke uses the term *kingdom of God* while Matthew primarily uses the term *kingdom of heaven*.) Luke bookends his narrative in the book of Acts with this announcement as well.

He opens Acts with the statement that Jesus "appeared to them over a period of forty days and spoke about the kingdom of God" (Acts 1:3), and closes his book with a summary statement that Paul, "proclaimed the kingdom of God and taught about the Lord Jesus Christ – with all boldness and without hindrance!" (Acts 28:31). This announcement of the kingdom of God stood in direct opposition to Rome's kingdom, the kingdom of the Caesars. To borrow a phrase from N.T. Wright, it was the message that Jesus is Lord and Caesar is not. It was a dangerous announcement! It is important to understand that Paul was not simply dropping in for some good theological debate; he argued persuasively for a dangerous and subversive message.

This went on for three months. As with every city where Paul entered the local synagogue, he desperately wanted his Jewish brothers and sisters to see beyond Israel's political kingdom and catch a glimpse of God's kingdom. This is what God had been up to all along, as he would later write in his letter to Ephesus. But this message was not only subversive to Roman ears, it was a message that threatened Jewish nationalistic hopes and exposed the power structure of Jerusalem's temple. So inevitably, to use Luke's word, those in the synagogue became *obstinate*, stubbornly clinging to those hopes and power structures. In fact, we are told that they did not just disagree with Paul, they publicly maligned the Way – another designation for followers of Jesus (see *Labeling Followers of Jesus* below). The Greek word being used is *kakologeo* and literally means to speak evil of or to pronounce a curse upon the whole idea. It does not just indicate a rejection of Paul's message, but the beginning of a public smear campaign against Paul and the Way.

III

LABELING FOLLOWERS OF JESUS

While Luke and the apostles may have tried to maintain an early identity within Judaism, it soon became necessary to distinguish between those who would continue in traditional Judaism and those who recognized Jesus as the Messiah. They were known by a couple of different names:

1. *Christians* – the term, so common today, was originally used by those outside the faith, possibly even in a derogatory manner. It literally means "belonging to Christ (messiah)." It was first used in Antioch (Acts 11:26), probably by Romans. The only other time it is used in Acts is by Agrippa II. It is used only one other time in the New Testament outside of Acts.

2. *The Church* – among followers of Jesus, the most common distinguishing label was simply the Greek term *ekklesia*, or church. In classical Greek, the term refers to a gathering of citizens. In the New Testament, it came to be used to identify local gatherings of these followers of Jesus, and then expanded to his followers collectively. Matthew even uses the term in

his gospel account, suggesting that even Jesus referred to *gatherings* of his followers.

3. *The Way* – several times in Acts, Luke uses this term to refer to followers of Jesus. It is not used elsewhere as a formal label. It was probably an early designation that served as shorthand for the primary message of Jesus.[6] Jesus himself was *the way*, the truth, and the life. John's message was one of preparing *the way* for the Lord. There are biblical references to *the way* of God, *the way* of righteousness, and *the way* of peace, among others, so that the Way was a simple summary of the teachings of Jesus and *a way* to identify his followers as well.

III

So Paul left them and took his twelve disciples with him (a familiar pattern of Jesus). He found some space in the lecture hall of Tyrannus and began daily discussions regarding this kingdom of God with anyone who wanted to listen. We know little about this lecture hall. We can imagine that it was a place large enough for a teacher or philosopher to gather a group of disciples and conducive for public lectures.

A longer reading in some manuscripts gives us a little more detail about setting up shop in this lecture hall. Some manuscripts add to the end of verse nine that Paul lectured "from the fifth hour until the tenth hour." Whether this phrase was original to Luke or added to provide some further detail is not known, but the scenario is a probable one. Paul rented or used the space from the fifth hour until the tenth hour – or from 11 a.m. to 4 p.m. In other words, he used it after normal business hours during the hot part of the day. This would have allowed Paul to get up before daybreak, engage in the business of tent-making to support himself, and then hold these daily lectures in a hall that had probably been used earlier in the day by another scholar or philosopher. This also would distinguish Paul from other teachers of rhetoric and itinerate philosophers, who earned their living traveling from town to town, peddling their rhetoric to earn a living. Paul was careful to avoid being seen in this light as a peddler of the gospel – an impression that he was clearly dispelling in his letters to the Corinthian church.

This lecture hall would serve as a base of operations for the next two years, but Paul's impact spread far beyond the walls of the lecture hall. Luke tells us that not only the people living in Ephesus heard of Paul's teachings, but "all the Jews and Greeks who lived in the province of Asia" (Acts 19:10). Ephesus, being the Roman administrative center of the province of Asia, would have had travelers from all over the region coming to the city to do business. As word spread, no doubt some would listen in on Paul at Tyrannus Hall and then take his teachings back to their own towns. But keep in mind *Team Ephesus*: Paul would also have been sending out his fellow-workers to nearby cities and towns to gauge receptivity and help support small gatherings of believers in the surrounding towns. Ramsay theorizes that all seven of the churches mentioned in Revelation were probably founded during this time period, and each would have had some communication with Paul and his team, even if Paul did not personally visit.[7] There is little question that most of the churches in the province of Asia were established in one way or another during Paul's time in Ephesus.

The reference to two years also helps us with our timeline of Paul's ministry and stay in Ephesus. Yet it is unclear whether these two years are in addition to the three months spent teaching in the synagogue or whether it is inclusive. Furthermore, Paul would later reference a three-year time period that he labored among the Ephesians.[8] It could be that the two years (and three months) covered three calendar years to which Paul referred, or that he lectured in the hall of Tyrannus for two years *and then* spent more time in Ephesus teaching in another venue or engaging in a different ministry task. Additionally, the absence of any more references to Priscilla and Aquila during these three years in Ephesus is curious.

IMITATION IS THE SINCEREST FORM OF FLATTERY

Paul not only distinguished himself from itinerate rhetoricians and philosophers by supporting himself through tent-making, but what also set him apart was the power of the Holy Spirit that accompanied his teaching. Extraordinary things were taking place through Paul's ministry: The sick were being healed and the evil spirits dispersed. Luke is being deliberate, noting that both illnesses were cured *and* that evil spirits were being exorcised. Paul was more than just an effective teacher; he was more than traveling healer. His teaching centered on the risen Jesus, and the Holy Spirit was one means of authenticating that central message. The spread of the gospel meant the retreat of the forces of evil.

This authenticating presence of the Holy Spirit was so formidable that Paul did not even need to be present for extraordinary things to occur. It seems that even handkerchiefs and aprons that had touched Paul were enough to get the job done: "God did extraordinary miracles through Paul, so that even handkerchiefs and aprons that had touched him were taken to the sick, and their illnesses were cured and the evil spirits left them" (Acts 19:11,12). While this may conjure up images of prayer hankies and other blessed chachkies being peddled by late night televangelists, this is not what was being alluded to. These handkerchiefs and aprons were part of Paul's apparel as a leatherworker. The handkerchief was a small towel used for wiping sweat from the face, while the apron was a workman's apron that protected his clothes. With this in mind, we must wonder if Paul ever got frustrated at the beginning of his workday at the mysterious disappearance of yet another apron or more towels. Perhaps Paul needed a sign that hung in my uncle's office: "Tool Rules: Don't touch them, borrow them, move them; Don't even look at them."

These distinguishing features are important to take into account as Paul's work would stand in contrast to the copycats of the day. The work of Paul in Ephesus was advancing in powerful ways, so inevitably others – even rivals – tried to replicate the formula. (Even today, if one church appears successful, it is only a matter of time before *the formula* is marketed, packaged for a conference, and replicated in numerous settings.) Of course, Paul would be the first to say there was no secret to his apparent success; it was the power of being *in Christ Jesus*. And that was available to all!

But some wanted the power *of Christ Jesus* without being *in Christ Jesus*. Exorcists would have been fairly common in Paul's day, and exorcism often accompanied the role of being a priest or prophet. So it is not surprising that some Jews were also going around driving out evil spirits. But what is surprising is that they began invoking the name of Jesus as their backing authority: "In the name of Jesus, whom Paul preaches, I command you to come out" (Acts 19:13). The authority one used to perform such exorcisms was a central component of the agenda being promoted. Historian Martin Goodman writes, "The procedure is taken so much for granted by the author of Acts that the only issue raised in the exorcisms described was the authority of the exorcist."[9] It is quite surprising then, that these opponents of Paul were invoking the name of Jesus, whom Paul was preaching, as their authority. Apparently, these exorcists were pragmatists above all else.

To emphasize that Paul's message was not merely reducible to a magic formula or invoking the right authority, Luke gives a humorous anecdote of bringing this trivialization of the name of Jesus to an end. We are told that seven sons of Sceva, a Jewish chief priest, were engaging in this deception. Whether Sceva was an actual chief priest is debated, given that we have already been told that one of the local synagogues had engaged in a smear campaign of Paul and his message. It would be difficult to imagine that Sceva had any authority in any such synagogue. Additionally, his sons could simply be a reference to his disciples.

So one day as this particular group of exorcists were attempting to drive out an evil spirit, the spirit answered back, "Jesus I know, and I know about Paul, but who are you?" Talk about a blow to your credibility! It is not the only time in the New Testament where even evil spirits recognize who the real authority is. As if that were not enough, the man with the spirit commenced to beat them senseless so that they ran from the house bleeding, without their clothes, and without their dignity or credibility. Luke, of course, is continuing to build the case that Paul was operating under true authority and through legitimate means, while the copycats were the ones stirring up trouble.

IN THIS WAY THE WORD OF THE LORD SPREAD

The account of how these exorcists came to be the ones *cast out* seems to be a turning point for Paul's work in Ephesus. As the story spread, so did the honor given to the name of the Lord Jesus and authority that accompanied Paul's message. Jew and Greek alike were struck with fear and awe. This fear was not an irrational fear or superstition. It was a term used by Luke to indicate the realization by both believer and non-believer alike that they were encountering the divine, much like one would react when approaching royalty. Conveying this same idea, Peter simply writes, "Fear God, honor the king" (1 Peter 2:17). One might disagree with Paul and his message but the message had to be taken seriously and respected.

In fact, in today's church vernacular, we might say that a bit of a revival broke out in Ephesus. This fear and awe prompted many to come forward and renounce the ways they had been living. We are not told whether Paul set up a revival tent on the outskirts of town. Actually, it is not really indicated that from the beating of the exorcists to this revival of sorts, Paul was actively involved in any of it. Little doubt Luke is emphasizing the movement of the Holy Spirit over and above Paul's actions, lest any should mistake Paul himself for the authority he represented.

However, a good old-fashioned scroll burning does take place! Those who practiced sorcery collected their scrolls and burned them publicly. In a pagan city such as Ephesus, where up to this point the goddess Artemis held predominant reign, many would have fallen into this category. The philosophers of the city might not have given much credibility to the power of the gods, nor would the city's Jewish population (though belief in magic was not uncommon even in many Jewish communities). The emperor-cult was the closest thing to a shared religious worldview among Gentiles, and in Ephesus, worship of Artemis also served as a common bond. Thus, the belief in sorcery and magic would have been quite common.

THE EMPEROR-CULT

When Octavian was named emperor by his adoptive father, Julius Caesar, in 42 BC one of his first acts was to have Julius Caesar deified, being declared a god. This would make Octavian, who would become known as Caesar Augustus, son of a god (hence the dangerous claim of Jesus to be the Son of God). This practice continued for the next couple of centuries. While most

Caesars waited until their death to officially be declared a god, some, like Caligula, openly claimed deification during their reign.

This practice of deifying Roman emperors and their subsequent worship grew in popularity throughout the empire. Temples were built all over the empire to facilitate their worship. This was especially growing in popularity during the time of Paul. Thus, when Paul asserts that there is one God, he is also asserting that this one God was neither Caesar nor even Artemis, for that matter.

III

The type of sorcery being practiced typically include the belief in demons and the ability to drawn on divine power through magic. If someone got sick, a family member might just as easily visit the local priest/magician as the local doctor. They might have even been the same person! The scrolls would have contained word magic, reflecting a belief that certain combinations of letters and words could provide the possessor with the ability to bring supernatural forces into play for their own advantage.[10] In other parts of the ancient world, magic incantation bowls, as opposed to scrolls, were used for the same purpose. Ephesus was so well known for these magic scrolls that some of them came to be known as the *Ephesian Letters* (see *Ephesia Grammata* below).

The value of the scrolls would have come from the potency of the magic words and phrases they contained. If they had proven effective in bringing a curse or protection on someone, they would increase in value. And valuable they were! Luke tells us that the value of the scrolls that perished in the flames that day was calculated to be around fifty thousand drachmas - a drachma being a silver coin worth about a day's wage. The text simply states fifty thousand *coins* or *pieces of money*, but a drachma was no doubt the silver coin being referenced. Even if we use our minimum wage of today, that comes close to three million dollars! (That's a lot of charred records - or scrolls.) Luke is not simply telling the reader that Paul was having a spiritual impact on the city, but that his message was having economic ramifications as well. We can almost feel tensions beginning to mount.

III

EPHESIA GRAMMATA

The image of Artemis was purported to have inscribed on it six magic words. These six words were copied onto scrolls and made their way around the region as far back as the fourth century BC. These words became so well known that the first century writer Plutarch refers to these scrolls as the *Ephesian letters* (or Ephesia Grammata), a reference attested by other ancient writers as well.[11]

There are several variations of these words that have been found in other places, such as Crete and Sicily. No one is quite sure what these words mean, leading to speculation that the words themselves were not supposed to have any meaning. Rather their purpose was that they were to be recited or chanted correctly, with their power coming from their sound. They would be similar to our terms "abracadabra" or "hocus-pocus." Artemis, along with the Ephesia Grammata associated with her, served as safeguards for the people of Ephesus.

And so it was that "in this way the word of the Lord spread widely and grew in power" (Acts 19:20). This phrase is one of Luke's phrase-markers that served to summarize a large section of narrative and allows the reader to rise above the canopy of the sub-plots, details, and vignettes, and take in a view of the forest: The message of Jesus the Messiah was spreading throughout the Roman Empire and growing in legitimacy and strength. Luke had already marked off an earlier section by simply stating, "So the word of God spread," (Acts 6:7) and concluded another section with, "But the word of God continued to increase and spread," (Acts 12:24). Perhaps reflecting Paul's own mindset, Luke was wrapping up the details of Paul's stay in Ephesus. But there was much drama to come!

THE END OF THE STORY, ALMOST

Having spent considerable time in Ephesus, Paul now made plans to return to Jerusalem, via Macedonia and Achaia. Similar to the conclusion of his second missionary journey, his plan was to leave Ephesus in time to pass through Macedonia, down to Corinth, and reach Jerusalem in time for Pentecost.[12] After that, he envisioned finally making the journey to Rome!

It was probably around the end of the year 55. Paul even sent two members of *Team Ephesus* ahead to make preparations in Macedonia. Timothy had accompanied Paul throughout his second journey and was now back in Ephesus. Erastus was from Corinth and had likewise joined Paul at some point in Ephesus. He would spend the spring and summer traveling through Macedonia and then spend the winter in Corinth. This would allow him to set sail for Jerusalem in the early spring of 57 and arrive in time for Pentecost.

Having sent Timothy and Erastus on their way, Paul must have reflected back on his time in Ephesus: A whole team of people was working for the advancement of the gospel, the Holy Spirit was moving in powerful ways, imitators had been exposed, paganism was being discarded to the flames, the church of Ephesus was growing in strength and legitimacy, no doubt along with several other smaller churches in adjacent towns, and the word of the Lord was spreading widely and growing in power. Paul was ready to pull up his tent-stakes, but then tensions would erupt and make for a stressful end to Paul's extended stay in Ephesus.

A CHANGE OF PLANS

Sounding like something straight out of a *Star Wars* movie, Luke (not Skywalker!) breaks the calm with the report that "about that time there arose a great disturbance about the Way" (Acts 19:23). Just as Paul was about to leave the gospel message in good hands, the message would face serious resistance, not from the Jews, but this time from the Greeks living in Ephesus. As the Holy Spirit encroached on paganism, the Way would collide with those who grew prosperous by advancing paganism. The result was a great disturbance. The account of what happens next is told in temporal terms, but as Luke has stressed throughout, this was nothing less than the clash of the spiritual forces behind both paganism and the Way.

The Temple of Artemis contributed greatly to the economy of Ephesus. Just as a modern-day sports team would draw fans throughout the region on game day, Artemis drew pilgrims from the region on a continual basis. And these pilgrims ate at local establishments, stayed at the inns, made offerings at the temple ... and purchased souvenirs - statuettes of the great image of Artemis and shrines of the temple in which she resided. These statuettes and shrines could be taken home and erected as part of household shrines, believing that they would bring protection and health to the home.

A number of these statuettes and shrines have actually been unearthed. The shrines depict Artemis seated in the temple accompanied by lions. Statuettes display Artemis standing with head crowned and covered in numerous symbolic designs. A distinctive feature seems to be her many breasts, perhaps symbolizing fertility, protection during childbirth, and guardianship.

An entire industry had sprung up around the production of these shrines. In fact, this industry brought in so much business for the people involved that a trade guild was formed around the production of these shrines. Trade guilds were similar to our unions of today. The workers organized, protected their industry, and formed powerful political and economic blocs (see *Trade Guilds in the Roman Empire* below). Most likely, the leader of the silversmiths' guild in Ephesus was a man named Demetrius. Luke identifies Demetrius as a silversmith who made silver shrines of Artemis. It is not known whether these silver shrines refer to the statuettes of Artemis, which have been found made of silver, or whether they refer specifically to replicas of the temple itself. Samples of these have been unearthed, but are made of materials other than silver. Regardless, the Way was becoming such a threat to the livelihood of these silversmiths that Demetrius called a meeting of this guild, along with other related trades, to do a threat-assessment.

TRADE GUILDS IN THE ROMAN EMPIRE

Similar to unions of today, tradesmen and craftsmen in the Roman Empire often found it economically advantageous to form corporations, or trade guilds, around a particular skill or industry. These guilds made it easier for craftsmen to protect their industry, set prices, and share trade skills. Trade guilds also held political sway in certain areas of the empire. In other areas, these guilds functioned more like the mafia, controlling and extorting local business districts.

Due to the practice of advertising a particular guild on stone inscriptions, more than a 150 trades have been identified, demonstrating the popularity of such organizations.[13] Scholar Jerome Murphy-O'Connor writes that in Ephesus alone, inscriptions have been found identifying the existence of such guilds as silversmiths, doctors, bakers, wine dealers, wool dealers, towel weavers, hemp dealers, cobblers, temple builders, surveyors, and bath workers.[14]

In his address to the various guild-members (no doubt Luke only gives us the bullet points), Demetrius makes note of three specific issues. First, the Temple of Artemis brought in a good business for their guilds. The specific word used here could even suggest that these shrines were making them all very wealthy! As long as the temple stood and the tourists showed up, there was enough demand to share the wealth.

Second, Paul's message was perceived as a threat to the Temple of Artemis. Demetrius was savvy enough to realize that Paul's message of the God of Israel being the one, true God and Jesus being the Messiah, essentially stripped Artemis of her divinity and power. Specifically, Paul, as he had done in Athens previously, was rejecting the widely held pagan belief in the power associated with idols. Demetrius went as far as accusing Paul of leading people astray with this message. Interestingly, within this accusation Demetrius attests to the rapid spread of the gospel with his claim that people were being led astray not only in Ephesus, but "practically the whole province of Asia" (Acts 19:26).

Third, if Artemis were to be discredited, then the guilds associated with the temple would be economically ruined. Demetrius actually placed the greater danger in Artemis being discredited over the fortune of the guilds. It is difficult to interpret how much of his speech was driven by religious devotion and how much was motivated by greed. As in most cases, it was probably a mixture of both, but the bottom line was money. What is clear is that their fortunes were tied to the fortunes of the temple. As with the second point, Demetrius also attests to the widespread popularity of Artemis in the province of Asia and throughout the Roman Empire. So what was to be done?

THE MOB HAS MANY HEADS, BUT NO BRAINS

It seems that the speech by Demetrius was quite effective, for the guild meeting soon turned into a frenzy that spread through the city like wildfire. The craftsmen began chanting, "Great is Artemis of the Ephesians" and soon the chant spilled out into the city streets. As mobs usually go, people began looking for a target for their fury. Unfortunately, two members of *Team Ephesus* happened to be in the wrong place at the wrong time. Gaius and Aristarchus became convenient targets. Being recognized as two of Paul's coworkers, they were snatched off the street and carried into the great amphitheater by a mob that moved as one entity. The scene in the amphitheater was utter confusion. The chanting continued, though now many different things were being chanted. Predictably, Luke reports that many did not even know why they were there; they were simply drawn into the entity and gawked at the spectacle of it all.

Understandably, when Paul received word of these events he was eager to appear before the crowd to defend himself and his friends. But some of the hometown disciples, perhaps with a better pulse on the rising tensions, restrained Paul from doing so. Even some of the local officials sent word that it would not be in Paul's best interest to face the mob. The fact that these officials were friends of Paul, perhaps disciples themselves, again tells us just how far the gospel message had advanced in Ephesus.

In an interesting move amidst the chaos, the Jews attempted to have Alexander speak on their behalf. We should not presume that the defense he attempted was on behalf of Paul. Rather it is more likely that, given the hostilities between the synagogue and Paul, the Jews were attempting to disassociate themselves with these followers of the Way. The crowd, however, simply lumped the Jews and Christians together as monotheists, and thus opposed to the idol-worship of Artemis.

This Alexander may have been quite the opponent of Paul. The name *Alexander* is a common one, so definitive connections can be hard to establish. But in both of Paul's letters to Timothy, who by the time of those writings had been given charge over the church in Ephesus, he warns Timothy of a man named Alexander.[15] In both cases he uses very strong language, summarized in the statement: "Alexander the metalworker did me a great deal of harm. The Lord will repay him for what he has done." If the connection is there, Alexander was a well-known nemesis, as both Luke and Paul chose to single him out. He would have been a Jew who became a disciple of the Way, then had to be excluded from the church for his blasphemous rhetoric (1 Timothy 1:20), causing great damage to the church. On the other hand, there were, no doubt, many *Alexanders* in Ephesus.

ORDER IS RESTORED

This scene in the amphitheater continued for two hours: "Great is Artemis of the Ephesians!" The crowd did not quiet until a city official made an appearance and addressed the issue. Luke identifies the official as the city clerk (*grammateus*), which brings up the political structure of a city like Ephesus.

Each province of Rome would have been governed by a proconsul. The proconsul was appointed by Rome and functioned as a governor, ruling from the capitol of that province. In this case, Ephesus was the capitol of the province of Asia. Under the eye of the proconsul, the city itself was governed by a two-house system: a council, which was led by the city clerk (*grammateus*), and an assembly of the people (*ekklesia*), which was led by a clerk of the people.[16]

So when Luke writes that the city clerk quieted the people, he is referring to a senior official of the city. This senior official, sounding very much like a politician, appeases the crowd while injecting some much-needed rationality into the frenzy. He began by reassuring the crowd that Artemis was known throughout the Roman world and Paul and his teachings were not about to supplant that notoriety (at least he uses this rationale to calm the crowd). In speaking of Artemis, he mentions "her image, which fell from heaven." It is not clear what is meant by this phrase (a single word in Greek). The word in general refers to something that was given by the gods, hence coming from the heavens. It could also refer specifically to a stone, which fell from heaven. Accordingly, some have speculated that the site of the temple may have been chosen because of a meteor that fell there. Ancient sources do not give us much of a clue and the language only serves to add to the mystery and the sense of the sacred that surrounded the Temple of Artemis.

Having calmed the crowd, the clerk then reminds the crowd that, in light of the widespread reputation of Artemis, the two men dragged into the amphitheater had not actually done anything wrong. They (presumably he was including Paul here as well) had neither directly attacked the reputation of Artemis nor attempted to rob her temple. Since temples also frequently served as repositories of great wealth for safe-keeping (including the temple in Jerusalem), robbing a temple was both a serious civil offense as well as a supreme act of sacrilege. Obviously, the notion that Paul and his team attempted something so blatant was ludicrous.

If there was no legal basis for the commotion, the mob scene and the illegal detaining of these two men could potentially be interpreted by Rome as a riot, and a riot in a Roman province brought swift and brutal justice. In 70 AD, Jerusalem would learn this the hard way. If there was something to pursue, Demetrius and his associates were free to file charges in a court of law. After all, the proconsul of Asia resided in Ephesus. If there was anything else to bring up, it had to be done in a legal assembly – an official *ekklesia* of the people.

Luke cites the role of the city clerk because, while his speech was not a legal ruling, it served as somewhat of an acquittal of Paul and his activities during his time in Ephesus.[17] It is ironic that this event demonstrates that it is the followers of Artemis that are forming mobs, gathering unlawfully, and throwing the city into an uproar, and not the followers of the Way. It was a common charged levied against the Way throughout Paul's journeys, yet this particular example served to expose the real culprits.

That this event left an indelible impression on Paul is clear from his letters to the Corinthian church. Assuming that Paul wrote 1 Corinthians just before he left Ephesus to inform them of his plan to visit (which seems clear from 1 Corinthians 16:5-9), then Paul alludes to this event a couple of times, which will be covered in detail in the next chapter. For now, it will be sufficient to stress that the danger that had arisen in Ephesus was very real to Paul.

With the upheaval behind him, Paul proceeded with his plan to leave Ephesus and travel through Macedonia, eventually reaching Corinth. He "sent for the disciples and, after encouraging them, said goodbye and set out for Macedonia" (Acts 20:1). Despite the danger, there is no clear indication that Paul was forced out of the city, as some scholars have asserted. While Paul had earlier been forced to leave Thessalonica on his second missionary journey, there is not a similar sense of fleeing Ephesus. In fact, the speech of the clerk indicates that Paul had a legal right to remain in Ephesus if he chose. Despite the near-death experience, Paul's time in Ephesus had been fruitful and successful. It was time to move on.

4 PAUL'S FAREWELL TO EPHESUS

Gaius ordered that a sacred precinct should be set apart for his worship at Miletus in the province of Asia. The reason he gave for choosing this city was that Diana had preempted Ephesus, Augustus Pergamum, and Tiberius Smyrna. But the truth of the matter was he desired to appropriate to his own use the large and exceedingly beautiful temple which the Milesians were building to Apollo.

- Dio Cassius, *Roman History*

L ike Ephesus, Miletus is now landlocked. Much of the site floods with the rains, yet rising above the marshy ruins is a well-preserved theater, which seats about 15,000 spectators. In many ways, the site resembles and rivals Ephesus, with its harbor, theater, bath complex, and adjoining temple precinct to Artemis' twin-sibling, Apollo. A ten-mile processional way joins Miletus with the site of Didyma and the Temple of Apollo. What is no longer visible at Ephesus can be visualized quite vividly at Didyma. The Temple of Apollo at Didyma was the third largest temple in the Greek world and patterned after the Temple of Artemis at Ephesus. One can truly get a sense of what the Artemis precinct must have been like by walking through the immense ruins at Didyma.

Acts 20 begins with the statement that "when the uproar had ended, Paul sent for the disciples and, after encouraging them, said good-by and set out for Macedonia." Paul had already sent Timothy and Erastus ahead to inform the churches of Macedonia of his arrival and travel schedule. Returning to our timeline, Paul probably left Ephesus sometime after Pentecost in 56 AD. He would have spent the remaining part of the year making his way through Macedonia, visiting the churches of Philippi, Thessalonica, and Berea. Luke says little about this leg of the journey, only that "he traveled through that area, speaking many words of encouragement to the people, and finally arrived in Greece," where he would winter in Corinth for three months.

His plan was to sail for Syria when the sailing season resumed after the winter months, but he caught wind of another plot hatched by Jewish leaders and decided it safer to backtrack the familiar roads of Macedonia, where he had plenty of friends to watch out for him. Seven of these friends, listed in Acts 20, would accompany him all the way to Jerusalem.

Since he wanted to reach Jerusalem for Pentecost, but could not sail directly from Corinth to Syria, time was now of the essence. He hurried back through Macedonia, spending Passover (April 5, 57) in Philippi, leaving him fifty days to travel to Jerusalem. Five days after departing Philippi he reached Troas in the province of Asia and remained there a week.

Here we pick back up on Luke's narrative. Noting the switch back to Luke's use of the first person, Philippi is apparently where Luke rejoined Paul on his journeys, which makes some sense as it was upon leaving Philippi on his second missionary journey that Luke began writing in the third person. In any case, Luke now inserts himself back into the story.

We went on ahead to the ship and sailed for Assos, where we were going to take Paul aboard. He had made this arrangement because he was going there on foot. When he met us at Assos, we took him aboard and went on to Mitylene. The next day we set sail from there and arrived off Chios. The day after that we crossed over to Samos, and on the following day arrived at Miletus. Paul had decided to sail past Ephesus to avoid spending time in the province of Asia, for he was in a hurry to reach Jerusalem, if possible, by the day of Pentecost. From Miletus, Paul sent to Ephesus for the elders of the church. (Acts 20:13-17)

Luke continued to recount the travel itinerary, making personal observations, such as Paul's preference to make the short journey from Troas to Assos by foot instead of sailing around the small peninsula. As each day passed, it became apparent that if they were to make Jerusalem by Pentecost, they could not afford to get detained any further. No doubt, if they had passed back through Ephesus, the believers would insist that Paul stay for a week or more, allowing them to refresh and encourage him before sending him off to Jerusalem. After having spent three years with them, it would have been discourteous for Paul to simply stay overnight and hurry out the next morning.

But he did want an update on his friends in Ephesus and to share some thoughts that had been brewing in his mind since he had left them. All of this serves to explain his decision to sail past Ephesus, avoiding a potentially awkward situation, and instead choosing to meet the elders of the Ephesian church in Miletus. Miletus would be the backdrop for a very heart-felt and transparent conversation between Paul and his longtime friends from Ephesus.

🏛

A SNAPSHOT OF MILETUS

Miletus shares much of the same history as Ephesus, though readers of scripture will be much less familiar with it. It was probably founded about the same time as Ephesus, around the sixth century BC, although the area was inhabited earlier. It is situated about thirty miles south of Ephesus along the coast. After being destroyed by the Persians, it was rebuilt by one of the Greek world's first urban architects, Hippodamus, who utilized the grid system for laying out the city. Miletus, along with Ephesus and ten other cities, formed the Ionian League, a loose alliance of city-states in the region of Asia Minor that not only shared some cultural similarities, but produced some rivalries as well. Miletus boasted four harbors and was home to influential early philosophers, known as the Milesian School.

It was this well-organized, flourishing city (along with Ephesus) that would come under Roman rule. Even though the glory days of Miletus were already in the past by the time Paul met the Ephesian elders on the beach, remains of a 15,000-seat amphitheater attest to the city's size and stature in the province of Asia during the time of the Roman Empire. It also boasted the region's first public bath house, a large temple to Apollo, and was known for its production of luxurious wool.

Miletus ultimately shared the fate of Ephesus, when over time the Maeander River silted up its harbors and it lost its status as an important port for commercial trading. Paul mentions visiting Miletus again in his second letter to Timothy (2 Timothy 4:20).

🏛

FROM THE FIRST DAY I CAME TO ASIA

When the Ephesian elders arrived, they spent some time catching up, both on the happenings at Ephesus and on the events of Paul's journey since leaving them. No doubt, Paul offered an explanation of why he summoned them to Miletus instead of stopping in for an extended visit. He, in no way, meant for them to feel slighted. After catching up, we can imagine Paul quieting the chatter of friends and side conversations; he obviously had something weighing on him that he wanted to share.

He began by reviewing his three-year ministry with them in Ephesus. His focus was not so much on *what* was accomplished at Ephesus under his leadership - they certainly needed no reminder of that – but rather *how* he led them. From day one, he led them with *humility* and *passion*. His work of spreading the gospel was not an easy one; it had its share of opponents. Yet Paul never domineered over the church, nor did he detach himself from the issues the Ephesians faced. They shed many tears together.

He had also led them *publicly*: "You know that I have not hesitated to preach anything that would be helpful to you but have taught you publicly and from house to house" (Acts 20:20). This was not a covert operation with secret meetings; his ministry was on display for all to witness. He preached in public places - his gatherings at the Tyrannus lecture hall were open to anyone who wanted to drop in - and the church met in homes in the midst of city life, not secretly on the outskirts of town.

Finally, his motivations were *pure* and his message was *clear* to any who would listen: Repent, turn to God, and have faith in Jesus. He was not trying to build a following for his own gain, but his goal was to add to the kingdom.

There are a couple of important reasons why Paul reminisced about the way he conducted his ministry in Ephesus. This was much more than merely shooting the breeze. Paul was being driven by a growing sense that tensions would boil over in Jerusalem, and that a showdown between he and the Jewish leaders could result in his imprisonment or worse. If Paul wrote Romans from Corinth the previous winter, as many scholars contend, then his tone changed drastically from the optimism he expressed to the Roman church: "After I have completed this task [of taking the contribution to Jerusalem] and have made sure that they have received this fruit, I will go to Spain and visit you on the way" (Romans 15:28). Compare that statement to the uncertainty he was expressing to the Ephesian elders. Perhaps the change in attitude can be attributed to the plot of the Jews (Acts 20:3) to seize Paul as he sailed from Corinth to Syria on his way to Jerusalem. The uncovering of this plot prompted Paul to change his plans, taking the land route back through Macedonia and Asia. Paul knew that his Jewish opponents would be waiting for him in Jerusalem, if they did not apprehend him sooner.

Paul's second concern was that if something did happen in Jerusalem, who would protect these young Gentile churches from the Jewish leaders who either denied that Jesus was the Messiah or would try to *Judaize* the Gentile believers? Paul had already chased these agitators[1] away from the seedling churches in the region of Galatia. Like birds perched in the branches, they would no doubt swoop in and consume the seed of the gospel should anything happen to Paul, leaving the churches unprotected. Paul, in fact, addresses this very danger later in his speech. Furthermore, if Rome got involved in a potential dispute taking place in Jerusalem, would it cast doubt on the legitimacy of the Way and spark a wave of persecution?

The reasons for concern become explicit with Paul's next statement regarding his intent to press on to Jerusalem, despite the unknown: "I only know that in every city the Holy Spirit warns me that prison and hardships are facing me" (Acts 20:23). The element of the unknown clearly weighed on him, but not for his own well-being; he considered his own life "worth nothing." He was more concerned that what might transpire in Jerusalem would have damaging consequences for the Gentile churches in Asia, Macedonia, and Achaia.

THIS IS OUR LAST GOODBYE

There are times when, in an effort to reinforce the spiritual pedestal we place scriptural figures upon (such as Paul), we can strip them of their humanity. Even when scripture itself is allowing us a glimpse of weakness and fear, we tend to explain it away or keep it at a distance. It strikes me that this is one of those times.

When one reads this speech, allowing emotions and tears to stain the pages of scripture, one gets the impression that Paul really was fearful - dare we say *scared* - about what would transpire in Jerusalem. Yes, Paul had been in prison, survived a stoning, beaten, and threatened. He has already stated that it is not his own life that he is concerned about. He wears his brave face well.

But when reading these next verses, would it not be more human to allow Paul to sit with dear friends and admit that he is scared about what Jerusalem holds for him? Even upon reading this, some may become uncomfortable with such an image. Yet it might help in understanding why Paul declares that he is certain none of them will ever see him again. It was a heart-rending statement, one that caused the Ephesians grief. But it ended up not being the case. As much as Paul believed that Jerusalem would be the death of him (why else would he make that statement?), we find out later that he almost certainly visited Ephesus again.

Fast-forward the story for a moment: After being released from prison in Rome, Paul and Timothy traveled through Asia and Macedonia. He left Timothy in Ephesus and then corresponded with him as he continued to touch base with the Macedonian churches. In his first letter to Timothy, he writes, "As I urged you when I went into Macedonia, stay there in Ephesus..." (1 Timothy 1:3). He would, in fact, see them again, but at the moment, it certainly felt like this was their last goodbye.

If it were to be the last time he saw them, Paul could declare that he had done everything in his power to announce the kingdom of God and warn people of the dangers of rejecting that announcement. This is the meaning behind the statement that "that I am innocent of the blood of everyone" (Acts 20:26). The prophet Ezekiel made a similar statement when he was told by God that as long as he warned exiled Israel of their unfaithfulness, he would not be held accountable for their blood, regardless of their response (see Ezekiel 3:16-19). Ezekiel's job was to sound the warning. No doubt Paul felt a similar burden and believed he had been faithful to the call.

Having been faithful to his call, he was now passing that same responsibility on to the Ephesian elders. They were now the overseers, appointed by the Holy Spirit, of this flock. They were now the shepherds over God's church. This imagery would also hearken back to Ezekiel's warnings to the shepherds (spiritual leaders) of Israel. This was a commissioning service!

As shepherds and overseers, they were to be on their guard. It would not take long for wolves to test the resolve of the shepherds and threaten the flock. As mentioned previously, this was one of Paul's very real concerns: If something were to happen to him in Jerusalem, who would hold their ground against the agitators - the wolves, the scavenging birds – who would descend on an unprotected community of believers? Paul had been at this long enough to know that sometimes the biggest threats are internal (just as many pastors today would be able to verify!). The responsibility that Paul carried for three years was now squarely on their shoulders.

Commissioning the Ephesian elders and committing their work to God, Paul left them with one last reminder. He had carried on his work in Ephesus without being a financial drain on the church. He had earned his own income: "I have not coveted anyone's silver or gold or clothing. You yourselves know that these hands of mine have supplied my own needs and the needs of my companions" (Acts 20:33,34). As mentioned previously, Paul was careful to avoid being seen as a peddler of the gospel. If he were rendered unable to safeguard his work in Ephesus, he wanted to reinforce to the Ephesian elders that his motive was not to profit from the church, or even to be compensated for his work.

It should be noted that Paul's refusal to accept compensation for his ministry work appears to be more of a personal decision and not a universal objection. Elsewhere, Paul does affirm the legitimacy of teachers getting compensated for their work.[2] But because of the itinerant nature of his calling, Paul personally did not want to have the gospel message convoluted with other philosophies or the Sophist teachers who traveled about marketing their wisdom. If he were detained, it would undoubtedly be one of the first accusations from the agitators: Paul was only in this for his own gain.

No, his only motive was to help the weak (those who had little faith or were new to the faith), following the example of Jesus himself: "It is more blessed to give than to receive." (This quote from Jesus is one of the few times in scripture where words attributed to Jesus are not directly quoted in one of the gospel accounts.) If there were ever any questioning of Paul's work in Ephesus, they need look no further than his own actions. In other words, "Follow my example, as I follow the example of Christ" (1 Corinthians 11:1).

With those words quoting Jesus, Paul and his friends knelt on the beach and prayed - for Paul himself, as well as for the church at Ephesus. It was an emotional scene as the elders said their goodbyes and then accompanied Paul to the ship. They would head back to Ephesus, but no doubt wondered if it could possibly be true that they would never see Paul again.

Even though Paul would return to Ephesus one day, his fears were not unfounded. His sea voyage would continue to Caesarea, where he then journeyed inland to Jerusalem in time for Pentecost. The growing threats against him materialized when he was apprehended in Jerusalem on trumped up charges of bringing a Gentile - an Ephesian, no less - into the inner courts of the temple. The remainder of the book of Acts recounts Paul's two-year imprisonment in Caesarea, where he appeared before the Roman governors Felix, and then Festus. Upon appealing to his Roman citizenship, he was then transported to Rome on a harrowing sea-faring journey that included a shipwreck and being stranded on the island of Malta. Paul spent two years in Rome under house arrest awaiting his trial. It was during this time that Paul wrote to his friends back in Ephesus, and produced the letter included in scripture known as Ephesians, which we will turn to shortly.

CONCLUSIONS FROM THE BOOK OF ACTS

So what groundwork does Acts establish for this letter to Ephesus? What can we conclude from Luke's account of Paul's three-year ministry in Ephesus? One of the aims of this book is to grasp Paul and his letters at a more contextual level before moving to present-day application. This will keep us from letting the text mean anything we want it to mean. To this end, it will be of assistance if we allow the following contextual points to add meaning to, and serve as a backdrop for, the epistle of Ephesians.

First, Ephesus, along with the Temple of Artemis, was one of the most influential cities in the Roman Empire. Along with being one of the largest cities in the empire, it also served as the Roman administrative center for the province of Asia. Before the city of Constantinople served as the bridge between Europe and Asia, Ephesus was the gateway to Asia and beyond. Trade routes from the east went through Ephesus and its port moved commerce to and from Rome, as well as to Greece, in the west. No wonder, even in Paul's day, Ephesus was seen "not as a land of sojourn, but as the desired destination: bustling and glamorous."[3]

The Temple of Artemis not only made Ephesus an influential cultural and religious center, but because of its dual role as a bank, it also made Ephesus the financial center of Asia Minor. Pagan worshippers were drawn to the temple's importance and Roman elites were drawn to the temple's wealth. Ephesus and Artemis were intimately linked in their collective identity. Thus, it is no mere footnote when Paul writes to the saints *in Ephesus*.

Second, Ephesus served as a base of operations for Paul's ministry to the whole province of Asia, and he had an entire team helping him with this ministry. Paul's three-year stay in Ephesus marked the longest amount of time he chose to invest in a single city while on his missionary journeys. Perhaps this road warrior wanted a place to hang his walking stick for a while. But he undoubtedly recognized the potential of reaching many of the smaller neighboring towns through teamwork and delegation. Instead of traveling from town to town, he could focus on the far-reaching influence of Ephesus, while concurrently developing the surrounding churches by having them come to him. This explains the numerous people that are linked to Paul through his time at Ephesus (and these are just the people we know of!). This has led some to speculate that Ephesians is actually a circular letter that would make the rounds throughout the whole province of Asia - an issue that will be addressed later.

Third, the church in Ephesus grew in strength and legitimacy during Paul's three years there, and was having a spiritual, philosophical, and economic impact within the broader culture. Luke's account of the events in Ephesus serves to reinforce his assertion that the word of the Lord was spreading widely and growing in power. Christianity was a legitimate expression of the messianic hope found in Judaism and this was being accepted at every level of society – rich and poor, slave and public servant, Jew and Roman. If Rome were to contest Christianity, it would have to contest it at every level. The impact of the church in Ephesus would continue to resonate for some 400 years, long after the apostle Paul had left town. The post-Pauline influence of the church in Ephesus will be covered in a later chapter.

Fourth, the mob scene at the amphitheater in Ephesus left an indelible impression on Paul. Luke devotes half of the chapter recounting Paul's time in Ephesus to this single event. If the allusions are correct, then Paul refers to this event in both of his letters to the church at Corinth (see below), and again in his first letter to Timothy. We might expect Paul to make further allusion to this event when he corresponds back to the Ephesian church. Having already covered this event in the previous chapter, as well as exploring it further below, we will not belabor the point at this time.

Fifth, if something happened to Paul in Jerusalem, the agitators would certainly test the faith of the Ephesians and Rome could potentially declare their faith an act of subversion. From Paul's perspective, he had spent the previous five years wresting control away from the Jewish leaders, leaving the Gentile converts unburdened by the minutiae of Mosaic Law and instructing them only in the essentials of the faith. Nevertheless, at every step of the journey those who insisted on Judaizing the Gentiles were not far behind. Yet, from Luke's perspective, a clean break from Judaism would jeopardize the legality of the Way within the Roman Empire. It would be a tightrope that would be maneuvered for the next 250 years before the emperor Constantine settled the matter for good.

Any discussion of Paul's letter to the Ephesians would, at the very least, need to keep these points close at hand. To disregard these points would be like reading Tolstoy and disregarding the impact of the Russian revolution on his writing. These points may or may not by explicitly mentioned by Paul in his letter, but they were certainly not far from his mind as he wrote Ephesians.

WHAT CAN BE LEARNED FROM THE CORINTHIAN CORRESPONDENCE?

It has already been mentioned that Paul's letters to the Corinthian church were closely tied to his stay in Ephesus. Paul makes it clear in 1 Corinthians that he was writing from Ephesus, probably in the fall of 55: "I hope to spend some time with you, if the Lord permits, but I will stay on at Ephesus until Pentecost" (1 Corinthians 16:7, 8). After he left Ephesus to go to Corinth via Macedonia, he wrote 2 Corinthians sometime in 56 to inform them of his change in travel plans: "I planned to visit you first so that you might benefit twice. I planned to visit you on my way to Macedonia and to come back to you from Macedonia, and then to have you send me on my way to Judea" (2 Corinthians 1:15, 16). The Corinthian correspondence as a whole is complicated by references to additional letters from Paul that are no longer extant. (1 Corinthians mentions both a letter from the Corinthians and a previous letter Paul had written to the Corinthians. 2 Corinthians mentions another letter that may have been written in between the two extant letters.)[4] So might this surviving correspondence written from Ephesus, or soon after departing Ephesus, give us some additional insights? Almost certainly, it does.

The first insight from the Corinthian correspondence only serves to reinforce the very real danger Paul felt from the mob scene at the Great Theater in Ephesus. It appears to be the very event Paul had in his mind when he wrote, "For it seems to me that God has put us apostles on display at the end of the procession, like those condemned to die in the arena" (1

Corinthians 4:9). The Great Theater in Ephesus almost served as his arena! He makes an even clearer reference to this event when he later writes, "If I fought wild beasts in Ephesus with no more than human hopes, what have I gained?" (1 Corinthians 15:32). Again, something happened in Ephesus that made him fear for his life and he could only recall the imagery of the arena to describe it. Writing later from the Macedonian leg of his trip, Paul again tells the church in Corinth, "We do not want you to be uninformed, brothers and sisters, about the hardships we suffered in the province of Asia. We were under great pressure, far beyond our ability to endure, so that we despaired of life itself. Indeed, we felt we had received the sentence of death" (2 Corinthians 1:8-9).

When we combine these images, what emerges is a picture of a Roman triumph. Roman triumphs were the rewards of military achievements in which the Roman emperor would victoriously march into Rome (or other cities) in an elaborate procession. This procession consisted of dignitaries, sacrificial animals, prisoners of war, and the emperor himself. When the emperor Caligula was planning his triumph, the biographer Suetonius writes, "Besides the captives and barbarian refugees, he selected all the tallest men of Gaul, men 'fit for a triumph' as he himself would say … who were to take part in the procession."[5] The fate of such prisoners is confirmed by Josephus, when writing of the future emperor Titus marching prisoners triumphantly into Caesarea Philippi during the Jewish war: "Here a great number of the captives were destroyed, some being thrown to wild beasts, and others in the multitudes forced to kill one another, as if they were enemies."[6] These triumphs declared in every imaginable way the glories of Rome and the humiliation of any who might try to challenge that glory.

THE TRIUMPHAL PROCESSION
The procession was part of the triumph that allowed the general public to take in the events of a military victory in the form of an elaborate parade. Long before the days of embedded reporters and television cameras, this procession was a living documentary – or propaganda, as the case may be - of what had transpired in distant lands. According to William Ramsay, the procession would typically advance in the following order:[7]
1. The Senate
2. A body of trumpeters
3. Carriages displaying the spoils of the war
4. A body of flute-players
5. White bulls or oxen to be sacrificed
6. Strange animals native to the conquered land, such as elephants

7. The arms and insignia of the enemy
8. The enemy leaders, followed by captives
9. Gifts given by foreign dignitaries and allies
10. The emperor on a horse-drawn chariot
11. The sons of the emperor and others on horseback
12. The army in marching order

The procession often ended with sacrifices at the Temple of Jupiter and the execution of the enemy king, as well as other captives.

There is little doubt that seeing his colleagues being dragged into the amphitheater and he, himself, being threatened, Paul considered himself to be someone nearly "fit for a triumph." It was why he wrote to the Corinthian church that, while in Ephesus, they were "put on display at the end of a procession," fighting wild beasts, and despairing for life itself. It would become his defining image to describe the mob scene at Ephesus.

A further word needs to be said about the description given in 1 Corinthians 4. When the entire passage is examined beyond the imagery of processing into the arena, we might question whether this passage is a description of Paul's entire time in Ephesus or more specifically, to his circumstances after the events at the amphitheater? Furthermore, might this passage indicate that Paul was forced to leave Ephesus?

To answer the first question, when we compare this brief description to Luke's three-year account of Paul's time in Ephesus, it does not seem to give the same impression. Paul certainly was not "homeless" for the two or three years he lived in Ephesus. He had a team around him, including people like Priscilla and Aquila who had a house of their own. He held daily meetings in the Tyrannus lecture hall. To revisit Luke's summary, after many spiritual victories in Ephesus, "the word of the Lord spread widely and grew in power." But the riot in the Great Theater seemed to change all that. For the few months Paul spent in Ephesus following the riots, he was mistreated, cursed, persecuted, and slandered. It was from this situation that Paul wrote to Corinth expressing the pitiful condition he found himself in after such a vibrant time of ministry in Ephesus.

As for the second question, was Paul now literally homeless and hungry, indicating that he was forced to leave Ephesus? It is actually difficult to find commentaries that relate this passage specifically to Ephesus, but some do conclude that Paul was essentially forced out of the city. For example, Jerome Murphy-O'Connor finalizes Paul's time in Ephesus by writing, "We are forced to assume that a sudden increase in the intensity of the hostility surrounding Paul eventually forced him to abandon Ephesus."[8] But given

Luke's account and the whole of Paul's correspondence with Corinth, this conclusion may reach too far. Luke ends by stressing the acquittal of sorts by the city clerk regarding Paul and his activities. Paul, himself, has time to correspond, to plan, and to linger in Ephesus until Pentecost. It is possible that he may have been briefly detained while officials sorted out the charges in the aftermath of the riot. However, Luke gives no indication that Paul was forced out of Ephesus. Rather Paul seems to be expressing his reaction to the riot and his ongoing status as a missionary who did not have the luxury of calling any one place home.

A second insight from the Corinthian correspondence relates to the collection for Jerusalem. As previously mentioned, the collection was a major point of emphasis on Paul's third missionary journey. He was anxious to strengthen relations between the Jerusalem church and the Gentile churches, and thus was urging the Gentile churches to set aside sums of money on a regular basis that he could deliver to the Jerusalem church and subsequently be distributed to the poor. Several references in the Corinthian correspondence (including two entire chapters of 2 Corinthians, chapters 8 and 9) remind us that the collection for the saints, as he would refer to it, was still a major point of emphasis.

This merits noting because while the Galatian churches, the Macedonian churches, and the church at Corinth are all linked to the collection, Ephesus is never explicitly linked to it. One might be tempted to conclude that the collection was not part of Paul's agenda for his three years at Ephesus. Yet it stands to reason that Ephesus must have participated. Surely part of what Paul was fostering among the believers in Ephesus was this discipline of, "on the first day of every week, each one of you should set aside a sum of money in keeping with your income," saving it up so that Paul could deliver it to Jerusalem (1 Corinthians 16:2). The only veiled reference to a collection at Ephesus is in the list of people that accompanied Paul to Jerusalem, presumably serving as representatives of their portion of the collection for the Jerusalem church. Among the people mentioned are "Tychicus and Trophimus from the province of Asia" (Acts 20:4). These two may have been put in charge of the funds collected from the Ephesian church and from the surrounding churches. Other references tie Tychicus specifically to Ephesus. This point of emphasis should not be forgotten when summarizing Paul's time in Ephesus.

A final insight - rather, an assortment of general insights - from the Corinthian correspondence can be found in Paul's personal comments at the end of the first extant letter to Corinth. Oftentimes, it is in these personal comments that Paul gives glimpses into everyday life and to the many otherwise unknown individuals who contribute to his work. 1 Corinthians 16 gives us several of these glimpses. Paul had sent Timothy (and Erastus) ahead to Macedonia and then they would continue on to Corinth (1

Corinthians 16:10). Apollos may have come back to Ephesus, at which point Paul encouraged him to accompany Timothy, but Apollos declined (1 Corinthians 16:12). Stephanas, Fortunatus, and Achaicus had arrived safely in Ephesus from Corinth and had updated Paul on the church in Corinth (1 Corinthians 16:17). It is here we also learn of the church in Ephesus meeting at the home of Priscilla and Aquila (1 Corinthians 16:19).

Among all these small insights, perhaps the most telling glimpse into the conclusion of Paul's time in Ephesus comes from this section as well: "I do not want to see you now and make only a passing visit; I hope to spend some time with you, if the Lord permits. But I will stay on at Ephesus until Pentecost, because a great door for effective work has opened to me, and there are many who oppose me" (1 Corinthians 16:7-9). Despite everything that had transpired in Ephesus, Paul still considered Ephesus an open door for the gospel to advance and he was not ready to abandon it because of some opposition. This paints a much different picture than one of Paul being forced out of Ephesus, even imprisoned. The fact that Paul intended to stay through Pentecost indicates that he was in Ephesus under his own volition and it was in his power to decide when he would leave.

Paul's account actually coincides well with Luke's account. Though the emotions from the riot were still quite raw when he writes to the Corinthians, everything considered, Paul was still hopeful that his work in Ephesus would continue to advance after his departure. Paul's own frustration with the Corinthian church cannot be discounted either when evaluating some of his word choices. It should not be surprising then, that writing from Macedonia some months later to the church at Corinth, Paul could draw upon that same imagery of a procession. Only this time, he has a different perspective: "But thanks be to God, who always leads us as captives in Christ's triumphal procession and uses us to spread the aroma of the knowledge of him" (2 Corinthians 2:14).

5 FOUR VITAL QUESTIONS

Though the archaeological site of Ephesus is impressive in part because of how much has been reconstructed, there is still much left to the imagination. Enough has been reconstructed to get a flavor of the city, yet the imagination is stretched to envision what it must have looked like in 55 AD. There is an area adjacent to the Great Theater where rock and marble pieces have been organized like a giant jigsaw puzzle dumped out over the landscape. Decorated marble fragments are all in one area, much like keeping all the edge pieces of a puzzle together. Stones with inscriptions are kept together in another area. Columns and capitals are grouped together. No doubt these pieces have all been recorded and entered into a database in the hopes that more of the great city can eventually be reconstructed. Until then, the giant puzzle remains.

Ephesians has traditionally been understood as a letter, correspondence from one person to another of a personal nature. When reading e-mail correspondence today, most people will not spend much time framing the context of the e-mail. Details such as whom the e-mail is from and when the e-mail was sent are so quickly processed that they scarcely register in our consciousness. Other details, such as who the recipient is (after all, it came to your e-mail account) and what the e-mail relates to (just read the subject line), are so plainly stated that they are incontrovertible. All this takes place in the second or two before the e-mail is opened and read. These details, however, are not so obvious when reading two-thousand-year-old correspondence, at least to us residents of the digital age.

So, while one of the aims of this book is an effort at contextualizing the letter to the Ephesians, it is still important to frame the letter in its most basic of contextual questions from the outset. To some, these four initial questions of context – who wrote it? to whom was it written? when was it written? and why? - may seem as inherent as reading your next e-mail. To others, these most basic of questions may open up an entirely new setting for the reading of scripture. But no matter where one may reside on the contextual spectrum, the answer to these initial questions will necessarily shape the reading of the text that follows. Answering these four questions is a good starting point whenever any study of scripture is undertaken, whether in personal devotion or in public teaching. And, as will soon be apparent, the simplest of these questions is fraught with debate, with each answer reworking the overall impression of the message.

WHO WROTE EPHESIANS?

In the opening line of the letter, the writer identifies himself as "Paul, an apostle of Christ Jesus." On the surface, this is perhaps the most straightforward of these four opening questions. We have already offered a biographical sketch of Paul in *Team Ephesus*, so a detailed outline of this Paul would only be redundant. This is, indeed, the same apostle who spent two or three years with the Ephesians and launched his ministry to the province of Asia from Ephesus.

As with any of these questions, if an author other than Paul is proposed, the meaning of the letter could change significantly. Modern scholarship has done just that, and today many scholars would assert that Paul was not the author of Ephesians. There are several issues normally raised in holding to non-Pauline authorship, and these are not inconsequential.

First, if Paul had such an intimate knowledge of the people of Ephesus, why does the content of Ephesians seem general and impersonal? We might expect a detailed list of people to personally receive greetings from Paul, such as in Romans chapter 16, or specific references to their circumstances, such as in the letters to Corinth. Second, the author uses many terms in Ephesians that are not used elsewhere in Paul's writings. However, this argument can be made for virtually any of Paul's letters, so this in itself is not overly significant. Third, many have noted the similarities between Ephesians and Colossians. The letters have a similar structure and share a similar message, leading some to believe that a later author may have used Colossians to construct Ephesians, using Paul's name to lend credibility to the letter. Finally, some have pointed to a different theology in Ephesians than we might expect from the apostle Paul.

Taken collectively, many today simply dismiss Pauline authorship of Ephesians. For example, Jerome Murphy-O'Connor, whose collection of ancient references to Ephesus I have drawn from extensively, dismisses Ephesians as one of those ancient works, "since Paul did not write to the church at Ephesus."[1] Murphy-O'Connor is certainly not alone. Yet there are voices who are not ready to abandon Pauline authorship. Summarizing this modern bias, N.T. Wright recently stated, "In the North American Pauline guild one is not allowed to use Ephesians or Colossians for arguments about what Paul really said because the academy has decreed that they are post-Pauline or deutero-Pauline ... but actually, I think that Ephesians and Colossians should be used as part of a construction of Pauline theology."[2]

So are we prepared to abandon the authorship of Paul? While some of the issues raised merit further investigation, none of them completely preclude Paul from being the author of Ephesians. Some questions are actually what we might come to expect if Paul was the author. For example, if Paul wrote Colossians and Ephesians from a Roman prison around the same time, we would expect to find a similar structure between the two letters. One need not have been "copied" from the other. Other explanations will become clear as we move forward, so that I, personally, am not ready to abandon Pauline authorship. To put it simply, since Ephesians identifies Paul as the author and Pauline authorship was not challenged throughout most of church history, the burden of proof lies upon the one denying the authorship of Paul, not on the one who holds to Pauline authorship. I do not want to oversimplify the answers to any of these questions; rather I only offer a rationale for why I have made the assumptions that will frame the context of Ephesians. There are many excellent commentaries that tackle each of these issues at length. Until definitive proof is offered otherwise, we are on safe ground assuming that Paul wrote Ephesians.

TO WHOM WAS EPHESIANS WRITTEN?

In the second line of the letter, Paul informs us that he is writing "to the saints in Ephesus," again providing what seems to be a straightforward answer to this second question. But settling this question will prove to be thornier than the previous one. Upon closer inspection, most English texts will have footnoted the word *Ephesus*, noting that some early manuscripts do not contain the phrase "in Ephesus." And this is no trivial footnote.

When pouring over extant manuscripts of the Bible, the general rule is that the older the manuscript, the more reliable its text. Thus, a biblical manuscript that dates back to around 400 AD is assumed to be closer to the original letter (and therefore more trustworthy) than a manuscript that dates to around 1100 AD. Though great care was generally given to the integrity of a biblical manuscript, over time copyists' errors could have been unknowingly passed on, editorial notes could have been inserted and confused with the text itself, or words and phrases may have been dropped for various reasons. The New Testament texts are incredibly accurate, but there are a few instances where scholars are unsure how the original text might have read. Unfortunately, the words "in Ephesus" happen to be one of those places.

The issue with those two words is that they are not present in the oldest manuscripts of Ephesians. One of the oldest texts of Ephesians dates back to 200 AD and one of the oldest complete copies of the New Testament, the Codex Sinaiticus, dates to the mid-fourth century. Neither of those texts contains the words "in Ephesus." Even earlier, writing in the second century, Marcion, whose theological beliefs were deemed heretical, identified the letter as being sent to Laodicea, though no manuscripts exist that actually contain Laodicea as a possible variant.[3] It was not until later that manuscripts of this Pauline letter began to be identified with the city of Ephesus. So the question, then, is why? Why did church tradition identify this letter with Ephesus while early manuscripts did not?

Some will maintain that, given the lack of allusion to the city and to the people of Ephesus within the letter and the omission of the words "in Ephesus" in the early manuscripts, the link with Ephesus should be dropped. Others, however, navigate around this omission by identifying Ephesians as a circular letter meant to be distributed to a number of cities in Asia Minor, Ephesus being one of them. Under this theory, in the same way that Revelation was addressed to the seven churches of Asia Minor, Paul wrote Ephesians intending it to be passed around to many of those same cities.[4] This would explain both the ambiguous language of the letter and the eventual link to Ephesus. For many, this is a satisfactory conclusion to the matter until new evidence may prove otherwise.

Although I do not disagree with this explanation, to leave the matter here and move on may be conceding too much contextual ground waiting to be unearthed in the letter. I believe the language of Ephesians, while at first glance seems ambiguous, actually fits quite well within the cultural context of the city of Ephesus that Paul called home for almost three years. I believe the text of Ephesians has not been mined to its depths because we are content to remain at the surface of what has been given the label of a circular, i.e. nondescript, letter.

So while on the surface, Ephesians may not contain clear landmarks that identify it with Ephesus, neither does it contain any markings that would identify it with another city, thus precluding Ephesus. Given Paul's investment in Ephesus and the number of letters written from prison or house arrest, it would be surprising if he did not communicate with his Ephesian friends during his imprisonment. (Of course, it is always possible that this communication has simply been lost, as some others surely have been.) And given what we know about Paul's time in Ephesus – that Ephesus served as a base of operations to launch a number of churches in the province of Asia – we might expect that a letter written to Ephesus would be circulated throughout the church communities of that region.

What I am proposing is that Paul wrote the letter of Ephesians to the believers in Ephesus. But he also understood that it was a letter that would be read to the other churches of the region as well. He understood that, like the official Roman correspondence of his day, to write to Ephesus was to address the entire province of Asia. The opening quote of this chapter is such an example: Josephus records that the Jews in the province of Asia were granted exemption from Roman military service. In order to inform all the people of the province – the Asiatics - a letter was sent by the Roman prefect Dolabella to Ephesus, because Ephesus was the metropolis – the chief city - of Asia. *To communicate with Ephesus was to inform the entire province.* This is just one example of this type of correspondence.

In the same way, Paul did not want to use language that would exclude the outlying Asian churches, but he would use images and references that most of those churches would relate to, including images specific to Ephesus. Colossians was written separately because, though it is part of the province of Asia, it is on the eastern edge of that province, somewhat isolated in the Lycus Valley, and there were some issues specific to their situation. Laodicea is also situated in this part of the province, and according to the Colossian letter, they also received a separate correspondence.[5]

Though the nuance is subtle, if Ephesians is simply a nondescript circular letter containing general exhortations and instructions, then we would not search for specific references to Ephesus within the letter. The context of Ephesus would have little bearing on the letter. But if Ephesians was written to the church in Ephesus, and would also be distributed to churches that closely identified with both the church and the city of Ephesus, then we would expect to uncover references that are specific to Ephesus, and understanding the context of Ephesus would contribute greatly to an understanding of these references. My hope is to uncover some of these specific references and put Ephesians back in its cultural context, a context that has been hesitantly skirted in recent years.

Perhaps a contemporary example will serve to draw out this important nuance. If I sit down to write a general, nondescript letter, such as one of those yearly updates you might receive around Christmas time to friends and family who live in various cities, I would probably not attempt to draw upon any references that might be specific to Chicago, Nashville, or Tallahassee - each of which I have called home at one time or another. Those references would be lost on the many friends and family who did not live in those cities. Incidentally, this is precisely the category that Ephesians too often is relegated to nowadays. At the other end of the spectrum, if I sit down and write an e-mail to a good friend who lives in Chicago, then I would probably include many references to our shared experiences, both of Chicago and of other places we have journeyed to together. But consider if I wrote an e-mail to that same friend in Chicago, and my intention was for that friend to pass the e-mail around to other friends and acquaintances in Chicago (let's say he prints out several copies of the e-mail to disperse), what level of detail would be expected? I would probably avoid references that are specific to our shared experiences (like a meal at a certain restaurant or a topic of conversation that we always engaged in), but I would draw upon images of Chicago that everyone there would understand. I might bemoan the Cubs, talk about Chicago winters, or make mention of the many great restaurants in the city. If you came across that e-mail (and didn't live in Chicago) and were expecting specific details, you may write it off as a piece of nondescript correspondence. But if I told you my intention for that e-mail and where it was originally sent, you might re-read it with a new understanding of the words and phrases I chose to employ.

Finally, it bears repeating that while early writings may not link this letter to Ephesus, church history would come to attach the letter to Ephesus, and there has not been any subsequent hard evidence to sever that attachment. There may have been good solid reasons why "in Ephesus" was eventually attached to the letter. So while the question, *to whom was Ephesians written*, is a complex one, the answer is of utmost importance as we proceed forward through the text.

WHEN WAS EPHESIANS WRITTEN?

By now it should be clear that the most basic of questions will have diverse and divergent opinions regarding an answer. This question is no exception. But if we build off conclusions drawn from the previous two questions, we can quickly narrow the possible answers. Clearly, for those who assume that Paul was *not* the author of Ephesians and that it was written later under his name, Ephesians could have been penned anytime in the late first to second century. But given that we are moving forward trusting Pauline authorship and building the case that Ephesians was written to Ephesus, our timeframe becomes much more specific.

The biggest clue Paul gives as to the date of his letter can be found in the fact that twice Paul identifies himself as a "prisoner" for Christ (Ephesians 3:1 and 4:1), and in a third instance of self-identification, he calls himself an "ambassador in chains" (Ephesians 6:20). Undoubtedly, Paul wrote Ephesians while in prison.

This narrows the possibilities to two timeframes: his imprisonment in Caesarea from 57 to 59, or his subsequent house arrest in Rome from 60 to 62. (Those who hold that Paul was imprisoned in Ephesus following the riot, such as Murphy-O'Connor, would add a third timeframe: his imprisonment in Ephesus in 55.) This is where some of the vague language of Ephesians may actually aid us in deciding between the two. If Paul had just said goodbye to the Ephesian elders at Miletus in the spring of 57, and then was imprisoned in Caesarea in the summer of 57, it seems improbable the he would have written an impersonal - as some would call it - letter to Ephesus so soon following his farewell. Ephesians seems to put more distance between the two events than a Caesarean imprisonment allows. A house arrest from Rome in about 60 or 61 would fit the circumstances better. Several years had passed since that meeting and he wanted to correspond with several churches, given the uncertain outcome of his trial drawing to a conclusion.

A couple other clues fit these circumstances as well, though by themselves they hardly settle the matter. Given that Colossians and Ephesians must have been written around the same time, house arrest from Rome fits the timeframe in which Colossians was written quite nicely. In Colossians and Philemon, Paul sends greetings from Epaphras, his fellow-prisoner. Epaphras likely founded the church in Colosse, and Paul's house arrest in Rome would have allowed people like him to visit, to be his "fellow-prisoner" for a time, and then go as they pleased. At the conclusion of Acts, Luke writes that "for two years Paul stayed there [in Rome] in his own rented house and welcomed all who came to see him" (Acts 28:30). There is no indication that this was the situation in Caesarea, where he was most likely confined to the Praetorium.

Finally, both Colossians and Ephesians indicate that they were delivered by Tychicus, further demonstrating that the two letters were written around the same time and should be dated to the time of Paul's house arrest in Rome. This link with both the letter of Colossians and the person of Tychicus also serves as further confirmation that Ephesians was intended, at the very least, for an audience in the province of Asia. As previously mentioned, Tychicus was most likely from Ephesus and, having spent some time visiting Paul, was leaving Rome with letters in hand for the churches in Ephesus and Colosse (and perhaps Laodicea as well). The fog is beginning to lift from our four vital questions!

WHY WAS EPHESIANS WRITTEN?

The question of *why* is a question less about dates, facts, and textual variants and more about the actual interpretation of the text. Having gathered all the relevant facts and taking our best shot at answering the previous three questions, we are now prepared to answer the more subjective question of why Paul wrote this letter. What was the main message he was trying to communicate to the church at Ephesus?

It is also helpful to understand that, on the surface, the question of *why* involves some circular reasoning. The answer will color how the letter itself is read. Yet, how can we answer the question unless we have first read the letter? We might be tempted to skip this final question, unless it is acknowledged that a clear and concise answer is as important to a correct reading of the text as other contextual issues regarding Ephesus, Paul, and the newly formed Christian church.

The way around this circularity is to consider the question of *why* similar to that of a thesis statement. An answer will be put forth here; it can then pass through the scrutiny of the text itself, and at that point, it can be tweaked and refined depending on how our statement faired with the actual text. This method has sometimes been referred to as *hypothesis and verification.*[6] A clear answer to this question will cause the text to fall satisfyingly into place, shedding light on every part of the text along the way. A clear statement of *why* is like well-illustrated, step-by-step instructions guiding one through the assembly of a new purchase. The result is a final product that resembles the picture on the packaging and there are no leftover pieces and parts leaving us to wonder if the whole framework will collapse in on itself. A poor statement of *why* might lead us to something that vaguely resembles an epistle of Paul, but there will be many superfluous concepts and ideas, leaving us wondering how they were supposed to fit or whether they were just some arbitrary and unrelated thoughts thrown in the box along with everything else.

This, then, should be the criteria for evaluating each of these contextual questions, culminating with the question of *why*: Will the text fall neatly into place leaving us with a valuable and relevant letter encouraging us on our spiritual journey or will the text leave us confused, with more questions than answers, leaving us with a curiosity that will sit on the shelf and collect dust?

Keeping these criteria in mind, it may be helpful to peruse some common responses offered to this question of why Ephesians was written. A standard response often found in versions of the Bible that include at least some brief commentary is that Ephesians was written to inform the church (*the church* often being the universal church, not specifically the Ephesian church) of God's purpose for the church: to bring all things under the headship of Christ. Along these same lines, the unity of the church is another common theme cited as the purpose of Ephesians. These responses may begin to draw out some of the themes found in Ephesians, but they are so general that they are of little value in shedding light on each part of the text, connecting the parts to the whole and to the larger context. There are many left over pieces. Another theme found in some well-known commentaries revolves around the idea of the Christian's riches in Christ.[7] This actually incorporates more of the contextual issues than may first appear, but this theme does not give a satisfactory answer to everything found in Ephesians. Again, we are left with some spare parts. Another commentary brings in the theme of cosmic reconciliation as part of the central message of Ephesians: Things in heaven and things on earth are being brought together into unity in Christ.[8] Taken collectively, some common themes are beginning to emerge; we are getting closer to the picture on the package.

Given our criteria - that the answer to *why* will cause the text to fall satisfyingly into place, shedding light on every part of the text along the way - I am putting forth a four-part statement behind the purpose of Ephesians. (To be fair, the themes cited above are usually expounded upon in more detail.) Paul wanted the church at Ephesus, which also represented the churches throughout the province of Asia, to understand four things: 1) God's plan is to bring all creation back under his authority; 2) this plan was revealed and accomplished through the death and resurrection of Jesus; 3) as Gentiles, they were part of this plan *from the beginning;* 4) so their response should be to fully embrace life as the people of God, knowing that victory had already been accomplished. There is obviously much more that can be said with each of these statements. That is the purpose of the rest of this book. But each statement is also an integral piece of Paul's message. With these four statements joined together, the text of Ephesians should now (hopefully) fall satisfyingly into place.

Having answered these four vital questions, we are now prepared to turn to the text itself. If we have correctly framed the context of Ephesians - that the Apostle Paul wrote this letter to the church in Ephesus from house arrest in Rome around 60/61 in order to clarify the plan of God, invite them, as Gentiles, into that plan, and encourage them to embrace life as the people of God – then the text will begin to paint a vivid picture, with many images and themes emerging from it. The final product will resemble the picture on the package! If not, then we will probably settle for some over-generalized platitudes from Ephesians, failing to see much evidence of Paul's handiwork or images of Ephesus in the text. The spare parts will be swept back into the box, and we will hope that what we are left with does not collapse with actual use.

6 A PLAN YOU CAN TAKE TO THE BANK

You know about the Ephesians, of course, and that large sums of money are in their hands, some of them belonging to private citizens and deposited in the temple of Artemis, not alone money of the Ephesians, but also of aliens and of persons from all parts of the world, and in some cases of commonwealths and kings, money which all deposit there in order that it may be safe, since no one has ever yet dared to violate that place, although countless wars have occurred in the past and the city has often been captured.
- Dio Chrysostom, *Oration*

From the upper area of the ancient city, Curetes street slopes downhill until you are standing directly in front of the Celsus Library. The street itself begins at the Heracles Gate, named after the reliefs of Heracles and Nike depicted on the structure. As you proceed down the street, marble statues would have lined either side of the path, some of which are still standing. These represented various donors, dignitaries, and civic leaders who helped establish Ephesus as a wealthy and influential city. Fountains and other structures would have also lined the street. Near the end of the street as you approach the Terrace Houses, part of the walkway is still preserved, revealing elaborate mosaic tile-work. One would be hard-pressed to walk down this street without getting a sense of the display of wealth that made Ephesus the leading city of the province of Asia.

We are now in a much better position to turn to the text of Ephesians itself. And remember, if our hypothesis is correct, then the text will unfold nicely in support of it. Paul begins this letter much like he begins most of his letters: with a traditional greeting and prayer. The details of this traditional greeting are easy to overlook, so it might be helpful to consider each of these elements in Paul's letters.

Formal letters of the first century followed a standard format and shared some common elements. Because Paul was writing a mixture of formal and personal letters with a spiritual emphasis, his correspondence would contain at least some of the following: an *introduction* (who wrote it and to whom), a *eulogy* (blessings or praise to God), *thanksgiving* (such as, "I thank my God..."), and a *prayer* (for example, "my prayer is this..."). For the most part in his writings, Paul tended to follow a standard format. Some letters, such as 2 Corinthians and Galatians, contain only a couple of these elements. Ephesians is the only extant letter to contain all four identifiable elements. As such, Paul uses the entire first chapter for a lengthy greeting (of course, the chapter divisions were not part of the original letter).

When I was in junior high school, I won a statewide essay contest sponsored by the local American Legion post. I, along with the other winners in various categories, was invited to the awards ceremony where we would each read our winning essay on the subject of freedom. To begin the ceremony, an elderly woman approached the podium to open with a word of prayer. She opened a book and began, "God in heaven, we are here to remember the life of Margaret Jones. We are gathered tonight to celebrate her life." She paused for a moment, and then muttered to herself (yet still into the microphone), "No, wait a minute, this is last month's prayer." Flipping through the pages in her little book, she landed on the right prayer and forged ahead with a more apropos benediction for the evening. As my mother tells it, she had to give me an elbow to the side to prevent my snickering from being even more distracting than the reading of the wrong prayer!

I have to confess that at times, I can treat these formal greetings of Paul like a dinnertime prayer. It might be a nice tradition to carry on, but the real meat and potatoes are getting cold if we spend too much time on it. A surface reading may appear as if Paul is simply reciting some nice sounding words and inserting them into a standard greeting – a eulogy here, an eloquent blessing there. But dally too long and the main course might get cold. However, in recent years I have come to appreciate these greetings from Paul as very personal, heavy with emotion, and incorporating all the courses that Paul will spell out at length in the remainder of the letter. Scarcely being a rote prayer before the main course, Paul is letting us sample each dish, whetting our appetite for what promises to be a satisfying feast. In this greeting, Paul is telling us everything we will need to know to navigate the rest of his letter.

EULOGY: THE PLAN OF GOD

Having identified some of the contextual details from these opening verses in the previous chapter, we now move to the eulogy. Far from the somber respects delivered at a funeral, a eulogy in scripture is a liturgical feature in which the writer offers praise and blessings to God. In Ephesians, this is delivered in verses 3 to 14 of the opening chapter, and this lengthy outburst of praise is even more dramatic in the original language, where this entire passage is one continual sentence. The praise in this opening line is unmistakable, as it literally reads, "*Blessed* is God ... who has *blessed* us ... with every spiritual *blessing.*" God is recognized as "the Father of our Lord Jesus Christ" and the extent of these blessings from God extend to the "heavenly realms."

The phrase in 1:3, "in the heavenly realms," is unique to Ephesians, at least as it appears in the Greek. In this letter, Paul uses a variation of the Greek word we would normally expect to find when we encounter the word *heaven.*[1] Most do not read much into this variation and attribute its use to stylistic preference, since the two variations can be used interchangeably. Regardless of which is used, the concept of the heavenly realms will become a theme in the book of Ephesians. So, rather than focus on small nuances, let us consider the larger question of what exactly do the heavenly realms refer to?

Too often, the idea of heaven from the New Testament has been used to refer to the place where we go after we die (and often, somewhere in outer space!). More recently, scholars such as N.T. Wright have demonstrated, quite convincingly, that heaven actually refers to "the place where the divinely intended future for the world is kept safely in store, against the day when ... it will come to birth in the renewed world."[2] In this sense, heaven is not a place where we go after we die, but is a realm under God's sovereign control, a realm that is not separate from the earth, but one day will encompass the whole earth. The primary content of Jesus' teaching alludes to this realm when he preached, "Repent, for the kingdom of heaven is near" (Matthew 4:17). So heaven is another way of referring to the *kingdom of heaven* or the *kingdom of God.*

This is notable, given the frequency of references to the heavenly realm in Ephesians. When Paul uses this term, he is not referring to the place that the Ephesian believers will go when they die, nor is he simply referring to the realm of the Platonic soul, beyond the physical world. Rather he is referring to the kingdom of God, which was announced by Jesus, began forcefully advancing during his life, death and resurrection, and will fully come to fruition one day, bringing renewal to the physical heavens and earth. It is the realm in which Jesus currently resides at the right hand of God; it is the unseen backdrop behind everything that is taking place in the world; and it is the place where these spiritual blessings spoken of by Paul are being kept for the believer. When Paul tells the Ephesian believers that they have been blessed with every spiritual blessing in the heavenly realm, he is not saying these blessings will be waiting for them when they die. He is reminding them that these blessings are available now and are held under the watchful protection of Jesus.

So what are these spiritual blessings? As he continues the eulogy, Paul lists four of these blessings, though they are hardly distinct from each other. Together they culminate in God's plan for the world. The first blessing is that God *chose* us before the creation of the world. We were chosen to be holy and blameless before God. These two descriptors, holy and blameless, hearken back to Old Testament times to describe an acceptable sacrifice. The animal to be sacrificed was to be without defect (blameless) and would become holy when placed upon the altar. In this way, the person offering the sacrifice would be acceptable in the sight of God. In other words, God's original design was that human beings would be sinless, and thus holy, as part of God's creation. That is what we were chosen for. But then we rebelled against that plan and messed things up.

As a result, God put another plan into place in which we would be *adopted* as legitimate children of God. Finding ourselves outside of God's family because of our rebellion, God decided well before hand (predestined) that he would bring us back into the family. And this is the second blessing. This adoption process was made possible by God's own son, Jesus. It was freely extended to us and God was more than happy to bring us back into the family.

But it did not come cheaply for God. In order to be adopted back into God's family, we needed to be *redeemed* - to have redemption through the shed blood of Jesus. This is the third blessing. Jesus would become the holy and blameless sacrifice, whose blood would cover our sin and rebellion, enabling us to enter back into God's good graces. This link between sacrifice and redemption would play well for the Jewish believers at Ephesus, but for the Gentile believers – some of whom were Greeks, some Roman citizens, some slaves – redemption would have meant something a little different.

Redemption refers to the process of setting a slave free and it often involved purchasing that freedom with a substantial amount of money. This is why Paul reassures the Ephesian church that their redemption was made possible "according to the riches of God's grace." It is one reason why the riches - or wealth - of God becomes another theme throughout the letter. The Jewish believer would immediately make the connection between redemption and the forgiveness of sins. Redemption had a deeper meaning of not simply political freedom, but spiritual freedom as well. But the Gentile believer would have needed help associating the process of setting a slave free with the forgiveness of sins. Hence, the death of Jesus was the price that had to be paid to secure their spiritual freedom. The price was indeed steep, but God was wealthy enough to redeem any and all who would accept his offer!

The final blessing could only come after we had been chosen (and subsequently rebelled), predestined for adoption, and redeemed back into God's family as children of God. Through Jesus, God *made known the mystery of his plan*, and with our new status, we were in a privileged position to understand this mystery. And the mysterious plan was this: God was bringing all things in heaven and on earth together under the reign of Jesus. God's plan, which was hidden for so many generations, culminated in the death and resurrection of his son, Jesus. And God was now actively at work bringing all creation back under Jesus' legitimate rule. There would no longer be a need to distinguish the heavenly realm from the earthly realm, because the two will come together as one in the kingdom of God. Artemis may have fallen from heaven, but heaven was now coming under the reign of Jesus; Rome may look like they are in power, but they too are being brought under the reign of Jesus.

All this will take place "when the times will have reached their fulfillment." In apocalyptic literature, this was a way of saying that there is a future certainty to this plan, but there is also a sequence of events already taking place that would lead to this certain outcome. It would take place in the fullness of time. Elsewhere, Paul had previously written that this fullness of time had already reached its culmination with the life of Jesus, even if the final outcome still lies in the future.[3]

So there it is. The mystery was now revealed. God was in the process of bringing all things together under the reign of Jesus. In this seemingly simple eulogy, Paul had clearly disclosed the plan of God for all who were ready to hear it. But there was one more misunderstanding that Paul needed to clarify, and this would become the heart of his letter to the Ephesians.

WHAT DOES ALL THIS HAVE TO DO WITH ME?

As Paul continues with his praise of God, verse 11 appears as if Paul is restating what has already been said. Certainly, Paul is no stranger to the allegation of rambling from thought to thought, abruptly leaving one subject and picking it up later. Indeed, we will encounter a "hold that thought" moment in Ephesians 3. But instead of being just some repetitive rambling, Paul is making absolutely clear a very important point that these Ephesians were seemingly struggling to comprehend. And speaking of a "hold that thought" moment, there is something that must be clarified to the modern reader so that we, ourselves, fully grasp the importance of what Paul is writing.

In verse 11, the terms *chosen* and *predestined* are repeated from earlier verses - Paul has already opened that theological can of worms. But it is only a can of worms from our modern perspective, because those terms (along with *election*) take us directly into the Calvinism-Armenianism debate (some may be more familiar with the terms *predestination* versus *free will*). It goes something like this: Do human beings have a free will to choose or reject God, or does God do the choosing for us? Is the doctrine of election a negation of free will? Can free will and predestination co-exists in one's theology? These are questions that make pastors and small group leaders scan the room for an exit or cause heated exchanges between otherwise congenial Christians.

But I believe when we examine the context in which Paul uses those terms, Paul is not having the same discussion that we are having. When we trace those concepts throughout the story of the Old Testament and into the New Testament, we arrive at an entirely different discussion. So let's redefine some terms, or rather let's recover some of their original meaning. *Chosen* refers to Israel's Old Testament status as the people of God; they were God's chosen people. *Election* is simply another word in English that means *chosen* (in Greek they are the same word). Thus, God's plan was to choose the nation of Israel for his people, and through Israel, bless all the nations and peoples of the earth.[4] When Israel failed to live up to that covenant, Jesus would come to be the embodiment of faithful Israel, keeping God's plan moving ahead. *Predestination*, then, refers to the fact that this plan of God was decided ahead of time, before the creation of the world. In other words, God was not being constantly caught by surprise, resorting to plan B, and then plan C, then D. From the beginning, God knew things would unfold the way they did, and God already had a plan ready to go. This is the conversation Paul is having.

"But what about God choosing some individuals for salvation and not others?" "Does an individual choose God or does God choose the individual?" Those questions fall under the modern debate, so let me repeat, that is not the conversation Paul is engaged in. It is common for commentaries on the book of Ephesians to use this opening chapter as a discussion on how an individual becomes saved. For example, *The Pillar New Testament Commentary* states, "There is clearly a corporate dimension to God's election. It is inappropriate, however, to suggest that election in Christ is primarily corporate rather than personal and individual."[5] But the corporate dimension is precisely what Paul is addressing here! And as long as we are engaged in the wrong conversation, we will continue to hotly debate these terms, wander down theological rabbit trails, and misunderstand Paul.

At the risk of belaboring the point, if the old categories continue to be used to explain Ephesians 1, then they must shed light on the rest of Paul's letter as well, causing the entire text to fall satisfyingly into place. But in my experience, the old categories often leave us with more questions than answers. Allowing Paul to use those loaded terms simply as they had been used throughout Israel's history leads us to much more satisfying results. For us moderns, this clarification is crucial as we move forward with Paul's own point of clarification for the Ephesian believers.

Returning, then, to the eulogy, Paul is repeating these terms not because he is rambling (and not because he is telling them how to get saved; he is addressing those already *saved*, to use that term), but because he has one more important point to make regarding this choosing. Through Christ, we were not only chosen to be blameless before God, but also that we would be "for the praise of his glory" – a phrase Paul uses three times in the opening chapter. The intended outcome of God's plan from the beginning - it was predestined - was that we would bring to God the recognition God deserves.

It is at this point that we reach an important detail in the text and this detail is a considerable part of the point Paul is trying to make. Up to this point (verses 1-12), Paul has been using the first-person personal pronoun *us* or *we*: God has blessed *us*, God chose *us*, he predestined *us*, etc. With all the contemporary emphasis on personalizing scripture, with the common phrase, "here is what this passage means to me," it is easy to read that first-person personal pronoun and includes oneself as part of the *us*. "Well sure, that must include me also," most Christians today would assume.

But if we let Paul simply say what he is trying to say, he is not ready to include us just yet. The Greek participle *proelpikotas*, which means, "to be the first to hope," makes it clear that up to this point, the *us* refers to the nation of Israel, the Jewish people. The nation of Israel was the people of God. The Jewish people, in the corporate sense, were the first to find hope *in Christ*, which is a title referring to Jesus as the Jewish Messiah (so the name *Jesus Christ* is actually declaring "Jesus the Messiah").

In effect, Paul, who remember was a Jew, has carried on throughout the entire first part of this letter about how much God has done for the Jewish people, how this Jewish Messiah had now come to the Jewish people, and about how God had chosen them (*us*, from Paul's perspective) from the beginning. Now if you were not a Jewish person – if you were a Gentile – what would be your initial response to all this? We might imagine that the predominantly Gentile Ephesians might be muttering something like, "Well good for you, Paul. We are all very happy for you, but what does all this have to do with us?"

For several years, I led a team to Guatemala to serve for a week in a local children's home. We always booked our airline tickets through one of the Central American airlines so we could get a direct flight from Chicago to

Guatemala City. For whatever reason, they routinely overbooked the flight and at least some of the team always got bumped up to first class. What kind of reception do you think I would get if I walked into the boarding area announcing to the largely Guatemalan passengers that I had gotten bumped up to first class, and I wanted them to know how roomy the seats were, how nice the meals were, and how rested I would feel after the flight? If I didn't get punched, I might get quite a few, "so what does all this have to do with me?" glares.

All this crescendos up to one of the main points of Paul's letter. About the time Paul might be getting a few of those "good for you, Paul" glares, he enthusiastically announces, "And you also were included in Christ when you heard the word of truth, the gospel of your salvation!" (Ephesians 1:13). *You* Gentiles are included as part of the *us*. This Jewish Messiah is for you as well. First class upgrades for everyone! When the Gentile Ephesians heard the gospel and accepted its invitation, they also were included among the chosen, as part of the true Israel. And quite astoundingly, Paul seems to be indicating that this radical inclusion of the Gentiles was part of God's plan from the beginning – it was predestined! (By the way, now might be an appropriate time for modern readers to include themselves among the *us*.)

This becomes the main thrust of Paul's letter to the Ephesians: God's plan is to bring all creation back under his authority, this plan was revealed and accomplished through the death and resurrection of Jesus the Messiah, and as Gentiles, they were part of this plan from the beginning. It could be supposed then, that for whatever the reason, the Ephesian believers needed to be reminded of this. Perhaps the "savage wolves" that Paul had previously warned them about (back in Acts 20:29) had made their way to Ephesus and were either trying to exclude them from God's plan, or convince them that they needed to Judaize in order to take part in God's plan. Regardless, Paul wanted them to know that it was always part of God's plan to include Gentiles as well. And when they heard the word of truth and believed, they were legitimate children in the family of God.

To make this point lucid, Paul further draws on the imagery of adoption and inheritance to convince them of their place in God's plan. They were given the Holy Spirit, who effectively marked them with a seal, guaranteeing the inheritance due to them as adopted children of God. The imagery is vivid. A seal distinct to the owner, and the waxy impression it would leave behind, was used to identify property, deposits held at the temple, or certify that a will was legal, among other things. The presence of the Holy Spirit among the believers in Ephesus acted as this impression, marking them as God's possession and heirs of the family fortune (see *Inheriting the Kingdom* below). Paul had previously introduced the Ephesian believers to the presence of the Holy Spirit and apparently needed to remind the next generation of believers there as well. If they could once again recognize the presence of the Holy Spirit as they gathered – through prayer, through healing, through insight – then they could rest assured of their place in God's family. The presence of the Holy Spirit among them trumped any other exclusionary claim or religious hoop to jump through. They were already in!

III

INHERITING THE KINGDOM

The Pauline concepts of adoption and inheritance are intrinsically bound together: Adoption was the means by which a wealthy person or a person of status selected an heir for his inheritance. It was not primarily a means by which a married couple could enjoy a child or additional children, or a benevolent act to give an orphan a home, as we might presume today. Nor was it even a particularly Jewish concept. According to Martin Goodman, adoption was "unknown in late Second Temple and rabbinic texts. A foundling might be fostered, but he or she could not take on a new identity as a full member of the foster family."[6]

In the Roman Empire, adoption was most notably the way in which the title of *Caesar* was kept in the family. It began with the original Caesar, who rose to the level of dictator for life in 44 BC. After the assassination of Julius Caesar, it was unclear who would lead or even how Rome would be led, because he had no surviving sons. The early Roman historian Suetonius recorded what transpired next: "But in his final will, he (Julius Caesar) designated as his three heirs his sisters' grandsons, Gaius Octavius to receive three-quarters of the estate, and then Lucius Pinarius and Quintus Pedius to share the rest. At the end of the document, he even adopted Gaius Octavius into the family and gave him his name."[7] Octavian would take the family name and the title of Caesar (Caesar Augustus), and his inheritance was nothing less than the Roman Empire!

From the time of Julius Caesar to Nero of Paul's day – over a hundred years - adoption was the means by which each predecessor inherited the empire. No ruler of Rome would have a living son of his own to succeed him until Titus succeeded his father Vespasian in 79 AD. This, then, is the language of adoption and inheritance, and it is important to keep this mind as we encounter these concepts in Paul's letter to the Ephesians.

III

For the believer today, this distinct presence of the Holy Spirit continues to act as a deposit, which guarantees our inheritance to the vast wealth of

God as well. We are simply the latest in a long line of believers being marked with a seal, receiving the gift of the Holy Spirit identifying us as God's possession, and anticipating the inheritance as children of God, until the time when God returns to claim, or redeem, what belongs to him. Paul reminds us one more time that all this will bring God the recognition God deserves.

Our inheritance is much more than an earthly kingdom, as some might have supposed in Paul's day. No, our inheritance far surpasses that of Caesar's treasury. And like then, too many today in the church assume that our inheritance has to do with some type of material prosperity in this lifetime, be it wealth, health, or leading a well-adjusted life of self-fulfillment. Others simply assume that our inheritance is a place that we will go when we die - once again, that misunderstood notion of heaven. The inheritance for the believer is nothing less than to share in the reign of God with Jesus when God's kingdom is fully established on the earth. As N.T. Wright points out, "God had promised the Messiah that he would give him the whole world for his inheritance. Now, it appears, this worldwide 'inheritance' is to be shared with all the Messiah's people."[8] Again, we are letting the Old Testament shape our concepts of all this: "Ask me, and I will make the nations your inheritance, the ends of the earth your possession" (Psalm 2:8).

THANKSGIVING AND PRAYER

The third common feature of Paul's letter, after the introduction and the eulogy, is thanksgiving: "For this reason, ever since I heard about your faith in the Lord Jesus and your love for all his people, I have not stopped giving thanks for you, remembering you in my prayers" (Ephesians 1:15,16). Only two of his letters do not contain some type of statement of thanksgiving to begin the correspondence. It is a simple enough statement. This giving thanks to God was sparked upon hearing of their faith and love, and it prompted Paul to lift them up in his prayers.

But this simple statement is also cited as being one of the reasons why some doubt that this letter was written for the church in Ephesus. The argument goes something like this: If Paul spent two or three years in Ephesus, founded the church there, and became closely involved with the people, then why is he acting as if he is just now hearing about their faith? Shouldn't he be well acquainted with their faith and love? So he must be writing to people with whom he is unfamiliar; he must not be writing to Ephesus. The late addition of the words *in Ephesus* only seems to bolster this argument.

However, this need not be the case. There are a couple of explanations as to why Paul might be using this kind of language. If Paul left Ephesus in the spring of 56 and he wrote the letter around 61, then he would have been five years removed from the people there. It could well be that the church had grown significantly and that there were many new believers, even some in leadership, that he had never met. If someone like Tychicus came to Rome to visit Paul, bringing word about how much the church in Ephesus had grown, then Paul might very well respond that he broke out in thanksgiving upon hearing about their faith, love, and response to the message of Jesus.

It could also be the case that Paul is using language that, to us might appear ambiguous, but to Paul would be inclusive, knowing that his letter would be read at other churches beyond Ephesus. Remember, to correspond with Ephesus was to correspond with the entire region surrounding Ephesus. Other cities of that region would be familiar with Ephesus, even though Paul might be unfamiliar with them. Of course, this one statement of thanksgiving is not proof positive one way or the other regarding the recipients of this letter. But this statement would fit with the proposal that Paul was writing to a region, with Ephesus being its chief city.

Finally, Paul reveals the content of this ongoing prayer - at each of the customary times of daily prayer - for the Ephesian church. His prayer is that God would give them the spirit of wisdom and revelation in order that they may know God even more. Certainly, God had already given them the Holy Spirit, who is the source of wisdom and revelation. Paul simply needed to remind them of what they already possessed. In a sense, he spends this first chapter reacquainting them with the Holy Spirit, just as he had done with them the first time he met them. This Spirit was not only a deposit guaranteeing their inheritance but the source of insight to be able to fully understand what was already in their possession. It is precisely because God has revealed himself that we are able to know him better.

Paul wants them to be enlightened by this Spirit. This enlightening of the heart is not in addition to the spirit of wisdom and revelation, as some translations suggest, but it is a restatement of this knowledge Paul wants them to fully grasp. He mentions three things specifically that he wants them to be able to "see with their heart" (literally, "the eyes of your heart"). It should be noted before we explore these three, that it can be misleading for us today to encounter a phrase like "seeing with your heart" and interpret it primarily as an emotion, feeling something deeply. For too many believers, to know God more is to feel God at deeper and deeper levels of the emotions. The heart, as Paul is using it, not only represents the emotions, but also the mind, the soul, and the will. Paul is not praying that they only feel something deeply, but that they understand something deeply and do something in response to that understanding. This will be seen throughout this letter: Deeper knowledge leads to different living.

First, Paul wants them to fully grasp the hope to which they were called. Paul has already revealed what this hope consists of: the plan of God to bring all creation back under his authority. If the Jewish people were the first to hope (*proelpikotas*), then as Gentiles, they were next in line, ready to fully share in God's plan. As we have already seen, this is the hope to which God had called them.

Second, Paul emphasizes again in his prayer that as adopted children of God - as being included in God's plan - they stood to inherit the riches of the kingdom. They would reign with God in this renewed creation. Paul uses this word, riches (*ploutos*) five times in his letter to the Ephesians. Only in his letter to Rome, a much lengthier letter, does he draw on this word so often. It is perhaps because the Ephesian church lay in the shadow of the Temple of Artemis, which served as a repository for unimaginable riches (see *Temples as Banks* below). This was language they could understand, imagery they could relate to. Ephesus was the wealthiest city in Asia and lest they think that they were giving up this lifestyle of the rich and famous in order to follow Jesus, Paul is subtly reminding them that the riches of Artemis were nothing compared to the riches of God's glorious inheritance for his people!

TEMPLES AS BANKS

In the ancient world, temples were not only edifices built to gods, but they also served as banks – not banks in the sense of paying interest on deposits and extending loans, but rather as depositories. What better place to store valuables than in a treasury guarded by a god! The treasury was usually situated as a separate room beyond the *naos* - the main hall that often featured a large image of the deity as its centerpiece. In other words, to reach the treasury, you literally had to pass by the god. Thus, "the more powerful the divinity, the greater the wealth of the temple."[9] By all accounts, there was an enormous amount of wealth deposited at the Temple of Artemis, leading Ephesus to be referred to at times as the bank of Asia. Julius Caesar wrote that, not once, but twice, his arrival in Ephesus prevented a rival from pillaging the wealth of the temple.

The temple in Jerusalem was no exception, except of course that there were no images of Yahweh in the temple. This would have been forbidden in Judaism. Apocryphal books record that "in the treasuries of Jerusalem are stored many thousands of private deposits not belonging to the temple account."[10] The design of modern-day bank buildings and stock exchanges, with their large, imposing columns in front, has actually descended from the architecture of Greek temples.

The picture of making a deposit at the temple and receiving a sealed certificate recording the amount of that deposit, which then allowed you to return and claim your possession at a later time, could explain some of Paul's word choice in Ephesians 1:13-14.

III

Finally, Paul reminds them of the great power of God that is available to the believer. Paul employs the first-person personal pronoun, us, as another reminder that they are no longer on the outside looking in. They are included as part of the believers. Through adoption, they constitute part of the true Israel. Paul uses the words *incomparable* and *great* to describe this power, which leads to two further questions: What is so great about this power, and incomparable, as compared to what? You see, the word for incomparable (*huperballo*) actually means to go beyond or surpass something else. Not surprisingly, Paul can hardly wait for a later point in his letter to address these questions.

As we have already encountered, the belief in magical powers was widespread. Paul witnessed firsthand the burning of magic scrolls in Ephesus (Acts 19:19) and this would have been no small event in the city. It was believed that Artemis gave the Ephesians the capacity to hold other powers in check. Yet there was always the fear that someone else might possess a more powerful form of magic or discover a word or phrase that might inflict a curse. Many of the believers at Ephesus would have come out of this background and would have continued to struggle with the fear of unknown forces that was so pervasive in the pagan culture of the region.

With this in mind, Paul does not simply mention that the God, whom they had believed in, possessed power – every deity encountered in their culture claimed some degree of magical power. Paul specified precisely what was so great about this power. It was the same power that God used to raise Jesus from the dead. To be sure, the challenge implicit in that statement is, "Can your god do that?" There may have been some corroborative evidence that other gods might be invoked to protect life if, say, the person wanting protection was still alive, or to inflict sickness, if someone grew ill, or even to take life, in the case where someone died. You may not have been able to prove causation, but circumstances may very well have led you to believe that there was a certain potency in invoking a god or a magic phrase. But who could produce evidence that another god could restore life to something that was dead? This was Paul's bold claim.

It is important to note that Paul is not asserting that Jesus had been crucified, died, and now somehow was only alive in a spiritual sense. Anyone might boast that their god could do that. Paul is asserting that Jesus was physically raised from the dead. There were many witnesses to this in Jerusalem and Paul counted himself among them:

For what I received I passed on to you as of first importance: that Christ died for our sins according to the Scriptures, that he was buried, that he was raised on the third day

according to the Scriptures, and that he appeared to Peter, and then to the Twelve. After that, he appeared to more than five hundred of the brothers and sisters at the same time, most of whom are still living, though some have fallen asleep. Then he appeared to James, then to all the apostles, and last of all he appeared to me also, as to one abnormally born.
(1 Corinthians 15:3-8)

Even now Jesus was still very much alive sitting at the right hand of God, a position of power, in God's kingdom.

Remember, the heavenly realms - the kingdom of God - is not a place that is separate from the earth, but is a realm where God's plan is safely being carried out under God's control. Thus, it is beyond the reach of all rule and authority, power and dominion, or any other name that could be invoked. That Paul is specifically addressing this pagan worldview, and not simply speaking in ethereal terms, Peter O'Brien, citing the work of Clinton Arnold, points out "several of the particularly rare terms in this petition appear in the magical papyri and inscriptions from Ephesus."[11] It was this power that surpassed that of, and was safely protected in a realm beyond the reach of, Artemis, the Ephesia Grammata, the emperor-cult, or even Caesar himself. It was a welcome reminder for the believer that Israel's God possessed incomparably great power, and that this power was at work protecting them and was made available to them through the Holy Spirit. Arnold concludes, "For those who lived in constant fear of the dreadful workings of evil spirits, this would have provided much comfort."[12]

In fact, all these things will be placed at the feet of Jesus as God moves his plan to fulfillment of bringing all things in heaven and on earth together under the reign of Jesus. Here, Paul draws on messianic language: "The Lord says to my lord, 'Sit at my right hand until I make your enemies a footstool for your feet'" (Psalm 110:1). By tying all this together, Paul is not only claiming that God's power trumps that of all other rulers and authorities, be it human rulers or magical spirits, but that God's plan includes subjugating these rulers and authorities under the reign of Jesus the Messiah.

And because believers have been adopted into God's family, the believer has a role to play in that plan to restore all of creation. As Jesus is reigning at the right hand in the heavenly realms, the church is the fullest expressing of that reign in the earthly realm. The church, with Jesus as its head, is where the kingdom of God is already advancing the reality of God's plan. It is where Jew and Gentile worship together, giving visible expression to this plan, with all the life-restoring power of God available through God's Spirit – to the praise of his glory!

AND ALL GOD'S PEOPLE SAID, "AMEN"

With this, Paul closes his opening prayer for the Ephesians. We can imagine that the initial hearers of this letter may have received this prayer, in whatever posture of prayer they might have taken, as if Paul himself was praying over them. As the Ephesian church eagerly awaited to hear what the Apostle had to say to them, they may have been kneeling, some with eyes closed taking in every word of this prayer, others standing with arms outstretched receiving this blessing. No matter what the posture, the church at Ephesus must have emerged from this prayer with a whole new purpose for gathering. God was bringing all creation back under His authority, this plan was revealed and accomplished through the death and resurrection of Jesus the Messiah, and as Gentiles, they were part of this plan from the beginning. Now that was a plan they could take to the bank!

7 A TALE OF TWO TEMPLES

I have set eyes on the wall of lofty Babylon, on which is a road for chariots, and the statue of Zeus by the Alpheus, and the hanging gardens, and the Colossos of the Sun, and the huge labor of the high pyramids, and the vast tomb of Mausolus, but when I saw the house of Artemis that mounted to the clouds, those other marvels lost their brilliancy, and I said, "Lo, apart from Olympus, the Sun never looked on aught so grand!"
- Antipater of Sidon, *Greek Anthology*

Having walked through the ancient city of Ephesus, my brother and I set out for the nearby site of the Temple of Artemis. We cut through an orchard and after crossing a busy road, followed the shaded walking path back toward the town of Selçuk. A sign pointing down a non-descript road indicated that the site of the temple was near. Otherwise it is easy to miss. A dirt parking lot and a couple vendors selling trinkets indicated that this was indeed the site. All that remains of what was once the largest temple in the Roman Empire is a single reconstructed column and its enormous footprint left imprinted in the earth. The footprint is now filled with water and is home to what seems to be hundreds of turtles. A stork's nest is perched atop the solitary column. What remains of the ancient wonder hardly inspires awe, but a trip to nearby Didyma to the Temple of Apollo helps overlay what would have been a massive temple precinct onto the verdant marshland. Didyma's temple was not quite as large as the temple at Ephesus yet the same architect designed them both.

III

My wife and I spent two years in Nashville, Tennessee while she finished her graduate studies at Vanderbilt University. During those two years, I was doing some consulting work from home, which came with the added flexibility of being able to spend considerable time researching the topic of Ephesus. In addition to utilizing Vanderbilt's library, I was also reading my own books on the subject, including one on the *Seven Wonders of the World*. Living adjacent to campus, as well as across the street from Nashville's Centennial Park, I spent many an evening taking the dog for a run past the football stadium and through the park, circling the full-scale replica of the Parthenon in Athens, Greece, which serves as the park's centerpiece. Today, most people would associate Nashville with the music industry, but back in 1897 the Parthenon replica was constructed for the Tennessee Centennial and International Exposition. Before it was known as "Music City", Nashville was known as the "Athens of the South" for its many educational institutions, and the Parthenon replica only strengthened the ties to ancient Greece. It is easy to see how it served as inspiration during those evening runs as I returned home to study more Greek gods, temples, and Hellenistic culture.

During the bulk of those two years, I never knew what was housed inside Nashville's Parthenon. I would ask a local every now and then, but all I would get was a shoulder shrug or a vague notion about an art gallery. So imagine my surprise while reading about the *Seven Wonders of the World*, when I ran across these words:

> *There is still a place in the world where you may walk into a temple and experience something of that ancient and alarming confrontation with a god ... [I]n Nashville, Tennessee, the good citizens built themselves a plaster Parthenon for a centennial exhibition ... [W]hen you push open those great bronze doors you find inside a statue so gigantic that your head is hardly level with its sandal straps. Yet here as well, standing under this reconstruction of Athena Parthenos – a third of the height of the Statue of Liberty and currently the largest indoor statue in the world – the temple's architecture is still friendly and accessible.[1]*

Here I was trying to comprehend what it must have been like to encounter Artemis of Ephesus, and not more than 500 yards away from my house stood Athena Parthenos in all her splendor! I had jogged by her temple numerous times a week and was totally unaware of her presence. And when I did finally explore the inside of the Parthenon, it was truly awe-inspiring!

Even though today a solitary column remains of Ephesus' wonder of the world, walking into the Parthenon in Nashville and starring upward at the huge figure of Athena must have been comparable to the experience of entering the Temple of Artemis. One would have been almost forced to bend the knee in order to take in the full scale of the goddess Artemis. Her presence cannot be underestimated in the city of Ephesus.

So we return to one of the key questions of the book of Ephesians: To whom was Ephesians written? If Artemis was such an imposing figure in Ephesus, why does Paul not mention the goddess or her temple by name? While I will not rehash those key points covered earlier[2], we might give the short answer, "for the same reason the Old Testament never mentions the great pyramids, or that the book of Romans never mentions the Pantheon." Or for that matter, for the same reason I lived in Nashville for two years and never knew about the statue of Athena in the Parthenon! New Testament writers were not writing travel guides or compiling lists of architectural wonders.

Additionally, we might argue that Paul would avoid giving these pagan gods and temples too much press, so to speak, since one of his primary messages was that the true god was the God of Israel, and was now available to all who would call on the name of Jesus. But if the Temple of Artemis was such a defining landmark to the Ephesians - indeed the entire region - then we might expect that Paul would borrow the imagery of a temple to convey his message to the Ephesians. This would be language they would understand. And that is precisely what we find in the book of Ephesians.

DIFFERENT BOATS, BUT UP THE SAME CREEK

Keeping in mind that Ephesians chapter 1 was Paul's prayer, we now come to some further explanation of the content of that prayer. Even though he has already announced back in 1:13 this predestined plan of God for Gentiles to be included among the chosen - part of the true Israel - Paul briefly returns to addressing Jew and Gentile separately. Fortunately, he does not linger here long. If unity in Christ is the end goal, the perceived ethnic divide has to be addressed as the starting point.

As for you, you were dead in your transgressions and sins, in which you used to live when you followed the ways of this world and of the ruler of the kingdom of the air, the spirit who is now at work in those who are disobedient. All of us also lived among them at one time, gratifying the cravings of our flesh and following its desires and thoughts. Like the rest, we were by nature deserving of wrath. (Ephesians 2:1-3)

Thus, Paul returns to addressing the recipients as *you*, excluding himself for the moment. He begins by calling on them to remember what it was like to be excluded from the people of God. If the Ephesian church was comprised of Gentiles who either did not understand that they were part of

God's plan or had forgotten their status as part of the true Israel, then pausing to remember their previous status may have helped reinforce their new status. Even though we are told in scripture that God will not remember our past sins - that is, hold them against the person who accepts God's forgiveness – remembering what our life was like without God can serve to solidify our new life with God. Three times in this chapter, Paul calls on the Ephesians to recall this life without God

Being a Jew himself, Paul may have been drawing from the frequent refrain in the Hebrew Scriptures to "remember that you were slaves in Egypt." In the book of Deuteronomy, numerous laws were given to the Israelites, followed by the reminder that they had just been redeemed from their exile in Egypt: "Remember that you were slaves in Egypt and Yahweh your God redeemed you from there. That is why I command you to do this" (Deuteronomy 24:18). Even though they were no longer exiles, their time of exile in Egypt was to shape their behavior and ethic as a people. (At least at the time of Deuteronomy, the Israelites were no longer in exile. By Paul's time, the belief was widely held that they were, once again, in exile as long as Rome was calling the shots.) This refrain would continue to echo throughout the Old Testament.

For the Gentile, the equivalent call to remember the time of exile in Egypt would be to remember life apart from God, exiled from the people of God. The "ways of this world" was their Egypt, and the ruler of the kingdom of the air was their Pharaoh. But no sooner does Paul call the Gentile Ephesians to remember their own time of exile, separated from the Jews, than he also gives the same ultimate diagnosis to the Jew as well. Real exile was never under the whip of Pharaoh or the sword of Rome. The real exile had always been under the grip of the ruler of the prince of the air, the spirit who is still at work among those who are disobedient. The real struggle had always been a spiritual struggle, which Paul will delve into further in Ephesians chapter 6.

It is with this shared diagnosis that Paul returns to inclusive language: "All of us also lived among them at one time." The Jew and Gentile had more in common than they realized. They were both slaves to their own desires and thoughts, subject to every craving that enticed. The Jews of Paul's day wrestled with the notion that they could find themselves outside of the covenant; they were Jews, after all! On the other hand, Gentiles wrestled with the notion that they could actually be counted as part of the covenant. They may have taken different paths, but apart from God, the same fate awaited both. Both groups found themselves deserving of God's wrath.

So it was with both groups, Jew and Gentile, drifting perilously close to the brink of destruction, that God tossed out a life preserver. God, because of his great love for *us* – both Jew and Gentile – intervened, making us alive with Christ. Paul, again, stresses the riches (*plousios*, from *ploutos*) of God's mercy in doing so. The extent of this mercy was demonstrated by the fact that this lifeline was extended not in response to a cry for help from either group, but it was extended even as both groups drifted aimlessly, dangerously unaware of their impending fate.

Here Paul begins to unpack the first part of the plan of God: God's plan is to bring all creation back under his authority, this plan was revealed and accomplished through the death and resurrection of Jesus, and as Gentiles, they were part of this plan from the beginning. Now that they had recalled their own time of exile apart from the people of God, he wants them to also revisit the good news: They were part of God's plan. And it was only by grace that this could be done. *It is by grace you have been saved!*

Verses 6 and 7 of Ephesians 2 contain, in abbreviated form, much of Paul's theology behind this plan of God. As part of Paul's prayer in chapter 1, he has already mentioned the power of God that is available to the believer, and it was this same power that God used to raise Jesus from the dead (1:20). But God did not just raise Jesus from the dead and elevate him to the place of authority at God's right hand. God raised us up as well – both Jew and Gentile – to that same place with the Messiah Jesus. Two main points can be made that will fill in some of the details of this abbreviated theology of the resurrection of Jesus.

First, when Paul writes that Christ had been raised, he is referring to the entire event of the actual death, bodily resurrection, and subsequent ascension to God's right hand in the heavenly realm. Returning to 1:20, he has already made this point during his prayer: "That power is the same as the mighty strength he exerted when he raised Christ from the dead." Neither first century Jew nor Gentile would have been overly impressed if all Paul were asserting was that Jesus had died at the hands of the Roman authorities and was now alive in a spiritual sense with God. Most people would have simply accepted that. It bears repeating that Paul is clearly boasting of God's power to physically raise the crucified Jesus from the dead, back to life. And after having ascended, he is still very much alive with God in the heavenly realm. This is a very different claim that anyone back in Paul's day, or in our own day for that matter, would presume to make.

In Paul's mind and in early Christian thought, the death and resurrection of Jesus affirmed him as the world's true messiah (hence Paul's use of the Greek title, *Christ*). With Jesus affirmed as Christ, death was conquered and no longer ruled. God raising Christ from the dead also signaled the beginning of the age to come. In the words of N.T. Wright, "Jesus' resurrection meant that the story of God, Israel, and the world had entered its new phase."[3] Thus, the plan of God was being revealed and was now moving forward to all who wished to understand and embrace it.

Second, when Paul writes that we also have been raised with Christ, he is further asserting that this raising up would foreshadow the destiny of those who accepted Jesus as Messiah. Again, Wright states, "Jesus' resurrection is the beginning of the 'end,' and the resurrection of all believers is (one feature of) the final end of the 'end.'"[4] Physical death would not be the end of the story, but would rather signal the full transition into the next chapter – the age to come.

Paul also gives us a glimpse into the role of the believer in this age to come - when God brings all creation back under his authority - when he informs us that we will not just be citizens of this new rule. Rather, we will co-rule with Christ, with all the wealth, power, and privileges of someone who stood to inherit a throne and a kingdom. The Ephesians would have been familiar with the examples of rulers such as Augustus, Caligula, and Nero, and their ascent to power, though God's kingdom would be markedly different from the harsh rule of emperors such as Caligula and Nero.

Not to be lost in all this good news, was the constant reminder that, as Gentiles, they (the Ephesian believers) were included as part of this ascent to the right hand of God with Jesus. They had gone from certain death, exiled from God's kingdom, to co-rulers. Perhaps the example of the improbable emperor Claudius would serve as a more apropos illustration of an unlikely ascent to power. They had come full-circle; the transformation was complete.

It was this radical transformation from exile to co-ruler that would serve to demonstrate just how wealthy God is in his administration of grace. In case they may have already forgotten to *remember*, this outrageous change of fate was all God's doing. It was his ultimate plan. It is truly a free gift from God.

The next couple of verses are no doubt familiar if you grew up in a church setting, as Ephesians 2:8-9 is one of the more oft-quoted scripture from the New Testament. It is undeniably a clear explanation of grace and how we should not confuse any of our own efforts as being a means of salvation. Yet, this free gift mentioned in these verses can only be fully appreciated when the whole plan of God, unpacked from the previous verses, is fully grasped. I wonder if too often nowadays, we hurriedly express this free gift of grace without taking people back to the beginning of why we are in such need of this free gift in the first place. Are we giving people enough time to remember? I am reminded of a quote from Brennan Manning on this subject, who writes that too many sermons are comprised of heavy-handed moralizing, guilt, and distorted images of god. Then he adds, "For many devout people who hear such sermons, the Good News isn't news and it isn't good."[5] The way Paul has unpacked this message of grace was truly good news. They had been reminded of the extent to which they had journeyed with God, from being exiles to co-rulers, from death to life. We must make sure that we are giving people the full picture of the good news – the gospel – of grace!

III

THE GOSPEL OF PIXODARUS

To the Ephesians, the concept of good news was not one that originated with the Apostle Paul. The idea that Paul was a bringer of good news (*euangelion*) would have allusions back to the very foundation of Ephesus and the Temple of Artemis. Vitruvius, who wrote in the first century BC, explains that when the temple was being designed, marble would have been shipped in from other locales at great expense. But one day, while a shepherd named Pixodarus was pasturing his sheep not far from the city, one of the rams struck a rock, chipping off a piece, revealing it to be marble. Pixodarus ran back to the city with the marble chip announcing the discovery of a nearby marble quarry. Vitruvius describes the response to the news: "Thus the citizens decreed him divine honors and changed his name. Instead of Pixodarus he was to be named Evangelus."[6] Even up to the time of Paul, sacrifices were made on a monthly basis at the quarry honoring the original Ephesian evangelist. But while Pixodarus' good news would help build the great columns of the Temple of Artemis, Paul's gospel would threaten its very foundations.

III

To the mostly Gentile church in Ephesus, this was what they would have been taught from the beginning when Paul arrived in Ephesus. But several years had passed since Paul's time there and Paul felt the need to remind them of what God was doing in the world. They were living in a new age, the age to come had already begun, and they were just as much a part of God's people as the Jewish believers, some of whom were no doubt a part of this church as well. Perhaps these Jewish believers also needed the reminder that they were not somehow elevated above their Gentile brothers and sisters. They may have been among the first to believe, but God's plan from the beginning was that Jew and Gentile would be brought together into the kingdom of God. No more *you* versus *us*!

Paul finishes this section by declaring that we - both Jew and Gentile believer - "are God's workmanship." It is often pointed out that this word *workmanship (poiema)* can refer to a work of art. Broadly speaking, the Greek concept of workmanship refers to anything made, be it a book, a poem, or a construction project. Paul uses this word elsewhere to refer to God's creation.[7] Here Paul is again using this word to refer to creation, only this time he is not referencing the Genesis creation. He is using it to refer to new creation. The result of God bringing dead things - in this case, Jews and Gentiles - back to life with Christ can be referred to as God's workmanship. Paul is also anticipating the new creation, or new person God is creating by bringing Jew and Gentile together, making the two one. So, in one sense, we are God's work of art. But what God created is much more than just a painting that hangs on the wall. God reclaimed what was destined for death and gave it new life. Perhaps it is better to say that we are God's prized reclamation project!

Before we leave this concept of workmanship, I want to offer another idea. I wonder if Paul wasn't contrasting God's workmanship with another piece of workmanship that would have been familiar to both Paul and the Ephesians. We have already established that the mob scene at the amphitheater in Ephesus left an indelible impression on Paul. This mob scene was prompted by the trade guilds that made shrines to Artemis. These shrines could have also been referred to as created things - works of art. Perhaps Paul chose this word *poiema* as a veiled reference to these shrines. But instead of simply offering up an alternative piece of workmanship to Artemis, Paul is pointing out the major difference between the two handiworks. At the end of the day, the Artemis shrines remained passive works of art. But as new creation, believers were quite active in reflecting the glory of their creator. As one writer makes the differentiation, "We are not only made in God's image but also to image God or to reflect Him."[8] Artemis may have her lifeless shrines, but Yahweh has created living, breathing shrines to the glory of God. We are God's living shrines!

The connection between God's workmanship and new creation is explicitly strengthened with the phrase that follows, "created in Christ Jesus to do good works." God had a purpose in mind for this new creation. The purpose of this newly created thing was to bear witness to the Creator, demonstrating the holiness of this Creator, at least in part by the holy way of life lived out by the creation. Indeed, *good works* was an expression that Paul often used to refer to godly behavior.[9] It is not to be confused with the works - or human effort - that Paul had just referred to in the previous verse as being insufficient for salvation. Our own efforts cannot save us, but through the gift of God's grace, empowered by the Holy Spirit, our new life in Christ can be characterized by godly living. This "good works" way of living will be spelled out by Paul at length in the second half of his letter, as he encourages the Ephesian church to respond to the plan of God by fully embracing life as the people of God.

Finally, Paul adds that these good works were *prepared in advance*. This is the same word that Paul uses in Romans 9:23, where he conveys a similar idea: "What if he did this to make the riches of his glory known to the objects of his mercy, whom he prepared in advance for glory." It was God's purpose for this new creation - or in the case of Romans, the objects of God's mercy

- to embrace a holy way of life. This is another instance where we can easily get distracted by a debate that Paul himself was not engaged in. Many interpretations today will read a "[strong] predestinarian thrust"[10] into this Greek word. But again, this is simply another way that Paul refers to the fact that this plan of God was decided ahead of time, from the beginning. Paul is not making the argument that the actions, i.e. good works, of each individual believer have already been scripted out, raising the question of whether or not we have free will. He is referring to the plan that God had in mind all along: to bring all creation back under God's authority, and as Gentiles, they were part of this plan *from the beginning*.

MR. GORBACHEV, TEAR DOWN THIS WALL

These being the words of President Ronald Reagan in a speech to the people of West Berlin in 1987, imploring the Communist leaders of East Berlin to remove the barrier that separated East from West. Two years later, that barrier would indeed be dismantled. No matter how famous walls may be, from the Berlin Wall to the Great Wall of China, the meaning behind a wall is usually rather straightforward: You are either inside or out. Unless you know the people inside you are not welcome past this point. Not to ignite a current debate, but it is one reason why I am uneasy with the border fence separating the United States from Mexico. It is not the way to tell your neighbors that you would like friendly relations with them. As a matter of foreign policy, nothing good usually comes from erecting walls.

Paul will draw on one final and powerful image in this section to help these Ephesian believers remember their previous status without Christ: the physical barrier that separated them, as Gentiles, from the inner courts of the Jewish Temple in Jerusalem. They were a people separated and excluded, and consequently, without hope and without God. But that was their former status. That had all changed. The barrier had been torn down. The time was now to fully embrace their new status as the people of God: "But now in Christ Jesus you who once were far away have been brought near by the blood of Christ" (Ephesians 2:13).

Paul calls on them, based on everything he has just previously written, to *remember* and reflect on that former status one last moment: "Therefore, remember." Remember that as Gentiles, you were not born into this status as God's people. Remember that you were referred to as the uncircumcised, that term being more or less a derogatory term by those who were circumcised as a physical sign of being part of Yahweh's covenant people. Remember that you were separated from Christ and excluded from citizenship. Remember that in this scenario, you were the foreigners, the people who had no hope of achieving a respected status. The Ephesians were by all accounts, separated – on the outside of the wall looking in.

(It should be noted, however, that Paul stresses that this circumcision was performed by human hands. In other words, Paul seems to be stressing that circumcision performed on the flesh is not a creation-work of God. So that while the Gentiles were not part of the circumcised, the Jewish people failed to realize that physical circumcision was only a sign of, and was no guarantee of, the supernatural new-creation work of God. Paul continues to draw heavily from this root word, *to do, to work, to create (poieo)*, in order to distinguish the workmanship of God from the workmanship of humans.)

But the status as outsiders was their former status. Through the blood of Christ - the death and resurrection of Jesus – the plan of God was revealed and as Gentiles, they were no longer on the excluded list. They had been brought near, able to enjoy the full benefits of insiders. Yet we must wonder how many of these Ephesian believers lingered on the outside, either not fully accepting their membership into the people of God or perhaps being told by agitators - "the circumcision" - that they still were not allowed beyond a certain point. Again, it seems to be a reoccurring theme that the Ephesian believers needed to be reminded of their inclusion in God's plan.

To return to a previous example, they had been given first-class upgrades, yet it seems that some of them were not fully embracing their new status. While they could have spent a layover in the first-class lounge, they were afraid that they might be embarrassed or commit some faux pas, exposing them as not really having earned their first-class status. So they were content to wait beyond the walls of the lounge with all the other passengers. And when the boarding call went out for first-class passengers, they waited behind to board with everyone else. (I remember one time getting upgraded. As I boarded the flight, I grabbed the boxed lunch from a cart on the jet bridge. When I sat down, the flight attendant grabbed the box lunch from me and said very seriously, "Oh, these aren't for you!") They may have been holding a first-class ticket, but they were not fully embracing their first-class way of living.

So even though Paul wants them to remember for the moment their former life apart from God, he will spend the remainder of Ephesians chapter 2 helping them also remember (perhaps explaining to some for the first time) their new status as part of the plan of God and what that new status would mean for them as Gentiles.

This plan of God was revealed and accomplished through the aforementioned death and resurrection of Jesus. In other words, it was in Christ that those who once were far away had been brought near. Paul can now spell out how the death and resurrection of Jesus truly incorporates the Gentiles as part of the people of God. He encapsulates his explanation with the statement, "For he himself is our peace, who has made the two groups one and has destroyed the barrier, the dividing wall of hostility" (Ephesians 2:14).

Peace was made possible when the two groups, Jews and Gentiles, became one – when cultural distinctions became secondary to their new identity of being in Christ. And this was no small accomplishment. Of course, it was not simply that the two groups had distinct cultures, but the two cultures often clashed. Hostilities went back a thousand years or more. When Israel entered the promised land of Canaan, God gave them the Mosaic Law as a covenant between God and the Israelites: "I will be your God and you will be my people." These laws would set the Israelites apart from the surrounding nations. The people of Edom, Moab, and the Canaanites were often described as wicked people without a sense of morality. In urging them to keep these laws, God said to the people, "You must not do as they do in Egypt, where you used to live, and you must not do as they do in the land of Canaan, where I am bringing you. Do not follow their practices" (Leviticus 18:3). It was through this covenant that Israel began to distinguish herself from the nations around her.

Yet far from promoting separatism or isolationism, this covenant was meant to lay the groundwork for the inclusion of other nations. Israel, as a nation, would serve as a kingdom of priests to other nations. Their collective moral example would serve to call others to a similar standard. It was all part of what God had originally promised Abraham: "… and all peoples on earth will be blessed through you" (Genesis 12:3), and later repeated through the prophets: "… for my house will be called a house of prayer for all nations" (Isaiah 56:7). But Israel spurned the part about being a blessing to other nations and pursued a policy of isolationism. By the time of Paul, the view from Judea was that if you were not a Jew, you were simply a pagan Gentile. Instead of building bridges, they erected walls.

It was in part because of this isolationism that, from a Hellenistic perspective, the Jews were a peculiar people with strange practices. Their monotheism did not jibe with the pantheon of the Romans and Greeks. Their refusal to accept the inevitability of Roman domination manifested itself in frequent rebellions and unrest. They resisted every attempt to make Jerusalem into a Roman city. Even when dispersed to places like Rome and Ephesus, the Jews were slow to integrate culturally, often keeping their own set of social mores, choosing to remain separate. "Jews were notorious for abstaining from the two main means of social intercourse with non-Jews": meals and marriage.[11] Thus, the view from Rome was that if you were not integrating into Roman culture, you were a barbarian.

This separatism and mutual suspicion created hostility. And perhaps nothing symbolized this hostility more than the temple in Jerusalem, with its dividing wall separating Jew from Gentile. Herod's Temple in Jerusalem was divided into four areas, each becoming increasingly exclusive on who could proceed forward. The outermost court of the temple was known as the Court of the Gentiles. It was in this area that Jesus drove out the moneychangers, perhaps in part because commerce had overtaken the one area of the temple that Gentiles were allowed to enter and worship. The next area of the temple was the Court of Women. Jewish men and women could proceed to this area, but Gentiles were prohibited from moving beyond the Court of the Gentiles, an act punishable by death. Jewish men could continue on into the Court of the Israelites, but only if they were ritually clean. The actual temple building itself was off limits to all but the temple priests. And of course, no one was allowed into the innermost Holy of Holies area, sectioned off by a large curtain, except for the high priest, and that was permissible only once a year.

THE DIVIDING WALL OF HEROD'S TEMPLE

When Paul writes in Ephesians 2:14 that Jesus has "destroyed the barrier, the dividing wall of hostility," he was not speaking of some metaphorical wall, rather he was undoubtedly referring to the literal wall in Herod's Temple, which separated the Court of the Gentiles from the Jewish inner courts. The first century Jewish writer Josephus describes this wall as being "a partition made of stone all around … upon it stood pillars, at equal distances from one another, declaring the law of purity, some in Greek, and some in Roman letters, that 'no foreigner should go within that sanctuary.'"[12] Two of these inscriptions have been discovered written in Greek, which confirm the description of Josephus. One is a complete inscription that reads, "No foreigner is to enter the balustrade enclosure around the temple area. Whoever is caught will have himself to blame for his death will follow."[13] Author Peter O'Brien points out that this wall was not just an architectural feature in Herod's Temple, but represented the Jewish view of the world: "The literal barrier in the temple which prohibited Gentiles from entering the inner courts where Israel worshipped was simply the outward expression of the Mosaic commandments."[14] Thus when Paul announced that Jesus was dismantling this dividing wall of hostility, the wall itself may have remained intact for another twenty or so years, but a sledgehammer was being taken to its very reason for existence.

So for Paul, nothing symbolized this hostility more than the wall that separated Jew from Gentile in Herod's Temple, even threatening death to those Gentiles who failed to mind their place in the temple. But Paul was writing to Ephesus. Wouldn't this reference to a wall in a temple in Jerusalem be lost on Gentile Ephesians? Are we reading too much into this metaphor? O'Brien concedes, "whether the Gentile readers of this letter, living in Asia Minor, would have recognized such an allusion is questionable", before concluding that "the real barrier was, in fact, the Mosaic law." And if the agitators were continuing to use Mosaic Law as a requirement for these Gentiles of Asia Minor to remain in Christian community, then this dividing wall of hostility very well may have been a reference to the Law.

Yet there remains an intriguing connection between the Ephesians and the Temple in Jerusalem that needs to be explored before we put the matter to rest. Return for a moment to that beach in Miletus where Paul commissioned the Ephesian elders before heading off to Jerusalem for Pentecost. Prior to that, Acts chapter 20 listed several people who were traveling with him at the time, including Tychicus and Trophimus from Asia Minor. Departing Miletus, Paul arrived at Caesarea in the spring of 57, and then made his way to Jerusalem. As mentioned previously, the growing threats against him materialized when he was apprehended in Jerusalem on fabricated charges of bringing a Gentile into the inner courts of the temple.

It would be this Trophimus who would be pegged by some Jews from the province of Asia as illegally accompanying Paul past the Court of the Gentiles, thus breaking Jewish law: "'People of Israel, help us! This is the man who teaches everyone everywhere against our people and our law and this place. And besides, he has brought Greeks into the temple and defiled this holy place.' (They had previously seen Trophimus the Ephesian in the city with Paul and assumed that Paul had brought him into the temple.)" (Acts 21:28-29). Paul would spend the next two years imprisoned in Caesarea, before being transported to Rome (including the shipwreck at the island of Malta). Paul would then spend two more years in Rome under house arrest, and it was during this time that Paul wrote the letter of Ephesians.

It was Trophimus the Ephesian then, that was caught squarely in the middle of Paul's arrest in Jerusalem and ensuing imprisonment from that spring in 57 to 61. Certainly, the charges were bogus, as it was revealed that the accusers had seen Paul and Trophimus together the previous day and had simply assumed that he must have accompanied Paul into the inner courts of the temple. Besides, Trophimus would have been the one in trouble and there is no mention of him being apprehended or questioned. Yet Trophimus must have felt threatened and left shaken that his association with Paul may have triggered Paul's arrest and imprisonment. It is not difficult to imagine that Trophimus returned to Ephesus and recounted to the church what had happened and why Paul was now in custody. And it is a mere hop from there to suppose that Trophimus must have explained to the Ephesian church the difference between the Court of the Gentiles and the inner court of the Jews at Herod's Temple and just what these charges entailed, as well as offering his own acquittal of his whereabouts while in Jerusalem, specifically within the temple complex.

Subsequently, the Ephesians may have had more understanding than other Gentile churches regarding the layout and restrictions of the temple in Jerusalem. It was only about three years later that Paul would write these words to them, reminding them that Jesus was dismantling these dividing walls between Jew and Gentile. Trophimus himself may have even been present when the church received this letter. Trophimus evidently accompanied Paul on some of his later travels after his release from Rome because Paul later writes to Timothy in Ephesus that he had to leave Trophimus sick in Miletus, too weary to travel.

Therefore, the wall separating Jew from Gentile in the Jerusalem Temple would serve as a fitting and meaningful image for Paul's "dividing wall of hostility." For Paul, this dividing wall encapsulated all of the symbols that had lead Israel down the path of isolationism - not only the wall, but the entire temple cult, the sacrificial system, as well as all that the law had come to represent. It is important to distinguish the intent of the Torah and the application of Torah, along with all its interpretations, which had come to be used as a means of separating Jew from Gentile. Elsewhere, the value of Torah is upheld and affirmed. Jesus clarified that he did not come to abolish the law, but rather to fulfill it and Paul later corroborates this view.[15] The death and resurrection of Jesus would bring an end to these symbols of separatism. God was bringing his plan back to its original intent: Jew and Gentile together would form the people of God.

Now, instead of hostility there would be peace, and peace would only come when the two groups found a common identity beyond ethnic, cultural, and geographic distinctions. By identifying with Jesus above all else, the two groups could forge a new identity, or as Paul states it, "one new person." This one new humanity is yet another allusion to new creation.

We can begin to follow the thread back through the letter thus far and untangle at least one of Paul's lines of thinking. The church is the body of Christ (Ephesians 1:23) here in this earthly realm, the physical representation of the risen Jesus, who is now in the heavenly realm. The church is also a new creation, part of God's plan to restore all of original creation back to the way God intended it (Ephesians 2:10). And it is this new creation - the church - that will give old rivalries a new unifying identity. Ironically, this hostility between Jew and Gentile was one factor contributing to the death of Jesus. But just as this hostility put Jesus to death, his death gave birth to the creation of something new, and through his resurrection and ascension Jesus was now putting to death the very hostility that led to his death in the first place. With the hostility between the two vanquished, they could now come together and embody this new creation. This is what is implicit in being the church.

Once more, Paul reminds the Ephesians that this message of peace is for "you who were far away": You who continue to think of yourselves as outsiders, holding a first-class ticket and yet content to fly coach (and eating the box lunch). Undoubtedly Paul drew heavily from the message of Isaiah, for Isaiah himself recognized God's inclusive plan long before Paul divulged its mysteries. Here he borrows a phrase from Isaiah 57:19: "'Peace, peace, to those far and near,' says Yahweh. 'And I will heal them.'" This actually picks up on Isaiah's earlier proclamation that "my house will be called a house of prayer for all nations." Through Jesus, there were no longer separate classes, courts, or paths to God the Father.

SURPASSING ALL BUILDINGS AMONG MEN

Chapter 2 concludes with Paul emphatically declaring that whatever their old status may have been - be it uncircumcised Gentiles, non-citizens of Israel or foreigners to the covenant - those labels were a thing of the past: "Consequently, you are no longer foreigners and aliens, but fellow citizens with God's people and members of God's household" (Ephesians 2:19). It was time to begin thinking differently - renewing their mind, to use a phrase Paul uses elsewhere – and fully embrace their new position. Two images are drawn upon to stress their new standing.

As opposed to being foreigners, they could now consider themselves fellow citizens with God's people. In the Roman Empire, citizenship was a preferred status, and came with its privileges. For starters, Roman citizens were exempt from paying many, if not all, taxes. Taxes were the burden of the conquered. Citizenship also meant that you could pursue the *cursus honorum* – the path to a future in Roman politics. It also entitled you to draw up a will, meaning your wealth stayed in your family upon death. (And, as Paul would discover, it also entitled you to a fair trial!) Essentially, citizenship moved you from being a nobody to the opportunity to become somebody. The definitive dream of a slave in the Roman Empire was to somehow, someday, become a Roman citizen. With that in mind, and with the barriers removed, the Ephesians could fully pursue their citizenship in God's kingdom.

And in contrast to being outsiders, separated from God without hope, they were now members of God's household. Similar to the example of citizenship, to be a member of a household meant refuge and protection.[16] You came under the jurisdiction of the *paterfamilias*. Your household and family name forged your identity. Paul will further draw on the example of this basic Roman institution at greater length later in his letter. But it is important to understand that both examples represent sweeping changes in status and identity in the Roman world.

However, if there was one concept that translated into any culture of Paul's time - be it Jewish, Greek, Egyptian, or Roman culture - it was the centrality of the temple. And there was no place this would have been truer than in Ephesus. As Murphy-O'Connor notes, "Artemis was part of the fabric of Ephesus, and the city was unthinkable without her. Ministry in Ephesus, Paul mused, was going to be very different."[17] So Paul would summarize his thoughts using language they could all relate to: the language of temple.

In the original language, this would have been much more observable than deciphering it from our English translations. Moving seamlessly from the images of citizenship to households, Paul then uses the root word *house* from *households* (*oikos*) to construct his final image of this section. This root word *oikos* is used four times in the final three verses to describe the construction process, which results in a completed temple structure. He also employs several other construction terms, making it clear the image Paul had in mind.

Construction begins by laying a foundation on which to build. In order to expand the temple precinct in Jerusalem, Herod had to enlarge the platform area, including using retaining walls to fill in valleys and utilizing a series of Roman arches to form a level foundation on which to construct his new temple. The foundation of the temple in Ephesus had to overcome the fact that it was constructed on a marsh. According to Pliny the Elder, in order to prevent the foundation from sinking, the area was first filled with charcoal, which would remain solid even when wet, and then covered with fleeces of wool.[18] If the foundation were not sound, then it would matter little what was constructed on top of it; it would not last long.

III

THE TEMPLE OF ARTEMIS

Pliny the Elder (23 AD to 79 AD) lived at the same time of Paul and left us one of the more detailed descriptions of the Temple of Artemis. In his own words:

The length of the temple overall is 425 feet, and its breadth 220 feet. There are 127 columns, each constructed by a different king and 60 feet in height. Of these, 36 were carved with reliefs, one of them by Scopas. The architect in charge of the work was Chersiphron.[19]

The dimensions of the temple were over twice that (both length and width) of the Parthenon in Athens. If you have had an opportunity to visit Athens and take in the Parthenon, a temple four times the size of the Parthenon would occupy much of the space atop the Acropolis. We can only imagine that the size of the Artemision was massive. It was larger than any other building in Rome, Greece, or Asia.

A large altar would have been found inside the structure. Pliny writes that various works of art also decorated the inside of the temple. Finally, a large statue of Artemis would have been the focal point of the inner temple. Among other things, the temple would have additionally functioned as a bank and a museum.

III

For this new structure God was erecting, the foundation consisted of the apostles and prophets. The apostles refer to the disciples of Jesus who would spread the good news after his death and resurrection, and Paul counts himself in this group as well. There is debate whether the prophets refer to the more traditional view of the Old Testament prophets, or rather to people other than the apostles in the New Testament who were also instrumental in spreading the gospel. Paul will use this phrase again in the next chapter (3:5) and his use there seems to support the latter. Regardless, it is clear that the groundwork for the faith of the Ephesian church had been laid by those who recognized the plan of God and went to great lengths to announce it.

With the foundation in place, the cornerstone (or capstone) is the piece that gives shape and guidance to all the other parts, or as Paul describes it, the part that joins the whole building together. This stone either refers to the squared cornerstone, by which the rest of the structure would be measured against, or the capstone of the roof. Again, there is debate as to which Paul is referring to, but it may suffice to say that in either case it refers to the most important piece of that particular structure. And in this new temple, the most important part is the person of Jesus. It is his life, death, and resurrection that give definition and meaning to the rest of the structure. Jesus as the cornerstone is common New Testament imagery and can also be traced back to the prophet Isaiah, "See, I lay a stone in Zion, a tested stone, a precious cornerstone for a sure foundation" (Isaiah 28:16).

It is interesting to note that Pliny recounts another story around one of the most important stones in the temple of Ephesus. The architect was having great difficulty getting the lintel settled firmly in place over the doorway to the temple. Contemplating suicide (this was no minor setback!) the architect went to sleep for the night. During the night, Artemis herself came to him in a dream and assured him that she would personally set the

105

stone in place. When he awoke the next morning, he found the lintel lying firmly in its proper place over the door. These images would have held much meaning for the Ephesians in particular.

Once the foundation has been laid and the cornerstone has been set in place, the structure can be completed. Stones joined together, columns erected, and all the intricacies affixed, it rises over time to reveal a magnificent temple. In Paul's example, the emergence of this structure occurs through the power and working of Jesus. In an age when buildings go up seemingly overnight, this image cannot be fully appreciated. Herod began construction on the Jewish Temple around 20 BC and it was still being worked on during the time of Jesus' ministry. Pliny indicates that the construction of the Temple of Artemis occupied all of Asia for 120 years! Temples did not go up overnight, so even 30 years after the death and resurrection of Jesus, it would have been appropriate for Paul to speak of the new temple (the church) still in the process of rising from its foundation.

We should also note that these are specific construction terms. Paul will draw on these again in Ephesians chapter 4 when he describes the church as a body, a living organism. But here, Paul is equating the church in all its glory with matching the splendor of any existing temple of his time.

And he cannot complete this image without reminding the Ephesians that "you too" are included in this magnificent construction project. God's plan – God's blueprint, to stick with the analogy – was being fully realized and they were no mere late modification. They were a part of this building project from the beginning. As Gentiles, they would no longer be confined to some outer court. God's spirit would indwell each of them just as much as God's presence had once filled the temple in Jerusalem.

OUR CITIZENSHIP IS IN HEAVEN

So what did it mean to be part of God's new temple and citizens of God's kingdom? Not citizens of Rome, as some of the Ephesians no doubt already were, or citizens of Israel as the Jews would have considered themselves, but as citizens of God's kingdom (or as Paul would write to the Philippian church, citizens of heaven). What did it mean to fully embrace life as the people of God?

Paul will spend a considerable amount of time throughout the rest of his letter answering that question. But some of the immediate benefits Paul had already pointed out were that as citizens of God's kingdom, the barriers obstructing them from full engagement, whether real or perceived, had been removed. Through grace, they were free to pursue the path that God had for them. They had in their possession the gift of the Holy Spirit, who not only was the source of wisdom and revelation, but also gave them full access to God's power. And their future with God was secure, having been made permanent members of God's household.

However, the Ephesian church had apparently forgotten much of this, which is why Paul was compelled to write them and remind them of their new status and identity. It was time for the Ephesian church to live in the full expression of their citizenship in the kingdom of God.

8 MYSTERY SOLVED!

Every year, two sets of Eleusinian Mysteries are held: the Greater in honor of Demeter and Core, and the Lesser in honor of Core alone. These Lesser Mysteries, a preparation for the Greater, are a dramatic reminder of Dionysus's fate, performed by the Eleusinians at Agrae on the river Ilissus in the month Anthesterion. They must then wait at least one year until they may participate in the Greater Mysteries, which are held at Eleusis itself in the month Boedromion; and must take an oath of secrecy, administered by the mystagogue, before being prepared for these.

- from *The Greek Myths*[1]

A s you survey the ancient agora in Athens, Greece, one of the more prominent structures is the Temple of Hephaestus. This temple is one of the most well preserved Greek temples still in existence. Another temple precinct can be found across the agora and up the slope, which leads to the steep cliffs of the Acropolis. Here you will find the scant remains of the Eleusinion. There is not much to look at today, especially if you have just witnessed the Temple of Hephaestus. Yet in its day, this would have been one of the more important temples in Greece. The larger Eleusinian temple complex was actually located outside of Athens, not far away at the site of Eleusis. A sacred way would have connected these two temples, and every fall a procession would begin at Eleusis and follow the sacred way, finishing at the Eleusinion in Athens. All this was part of the Eleusinian Mysteries, a mystery religion that flourished for over a thousand years.

III

Everybody loves a good mystery. From crime dramas on television to the murder-mystery genre of books and movies, our culture loves the twists and turns that a good mystery traverses. We engage with the main character as he or she follows the clues, interprets the signs, and runs the tests, eventually cracking the case putting all the pieces together. Mystery solved!

I remember one movie that created quite a buzz when it was released was the movie *The Sixth Sense.*[2] If you had not figured out what was *really* going on in the movie by the last five minutes, your mind was blown when the mystery finally gets revealed. People could not wait to ask their friends if they had seen the movie and if they were able to figure it out before the ending. The great thing about that movie was that most moviegoers were not able to figure out the plot until the startling revelation at the movie's conclusion.

Yet for the people of Paul's day - be they Greek, Roman, or Hebrew – the word *mystery* had a very different connotation. A mystery was hidden knowledge only understood by those who had gained special insight through some spiritual experience. Many of the pagan religions offered its adherents insights into the spiritual world and its secret mysteries. Not surprisingly, many of these became known as *mystery religions.*

According to Ronald Nash, mystery religions had five basic traits.[3] First, a central component to each was that of the annual vegetation cycle. Crops and vegetation were planted in the spring, grew during the summer months, were harvested or began to die in the fall, and then were reborn again the next spring. Second was the importance of a ceremony or initiation rite. Only after initiation could the secrets and mysteries be revealed to those who made it through. The first rule of most mystery religions was that you did not talk about the mystery religion to those on the outside. Third, there was normally a central myth having to do with the death and rebirth of its deity. Next, these religions were not so much about correct actions and beliefs as they were about emotional experiences. And finally, the goal was some type of mystical experience that would ultimately bring about salvation and eternal life.

One of the most well-known of these mystery religions was the Eleusinian Mysteries. Located not far from Athens, the city of Eleusis was home to a temple to Demeter and the cult that went along with it. The ceremony involved activities such as bathing in the ocean, sacrificing a sow, a ceremonial procession to the Eleusinion in the city of Athens, fasting, and the consuming of a barley drink called *kykeon.* It is speculated that this drink had a hallucinogenic effect, creating some of the ecstatic responses from worshippers. In addition to a temple to Demeter, the site also housed a temple to Artemis, informally linking the temple precinct of Eleusis to the city of Ephesus.

The Eleusinian Mysteries was an active religion for nearly two thousand years. Its initiates ranged from such figures as the Greek hero Heracles to the philosopher Cicero to the Roman emperor Julian. Yet, its secrets were remarkably well kept. If the details seem hazy, it is because there is much that still is not known about the specifics of the cult.

THE MYTH OF DEMETER AND CORE

Demeter was the Greek goddess of the harvest and agriculture, and by extension is sometimes referenced as a fertility goddess as well. She was the daughter of Cronus and Rhea, and among her children was a daughter named Core by her brother Zeus. (Sexual boundaries did not really apply to the Greek gods and goddesses.) The central narrative around Demeter involves the search for her daughter when Core went missing.

Core disappeared when she caught the eye of Hades, king of the Underworld. One day while picking flowers – presumably at the site of Eleusis – Hades opened the earth, abducting Core down into Tartarus. Demeter frantically searched for Core and became enraged when she learned that Hades was behind the abduction. In her anger, Demeter prevented the earth from producing crops until Zeus relented and ordered Core to be reunited with her mother. But Core had already eaten a pomegranate from the Underworld - tasting the food of the dead - essentially preventing her return to the earth.

In order to persuade Demeter to return the land to fertility, a compromise was struck. Core would remain with Hades, becoming queen of the Underworld and taking the name *Persephone*. In return, she would be allowed to leave Tartarus and visit her mother Demeter for an allotted time each year. Thus, every year when Persephone is reunited with Demeter, the earth yields fruit and flowers bloom. But when their time together comes to an end, Demeter's joy also departs, leaving the earth cold and barren until her return the following year.

The story of Demeter and her search for Core has been an enduring myth in Greek culture and gave rise to the Eleusinian Mysteries.

So why all the talk of movies, mysteries, and secret religions? As the third chapter of Paul's letter to the Ephesians begins, the language of mystery becomes frequent and, as previously mentioned, it will be important to hear these words as an Ephesian would have heard them. Paul uses the word *mystery* in his letter to the Ephesians with greater frequency than any other letter. (A close second is his letter to Colosse, which was written around the same time as Ephesians, as well as being written to a similar people.) Chapter three in particular contains half of the occurrences of the word. In addition to the word *mystery*, Paul also employs similar mystery language terminology, such as *revelation, hidden, knowledge,* and *power.* It is clear then, that Paul is purposeful with his language in order to communicate his message. So are you ready to solve the mystery?

DE-MYSTIFYING A MYSTERY

Previously, we noted that Paul could ramble at times and be prone to a "hold that thought" moment every now and then. It is here at the beginning of Ephesians chapter 3 that Paul has one of those moments. He begins with the phrase *for this reason,* but then abruptly pauses as if he is not yet ready to move on to the next thought. In fact, he hits the pause button after the word *Gentile*: "*I, Paul, the prisoner of Christ Jesus for the sake of you Gentiles.*" Perhaps as Paul wrote the words *you Gentiles,* he wanted to emphasis one more time the good news that was being revealed to them – not just the Jews, but to the Gentiles. He will pick his train of thought back up in Ephesians 3:14.

It is also this opening phrase of chapter 3 where Paul offers a clue as to where Ephesians may have been written from by identifying himself as a prisoner of Christ Jesus. This is the first of three times (the others being 4:1 and 6:20) that Paul makes reference to his imprisonment. We previously noted that this narrows his location to two places and timeframes: his imprisonment in Caesarea from 57 to 59, and his subsequent house arrest in Rome from 60 to 62. Because of the impersonal nature of the letter – there seems to be some distance between Paul's stay in Ephesus and the letter - the house arrest from Rome in about 60 or 61 seems the better choice.

But back to the mystery and picking up Paul's unfinished thought. Paul had previously revealed this mystery to them, as he notes here, "I have already written briefly." Yet before he moves on to other subjects, he feels the need to emphasize one more time just what this revelation means to them as Gentiles. And he also wants to take a moment to stress his role in this revelation.

Since Paul had already briefly mentioned this mystery, this particular moment in his letter is not so much about the big announcement as it is restating and making clear just what the big announcement entails. Back in Ephesians 1 during his opening eulogy, Paul revealed the mystery to be that

God was in the process of bringing all things together under the reign of Jesus. Here Paul reiterates the mystery using marginally different language:

This mystery is that through the gospel the Gentiles are heirs together with Israel, members together of one body, and sharers together in the promise in Christ Jesus.
(Ephesians 3:6)

Both accounts reveal the plan of God to be about bringing creation back under the reign of Jesus. But here the emphasis is on the inclusion of the Gentiles as part of that plan. Remember, when Paul expressed this plan in the opening of his letter, the Ephesians were not ready to accept that they had any part in that plan. Paul then goes to great lengths to help them understand that this was not just a Jewish plan, but a collective Jew/Gentile plan – they were part of it. So it is not surprising that before Paul continued, he wanted to give the Ephesians a fresh opportunity to hear the revelation of this mystery again, armed with the assurance that this mystery included them.

Beyond simply restating the mystery, Paul also uses this interlude to explain how he himself arrived at this secret knowledge. He was no mere pagan mystagogue pitching a rival religion. Perhaps it occurred to Paul that in the midst of using all this mysterious language – word choices they would undoubtedly resonate with – he needed to clarify that this message did not originate with him, nor did he possess some magical ability to receive revelation from the gods that was beyond the reach of ordinary people. He was not offering secret initiations nor peddling ecstatic experiences. He wanted to pull back the curtain for a moment so that his role was not misunderstood.

To avoid some potential misunderstanding, Paul uses the term *administration (oikonomia)* to describe his role in this plan of God. This term is where we get our English word *economy* and it is used in relation to the running of a household. A head servant or slave might be in charge of the household economy, ensuring that other servants were getting their tasks done and overseeing the smooth operation of the master's household. So, as a servant of God, Paul saw himself as having ongoing tasks and responsibilities to ensure that this mystery was made known and understood.

This administration would be in contrast with the role of an oracle, who would simply dispense secret knowledge - often cryptically - with no real responsibility of how that knowledge would be utilized. Paul was not peering into the future and washing his hands of the outcome. He had work to do, people to visit, and places to go. In revealing this secret knowledge to them, Paul also felt the personal responsibility to make sure they understood what was expected of them and how they were to respond. This all fell under his duties of administration.

Interestingly, he also assumes that they had heard about his role previously, "Surely you have heard": Paul is not wondering if they have heard all this before, he is quite certain they have. This might be another clue to the recipients of his letter. Paul was writing to people with whom he knew there was at least some familiarity. He invested much time in Ephesus and knew some of the recipients personally. Yet some time had passed and there would have been others with whom he had not interacted. Again, to address Ephesus was also to address the larger region associated with Ephesus.

So even though there was some divine revelation involved in Paul's receiving (see the Damascus Road encounter in Acts 9!) and deciphering this mystery, part of Paul's task could be said to de-mystify God's plan for those involved. He wanted to make sure they understood their role and response to the plan of God:

In reading this, then, you will be able to understand my insight into the mystery of Christ. (Ephesians 3:4)

It may have been a mystery to those in previous generations, but Paul did not want the shroud to remain. This was not knowledge that was only for a select few initiates.

It also merits mentioning that even though Paul indicates that this plan of God was not made known to previous generations, neither was it a foreign idea in the Hebrew Scriptures. In his letter to the Romans, Paul writes:

As it is written: "Therefore I will praise you among the Gentiles; I will sing the praises of your name."
Again, it says, "Rejoice, you Gentiles, with his people."
And again, "Praise the Lord, all you Gentiles; let all the peoples extol him."
And again, Isaiah says, "The Root of Jesse will spring up, one who will arise to rule over the nations; in him the Gentiles will hope." (Romans 15:9-12)

This was just a sampling of scripture from Deuteronomy to Psalms to Isaiah where it was acknowledged that the Gentiles were to be a part of this plan. It was not made known to previous generations only in the sense that it was overlooked and not fully embraced, even though the idea was out there. The clues were there to be deciphered. Perhaps this further contributed to the mysterious aspect of the plan of God.

So the first step of this de-mystification process was for Paul to make clear that the only reason he understood and had access to this hidden knowledge was through the gift of God's grace given to him. If they were crediting Paul with any sort of remarkable power or ability, it was only the power of God working through him - the same power that God used to raise Jesus from the dead.

The next step, then, would be to encourage a response to this knowledge. Unlike times past where this plan of God may have been recognized but not acted upon, Paul considered it his calling to ensure that it no longer remained a mystery: "This grace was given me: to preach to the Gentiles the boundless riches of Christ, and to make plain to everyone the administration of this mystery" (Ephesians 3:8,9). Once more, Paul is careful to minimize his own abilities and merits in the administration of this mystery – he considered himself among the least of the saints. Elsewhere, Paul makes clear that this humility stemmed from his previous life as a persecutor of the church: "For I am the least of the apostles and do not even deserve to be called an apostle, because I persecuted the church of God" (1 Corinthians 15:9). But in revealing this mystery, Paul wanted the Ephesian church to respond to the power of God, and not be distracted by or misunderstand his own role in this revelation. Again, Paul was not out to offer secret initiations or peddle ecstatic experiences.

Having demystified his own role in understanding this plan of God, Paul turns next to explaining how this plan is now unfolding, including their part in what God was doing. He recycles many of his same thoughts from his opening prayer in Ephesians 1. Whereas previously this mystery remained hidden, now it would be announced to the rulers and authorities in the heavenly realms. And this is where the Ephesian church entered into the plan. It would be through the church that this announcement would take place. Certainly, the church here refers to the universal church – the people of God. But Paul wanted the Ephesians to grasp that, as Gentiles, they were part of the people of God and that their church in Ephesus was certainly part of this announcement project. Perhaps Paul even had the many different expressions of the church in mind when he refers to the wisdom of God as *manifold* or *diverse* in 3:10. The full expression of God's wisdom would need the manifold expressions of God's church.

As previously mentioned, the concept of the heavenly realms is an ongoing theme in the book of Ephesians. Remember, when Paul uses this term, he is not referring to a separate, far away realm beyond the physical world. Rather he is referring to the kingdom of God - the unseen backdrop behind everything that is taking place in the world. It is the realm that God was bringing back under the authority of Jesus.

Thus, when the church is said to announce this plan to the rulers and authorities, it is not only its physical representatives standing before the governors and the rulers of the day (just as Paul would stand before Caesar and many other rulers), it was also the authority of the church making this announcement to the spiritual powers behind these rulers. In one sense, Paul was reflecting Greek philosophy, which held that it was the spiritual world that was of importance. The material world was something that needed to be overcome. Yet at the same time, Paul is challenging this same philosophy by acknowledging that the spiritual and the material realm interact with one another and what happens in one can affect the other.[4] It is not, as we will see later in Ephesians 6:12, that the spiritual realm is all that matters, but that the spiritual realm is where the real battle is taking place and that what happens in the physical realm can affect the spiritual.

God's plan was being kept secure in the heavenly realm, but there was an earthly component to it as well. This plan was being announced before literal rulers and authorities, but there was a larger spiritual dimension with all its implications. N.T. Wright maintains that it is the coming together of Jew and Gentile to form the church that "is the sign to the principalities and powers that their time is up … The church is constituted, and lives its life in public, in such a way as to confront the rulers of the world with the news that there is another king named Jesus."[5] This was the role of the church: to publicly announce the plan of God to the world.

And it is precisely because this plan was fulfilled in the person of Jesus that the church can have confidence in this announcement. The ultimate outcome is certain. Paul's words that "we may approach God with freedom and confidence" (Ephesians 3:12) are often used today in reference to the prayers of individuals. And certainly that aspect can be applied to these words. But in the flow of the narrative in which Paul is writing, these words more so apply to the church in announcing the plan of God. The church can confidently make the announcement knowing that God is fully behind it. In fact, in classical Greek the word *freedom* (*parresia*) denotes more a freedom of speech and may tie back to 3:10 and the church's role in making known the plan of God.[6] Whether it is the church announcing or the individual believer praying, we have unrestricted access to the throne of grace!

By now the fog should be lifting from the mystery. Even though Paul was administering this plan, his role was also to de-mystify it for those involved, namely the church. The church's responsibility was to respond to the plan of God and announce it to the surrounding culture.

Therefore, when Paul encourages the Ephesian church "not to be discouraged because of my sufferings for you" in 3:13, he is offering them comfort from a much larger perspective. Paul understood that suffering – in this case, being imprisoned – came with the role of being the *plan administrator*. And in many ways, his suffering was a sign that he was being faithful to his role. Furthermore, as the church they were also participants in this plan of God. So if Paul viewed his suffering as a sign of faithfulness (he refers to the purpose of suffering about thirty times in his letters), then they should certainly share in that glory. Just as sports fans celebrate – or share the glory in – their team's accomplishments, even though they were not the ones playing the game, so followers of Jesus can glory in his victory on the cross.

THE GLORY OF ROME

Ravi Zacharias, a well-known apologist and speaker, has often said that the highest pursuit for the Hebrews was light, for the Greeks it was knowledge, while for Rome the highest pursuit was glory. Glory (*doxa*) is one of those words that has a wide range of meaning. Therefore, depending on the context and audience it can denote slightly different images.

When people nowadays read the word *glory* in scripture, ideas such as majesty, supernatural power, worship, honor, and even heaven come to mind. But for the Roman Empire, glory was much more specific. It had to do with the ambition of a single great world empire. Romans believed that if the world came under the power and influence of Rome, the *Pax Romana* would be established. Peace would reign (as the term suggests), the arts would flourish, people would be educated, and the barbarian world would benefit from the superior Hellenistic culture. The reigning Caesar was the embodiment of that ideal in the Roman Empire. Thus, any advancement of this ideal was for the glory of Rome and for Caesar.

While *glory* has a broader meaning throughout scripture, it perhaps translated well to people who lived under Rome's control that the mystery Paul was revealing was for God's glory. God was bringing all creation back under the sole reign of Jesus, and when that happened, creation would once again flourish and usher in a time of peace.

BUT I DIGRESS …

Paul began Ephesians 3 with the phrase, "For this reason." After deviating into the mystery of the plan of God, he now returns to what he initially intended: a second prayer for the Ephesian believers. He does so by repeating that same phrase. His first prayer was covered in Ephesians 1:15-23 and he will reemphasize much from the initial prayer.

Having just written that *we* - the Ephesians could do this as *freely* as Paul - can approach God with freedom and confidence, Paul does just that, kneeling before the Father on their behalf. He also uses a play on words, indicating that all families (*patria*) derive their name from God the Father (*pater*). The same Greek root word is used for both. The interaction between the heavenly and earthly realm is also used by Paul to further emphasize God's reign over both. It was important that the Ephesians understand that the spiritual realm, which it seems was a source of a good bit of apprehension for them, was not outside of the realm of what God was accomplishing.

I pray that out of his glorious riches he may strengthen you with power through his Spirit in your inner being, so that Christ may dwell in your hearts through faith. And I pray that you, being rooted and established in love, may have power, together with all the Lord's people, to grasp how wide and long and high and deep is the love of Christ, and to know this love that surpasses knowledge - that you may be filled to the measure of all the fullness of God. (Ephesians 3:16-19)

In this second prayer, Paul offers two petitions on their behalf. The first is for the strengthening of their faith. Paul was doing all he could to remind them of their new status and identity, but they would need the ongoing and unending power of the Holy Spirit to live in the full expression of their citizenship in the kingdom of God. So Paul prays for strength and power in their inner being, or the person within them. In other words, if they were to live in the full expression of their citizenship, it would have to come from the very fabric of who they were – their identity - and not simply from some information Paul would pass on to them. Paul had instructed them of all this when he lived among them in Ephesus. He was now reminding them of their identity several years later, still waiting for it to sink down to the level of their inner being.

One of the emphases of his first prayer was the riches or wealth of God. So it was only natural that Paul now draw on those riches as a source of power fully available to them. The inheritance was already available to them as a benefit of their adoption; they only needed to draw upon it.

Likewise, he mentions Christ dwelling in their hearts – their inner being. If they are being built into a holy temple, as Paul has already written, then it only stands to reason that Christ would live there. By the same token, he is not intimating that Christ is currently absent, but that he wants them to fully live in the reality that Christ already dwells among them as they are being built together to form a holy temple (Ephesians 2:22).

But wealth and power, even in the spiritual sense, are nothing unless they are grounded in love. So the second – and more vital – aspect of Paul's prayer here is that they truly understand and are filled with the love of Christ. He prays for the power to grasp this love even though he reminds them up front that they have already been built on a foundation of love. He employs both a farming term (rooted) and a construction term (founded) to stress this. He is not praying for them to understand Christ's love so that they can mystically obtain it. He is praying that they fully grasp what they already have in their possession.

And what they already have is beyond human comprehension. In describing the expanse of God's love Paul covers the width, length, height, and depth. This could be a further elaboration of the manifold wisdom of God referenced back in 3:10. It is another way of saying that God's love extends to all realms – the heavenly and earthly realms. No location or realm is beyond God's reach. This fits well with contrasting God's love and power with the magical powers and spells alluded to throughout this chapter that were commonplace in Ephesus.

Throughout this entire section, Paul is careful to keep the tension between making plain the plan of God and yet still retaining a certain amount of mystery around its unfolding. He is using the language of mystery that the Ephesian culture would have recognized, yet he is trying to de-mystify the work of God. God's plan has been hidden from previous generations, yet it is there for all who would see it. Paul himself understood this mystery by means of unique revelation, yet he is the least of all God's people. For their part, he eagerly wants the Ephesians to take hold of what is already in their possession, to claim the inheritance that has already been credited to them.

It seems only fitting, then, that he concludes the prayer with a couple more tension-filled requests: to *know* the love that surpasses *knowledge* and to be *filled* with the *fullness* of God. This is Paul's way of giving the Ephesian church access to something that seems at times inaccessible to them. He did not want their faith to become just another mystery religion, nor did he want to remove all the mystery from their faith.

A RELIGION WITHOUT MYSTERY MUST BE A RELIGION WITHOUT GOD

Perhaps this is some of the same tension we can feel today in our churches. How do we make God accessible to people without removing all sense of mystery and holiness? In an attempt to make God relevant and reach a wider audience, some churches can remove most of what is sacred and holy. On the other hand, there have been periods in church history that held God to be so holy and beyond that God became inaccessible to ordinary folks. This is the struggle of trying to capture the manifold wisdom of God. Perhaps both approaches are needed and serve to balance each other out.

Paul concludes with a typical blessing at the end of a prayer, reiterating the power of God "to do immeasurably more than all we ask or imagine" and giving God all the praise and glory. This benediction not only closes out the prayer in chapter 3, but also concludes the first half of Paul's letter to the Ephesian church. He has spent a good many words unpacking the plan of God and making sure they understood that they were included in this plan. He has reminded the believers of all they possess in Christ and has encouraged them to live in the full expression of their citizenship in the kingdom of God.

But what does that look like on a daily basis? What did it mean to live as citizens of God's kingdom as they left the gathering and went back to work, as they kept their households, or as they rubbed elbows with the surrounding pagan culture? This is what Paul will address in the second half of his letter: a proper response to their citizenship, to fully embrace life as the people of God, knowing that victory had already been accomplished.

9 GROW UP!

All cities worship Artemis of Ephesus, and individuals hold her in honor above all the gods. The reason, in my view, is the renown of the Amazons, who traditionally dedicated the image, also the extreme antiquity of this sanctuary. Three other points as well have contributed to her renown, the size of the temple, surpassing all buildings among men, the eminence of the city of the Ephesians and the renown of the goddess who dwells there.

- Pausanias, *Guide*

The structure most often associated with photos of Ephesus is the Celsus Library. Its façade is elaborate and impressive, but the structure itself post-dates Paul's time in Ephesus. Just to the right of the library is the Mithridates Gate, which serves as the south entrance to the large commercial agora. An inscription above the triple-arched gate begins, "To the Emperor Caesar Augustus son of a god, the high priest." We walked through this gate and into the sprawling agora area. If you turn to your immediate right as you enter the agora you will see several arched rooms that have been gated shut to protect various artifacts unearthed at the site. These rooms no doubt served as shops built into the wall that enclosed the agora. Confined in one of these rooms against the back wall, we could see a large statue of Artemis. The statue is the distinctive image associated with Artemis: a large headdress, ornately decorated clothing, with a number of egg-shaped objects adorning her front. There is no consensus as to what these objects are: eggs, dates, or perhaps breasts. No doubt this image was a common one during Paul's stay at Ephesus. Even today, her image can be found in many of the souvenir shops around the town of Selçuk.

121

It is worth revisiting the main theme of Paul's letter and where he has taken the Ephesian church thus far through the first three chapters of his letter. The landscape will be much different in chapters 4 through 6. We summarized Paul's main theme in four statements:

1) God's plan is to bring all creation back under his authority.

2) This plan was revealed and accomplished through the death and resurrection of Jesus.

3) As Gentiles, they were part of this plan *from the beginning*.

4) So their response should be to fully embrace life as the people of God, knowing that victory had already been accomplished.

Paul has spent roughly half of his letter building his case for the first three statements. He has revealed the mysterious plan of God in Ephesians 1:10 and restated it in Ephesians 3:6. He has clarified the saving role of Jesus as part of this plan in Ephesians 2:13. And he has spent considerable time throughout each of the first three chapters convincing the Ephesian church that they were part of this plan and, as Gentiles, counted among the people of God.

It is only after Paul has made certain that the Ephesians are convinced of their inclusion in the plan of God that he can proceed to the last statement: Their response should be to fully embrace life as the people of God. But what would that lifestyle look like? How would it differ from the pagan world surrounding them in Ephesus and in the wider Greco-Roman culture? The second half of Paul's letter will address these questions.

WALKING THE WALK

Ephesians 4 begins the same way Ephesians 3 began, before Paul paused to further clarify his own role in this plan of God: "As a prisoner for the Lord…." Paul is about to strongly encourage the church to embrace this distinctive way of life and he is not doing so from an ivory tower or lavish corner office. He is doing so as a prisoner under house arrest. He is not asking anything of them that he has not been willing to risk his own freedom to live out. He has walked the walk and it has led him to chains, surrounded by Roman guards.

The next phrase introduces the final point of Paul's four statements: "I urge you to live a life worthy of the calling you have received." Two words provide a clue as to the force of this last statement.

The first word is the English word *urge* (*parakaleo*). This word can have a range of meaning, from politely asking something of someone to downright demanding it, depending on the context. Because of the case Paul has built up to this point, it carries more of the forcefulness of *strongly encouraging* a response from another person. It falls just short of putting one's foot down. A professional coach was once heard to announce that there would be an optional team meeting … which everyone WILL attend! Similarly, Paul may be asking, but there is no question as to what he expects of his audience.

The second word is actually the root word of the previous one. It is the word *calling* (*klesios*, from *kaleo*). It is used twice here and the force would be much more evident in the original language. In essence Paul writes, "I am calling you to the calling to which you have been called." He first mentioned this calling in Ephesians 1:18 and will refer to it again shortly. In classical Greek, there was a legal aspect to a calling: a legal summons was issued calling you to court. It was not an optional appearance if your schedule permitted. So, as the people of God, this was their calling; it was not an optional way to live for the hard-core believers. It was an expectation of all believers.

Paul then begins to build a framework for this way of living life, or walking, the term Paul prefers. What immediately follows is not the actual calling, but the outlook necessary to live out this calling. He will pick up the calling again in Ephesians 4:17. The framework could be stated in this way: An understanding of your unique gifts, while keeping unity with other believers, is the pathway to spiritual maturity. To put it more succinctly, diversity within unity can lead to maturity.[1] And becoming mature followers of Jesus was the essence of their calling.

We start with unity. Unity implies oneness of belief and purpose. But remember that in the context of Paul's letter to the Ephesian church, unity refers to Jew and Gentile living together under the reign of Jesus. Recall from chapter 7 that the dividing wall of hostility had been torn down. Jew and Gentile together would form the people of God. They would now be a unified people.

As you might imagine, being a unified people comprised of ethnic groups that were previously hostile enemies would require some attitudinal changes. Imagine today if the leaders of Palestine and Israel raised hands together announcing that the two were now unified. Little doubt, there would need to be some radical changes in perspective for that unity to become more than just lip service. So Paul begins with three attitudinal changes that would need to take place: they would need to learn to be humble, gentle, and patient.

These are not characteristics that you will find in many books on leadership today (even among church leadership books). These attitudes were equally as counter-cultural in Greco-Roman culture as they would be today. The first attitude, humility, was actually regarded as a weakness in Roman society, referring in part to the condition of a slave. Plato utilized this word in both a positive and negative sense. Possessing a little humility might have been acceptable, but being characterized as a humble person was not a compliment. In general, humility was not something that would have been commended.

In much the same way, gentleness was also viewed primarily as a weakness, implying a lack of courage. Even in the Old Testament, it was often used to describe the condition of the poor or oppressed. So it is significant that here Paul asks believers to voluntarily take on the attitude of gentleness.

The third attitude, patience, is a word that was rarely used outside of religious writings. Within ancient religious texts, the meaning of patience is much closer to that of *endurance* or *perseverance* than one's ability to wait an extra five minutes without fussing and fuming, as we might regard it today. Elsewhere, in Galatians 5, Paul includes gentleness and patience as two attitudes of the fruit of the Spirit. It is important to recognize that while we may look upon these as desirable traits of spiritual people, they would not have been recognized as all that desirable in Paul's day.

So what was to unify them? Paul has already mentioned a couple things that Jew and Gentile now shared in under the reign of Jesus. Together, they would form one new body, a new person (Ephesians 2:15,16) and there was one Spirit by which they had access to God (Ephesians 2:18). But now Paul wants to stress just how much they truly shared in order to minimize the differences.

There is one body and one Spirit, just as you were called to one hope when you were called; one Lord, one faith, one baptism; one God and Father of all, who is over all and through all and in all. (Ephesians 4:4-6)

One of the most effective ways to overcome differences is to identify higher-level commonalities and goals. Two sides that normally do not get along may set aside differences if a larger, overarching purpose can be identified. Thus, seven times Paul stresses their commonalities, the higher-level purposes that bind them together. In addition to being part of the same body and having access to the same Spirit, they also shared one hope. God's saving purpose was to bring all creation back under his authority, and this was now their hope. This is not a *wishful thinking* kind of hope, but an expectancy that God's purpose will reach its fulfillment. They now shared in this expectancy as they watched God's plan come to fruition.

Together, as part of the church, they fell under the same lordship of Jesus. It was their faith in the faithfulness of Jesus that enfolded them into the church. There were not separate pathways into the people of God – one for Jews and another for Gentiles. Nor were there separate initiation rites. They shared one baptism, an issue that Pricilla and Aquila had already tackled after one of Paul's first visits to Ephesus (see chapter 2). Finally, to complete the Trinitarian thrust of Paul's example (Spirit – Lord – Father), he finishes with the God who is one. This is another example of something that we can take for granted and miss the oddity it would have been to worship only one God!

III

PAGANISM AND MANY GODS

In the Old Testament and the New Testament alike, the writers of scripture are constantly asserting that there is one god and that God is Yahweh. While this may not sound bizarre to us today, throughout the pre-Judeo-Christian world this would have been an outlandish assertion. It was not simply the primacy of Yahweh over another god, be it Baal, Amun Ra, or Artemis. It was the theological position that as a people, first as Israel and later under Christianity, they would limit themselves to *only* one god.

In the pagan world, even while one god may have ascended to a higher status than other gods, it was still held that there were many gods in many different roles. Zeus may have been at the forefront of the Olympic pantheon, but numerous other deities were constantly at work behind daily events. Artemis ruled supreme in Ephesus, but by no means was she the lone god of the Ephesians. The scandal of the Egyptian Pharaoh Akhenaten was not the elevated worship of the Aten, but rather that the Aten would become the only deity to be worshipped, albeit briefly. For this reason, early Christians were even referred to as *atheists* because they rejected the worship of many gods.

So while the Temple of Artemis was the centerpiece of paganism in Ephesus, emperor worship was taking on an elevated role as well. In the agora, the remains of a temple to the Egyptian god Isis have been identified. Images of Nike and Heracles are still visible at the site today. Ancient writers mention a temple to Apollo that once stood in Ephesus and we have previously alluded to participation in the mystery religion of Demeter, covered in Chapter 8. There is little doubt that the Anatolian goddess Cybele was still being worshipped in Ephesus as well.

Participation in these varying religious activities was not mutually exclusive. Participants were not alleging that their deity was the only deity. This is why Paul's words would have been so foreign and challenging to the typical resident of Ephesus.

III

Paul's repetition of the oneness of God sounds very similar to a central Jewish confession of faith - the Shema. Known as *the Shema*, after the Hebrew word *hear* that begins this confession, it is found in Deuteronomy 6 and would become a daily recitation for the Israelites:

Hear, O Israel: Yahweh our God, Yahweh is one. Love Yahweh your God with all your heart and with all your soul and with all your strength. (Deuteronomy 6:4-5)

The primary thrust of this confession is the oneness of God. Yahweh is one; Yahweh is not many. Yahweh would not be worshipped alongside many other gods, nor would it be enough to give Yahweh an elevated position among other gods. They would worship only one God, and it would be Yahweh. No other gods should even enter the picture. The mystery of the Trinity (Father, Son, and Spirit) does not change the oneness of God. God is still the three-in-*one*.[2]

But just as Paul utilizes the oneness of God to stress the unity that should now mark the Ephesian church, he next turns to stressing the diversity of gifts within the church. Unity does not equal uniformity. And he again turns to a theological illustration to make his point.

Paul begins by reminding them that, even though they are to be unified (Jew and Gentile worshipping together), God has given each individual member a unique gift that would begin to define their marching orders as they walk this path toward spiritual maturity. He refers to these gifts in this context as *grace*, which simply means a *free gift*. Paul himself was the recipient of a specific grace: to bring the good news to the Gentiles (Ephesians 3:8). So just as Paul was the recipient of the grace of God's forgiveness, he also received a grace of preaching, which accompanied forgiveness.

It is curious that in so many churches today, the emphasis is on grace - referring to forgiveness of sins. But too often the message ends there. *You are forgiven, but so that you don't fall into a works-based legalism, don't exert too much spiritual effort.* Yet the grace that Paul and other New Testament writers emphasized not only encompassed forgiveness, but also included the subsequent dimension of a personal calling. The free gift of grace is appended by another grace: a unique gift equipping the believer to pursue his or her calling within the body of Christ.

In order to demonstrate this, Paul turns to a passage from Psalms:

When you ascended on high, you led captives in your train; you received gifts from men, even from the rebellious - that you, O Yahweh God, might dwell there. (Psalm 68:18)

Psalm 68 is a picture of God ruling from the heavens caring for the downtrodden and scattering the powerful. Mount Sinai, where Moses received the Ten Commandments, is pictured as God's former earthly place of rule while the nation of Israel was being established. God, here, is depicted as descending from Mount Sinai and, after driving away the opposition, ascending on high making Jerusalem the new seat of power. The procession that follows would normally be both prisoners of war and the victorious army. Conquered kings would pay tribute to the victor and the victorious army would offer the spoils of war to the triumphant king. It is similar to the image of a Roman triumph discussed in Chapter 4.

Yet there is one startling difference between the passage from Psalm 68 and the way Paul applies it here in Ephesians 4. In the Psalm, Yahweh God is rightfully *receiving* tribute and treasure from the spoils, but as Paul applies it here to the Ephesian church, Jesus is the one *giving* gifts to those in the procession. *Why is the king the one passing out gifts?*

A couple of explanations have been set forth to account for the discrepancy in Paul's quotation of Psalm 68. Among them, commentators have pointed out that it was not uncommon in early Jewish interpretation to rephrase the text to fit the context or in light of perceived messianic fulfillment.[3] This may be the case here, as Paul would have seen Jesus as the culmination of many Old Testament writings.

Along this same line of interpretation, Psalm 68 itself may imply both the receiving and the distribution of gifts by the king. Earlier in Psalm 68, verse 10 states, "Your people settled in [the land], and from your bounty, O God, you provided for the poor." After the enemy had been conquered and tribute paid to the king, part of the bounty would be customarily distributed by the king back to his people. Previously in his letter, Paul already stated that the battle has been won through the death and resurrection of Jesus (Ephesians 1:19-23). God is victorious! So it stands to reason that now is the day and age (post resurrection and ascension) where Jesus distributes the spoils of the battle to his people – a peace dividend of sorts.

But before turning to the substance of this peace dividend, Paul adds a few more brush strokes of color to his already distinct interpretation of this verse from Psalms:

What does "he ascended" mean except that he also descended to the lower, earthly regions? He who descended is the very one who ascended higher than all the heavens, in order to fill the whole universe. (Ephesians 4:9-10)

Sometimes, we might wish that Paul had left well enough alone! Paul wants his readers to understand the origin and meaning behind these peace dividends, but raises more questions in the process. Just as God had to descend from Sinai, scattering the enemy and freeing his people along the way, in order to ascend to Jerusalem, so too Jesus must have had to descend if he is now ascended to the heavenly realm, as Paul has already asserted.

The statement that remains unclear - to present-day readers at least - is: to where did Jesus descend? Is Paul simply reminding the church that in order for Jesus to ascend to the heavenly realm, he also had to descend via the incarnation to the earthly realm, and in so doing conquered sin and death? Or is Paul teaching that in his death, Jesus descended to Hades before ascending to the heavenly realm, as some have interpreted this. The Apostle Peter makes a similarly indistinct allusion in 1 Peter 3:18-19, a reference to Christ preaching to the spirits in prison after his death. Yet, in the absence of any further clarification by Paul, we must be careful not to extrapolate a belief from Paul that he does not clearly express. In light of the context of this letter to the Ephesians, it makes more sense that Paul is referring to the incarnation and subsequent ascension of Jesus. On the heavenly-earthly spectrum, the earth unquestionably inhabits the *lower region* of that spectrum.

These peace dividends, then, are a result of Jesus descending from the heavenly realm to the earth, conquering his enemies, and returning to the heavenly realm, where he now fills all things in every way. It follows the same journey attributed to his Father God in the Hebrew Scriptures, from Sinai to Jerusalem. This journey ushers in a new age where hostilities have ceased between Jew and Gentile and these fellow-citizens are being equipped to serve in a time of peace.

The specific gifts that Paul mentions here are sometime referred to as *the fivefold ministry of the church*: apostles, prophets, evangelists, pastors, and teachers. These are all types of leadership roles within the church. So, is Paul saying that everyone has been given a leadership role? After all, he just mentioned that to each person grace has been given, before expounding on where these gifts originated. It is helpful to take a step back to follow his line of thinking.

Remember that Paul's primary message is that Jew and Gentile have been reconciled to form one new body, which is the church, of whom Christ is the head. Each member of this body has a unique function and role to carry out. Christ himself has distributed these roles so that each person can embrace life as the people of God. In order for each member to discover his or her role, he has also *gifted* leaders of his church, whose job it is to equip the members to carry out the work. So these five leadership roles are not the graces – the gifts - that Christ has distributed. They are specific roles in order to equip everyone else to embrace their gifts. Christ distributed gifts and is the head of the church; the church is led by people uniquely conferred to help the members of the church understand their roles. Working together, then, the church functions as one body, even though each member has a unique gift functioning in a specific role.

As it relates to this fivefold ministry, Paul may have had his own role of the administration of the gospel in mind. He has already made clear in the previous chapter that his gift was specifically the ongoing tasks and responsibilities in ensuring that the church understood this mystery.

Elsewhere, Paul lists a variety of gifts that are not unique to church leadership, but are examples of what each member should explore and develop.[4] Here he has chosen to focus explicitly on the leadership structure of the church. It could be that having left behind a strong leadership structure in place at Ephesus, he wanted to validate the current leadership already there. There was no need to rehash a lengthy list of spiritual gifts to the Ephesians; they only needed to trust the current leadership in Paul's absence.

To summarize, the fivefold ministries listed are not the peace dividends distributed to God's people, but rather the leadership structure that will equip God's people for works of service, so that the body of Christ may be built up. In this way, the church can be a unified body, reaching maturity, while allowing individuals to live out their specific function within the people of God.

The goal of all this is the full engagement of life as the people of God, what Paul is defining as spiritual maturity. The body must not remain in an infantile state indefinitely. If Paul is trying to emphasize the importance of spiritual maturity, here is where the metaphor of the body runs into some limitations. The human body will not stay in the infant stage for long. Whether malnourished or well fed, directionless or driven, the human body will grow toward maturity (though mentally and emotionally we know that a fully-grown person can still be infantile and immature).

Therefore, Paul introduces a new metaphor to complete his point. The words Paul chooses here in verse 14 paint a very specific picture: a boat being tossed about by the waves (*kludonizomai*) and blown about by the wind (*periphero*). James, the brother of Jesus, uses this same word of being sea-tossed in his letter (James 1:6). Failing to grasp the fourth and final statement of Paul's message to the Ephesian church is like setting sail in a vessel that has no sail or rudder: you may not stay in place very long, but you will have no control over where you are going. We would say today that you are dead in the water, left to the elements, where you will eventual run aground or sink.

Additionally, Paul adds that you will be susceptible to every gust of wind that happens to blow by. The wind here is identified as rival philosophies that are contradictory to the life Paul is encouraging them to pursue. Because he stresses the trickery and deceit involved in these teachings, he probably does not have the agitators in mind from Chapter 4, who were trying to Judaize them. He is most likely referring to pagan philosophies. He uses some of this same language in Ephesians 6 when describing the schemes of the devil. Paul had worked tirelessly to distinguish the gospel from any number of *philosophies-du-jour*.

PHILOSOPHIES OF THE GREEK WORLD

Religion and philosophy frequently crossed paths in the Hellenistic world of the first century. Unlike Judaism or Christianity, which contain elements of both religious practice and a philosophical worldview, pagan religious practice did not preclude adopting a worldview of any number of philosophical schools of the day. One could engage in an assortment of religious practices, while espousing a worldview heavily influenced by such notables as Plato and Aristotle. Among the philosophical worldviews of the day:

Epicureanism. Epicureans regarded the pursuit of pleasure as the ultimate good. Today it is often linked with the phrase, "Eat, drink, and be merry." Yet practitioners did not live lives of indulgence and excess, as many assume. True happiness came from a life of moderation and justice. Its founder, Epicurus, rejected Platonic thought and held that the material world was all that could be understood. There was a huge knowledge gap between the material and the divine.

Skepticism. The Skeptics grew out of Plato's teachings. Though the term skeptic may have a negative connotation today, Skepticism held as its objective an intellectual understanding of the world. The starting point, however, was unbelief. Only through careful examination could one arrive at a place of belief about the world. What others took for granted, the Skeptics questioned. There may have been such an idea of truth, but it did not yet exist in its purest form. Therefore, one should avoid making claims of truth.

Sophism. We have already been introduced to Sophism via Apollo in Chapter 2. As a school of thought, it stressed the memorization of certain rhetorical formulaic devices in order to persuade others of an argument, frequently political in nature. The development of skill was the end goal, rather than discovery of truth. It often valued the ability to gather followers by any means, regardless of the validity of the cause.

Stoicism. Stoicism emerged from the teachings of Aristotle. Stoics believed the only good was a life of virtue and peace, developed through the understanding of nature. There was a *logos* – an order to the world - that embodied all things, and when perceived through the senses, one could come to live in harmony with nature. Stoicism placed a high value on morality.

It is not difficult to identify points of contact from these philosophical worldviews with Paul's message of Jesus, while at the same time recognizing the many ways these teachings stood in stark contrast with the gospel.

III

How, then, do you keep from being lost at sea? Or returning to Paul's preferred image of the body, how do you keep from getting stuck in an infantile state and proceed on toward the maturity of adulthood? Maturity comes through the truth spoken in love. Truth is the rudder that guides through a sea of empty philosophies.

As I have written elsewhere, speaking the truth in love is more of an art form than a science - a delicate balance that, as followers of Jesus, we must strive for in our words.[5] Words that contain both truth and love provide valuable nourishment for others and ourselves. Yet it is rather easy to leave one of these two ingredients out of our words. Some people speak the truth quite freely, but love is absent. Their words are not delivered with gentleness.

Other people extend love quite easily to those around them. They are often encouraging and make others feel good about themselves with their words. But when the truth does need to be spoken, they shy away from it, often settling for the approval of those around them. Truth is skirted if there is a possibility that it may bring disagreement, tension, or rejection.

The truth is that on the truth-love continuum, most of us lean more toward one than the other. Some of us are truth-tellers, while others of us are grace-givers. One comes easily for us while the other is a bit more difficult to muster up. In many cases, there needs to be some thought and intentionality to our words in order to embody speaking the truth in love. But finding that balance is part of growing up toward maturity.

Paul concludes this image of the body growing toward maturity by placing Jesus as the head. With every part fulfilling its function – joints, ligaments, and the like – the body grows in strength and stature, working as a single unit. It is being nourished by love, under the direction of Christ. This is Paul's deeply held desire for the church at Ephesus.

With all this talk of gift gifting and metaphors of the body (or drifting at sea), it is key to understand the issue Paul is addressing. Yes, they are part of the plan and people of God. But now what, if anything? Paul is answering the all-important question: Isn't it enough to be part of the people of God – to simply become a Christian? Why the need to pursue spiritual maturity? This is an equally important question for the modern contemporary church, where often the stress is on evangelistic outreach, while discipleship is relegated to elective studies.

The answer, of course, is that the plan of God involves Jew and Gentile functioning together as one, not simply residing in separate parts of the same kingdom. Paul did not use the image of a walled city to describe the kingdom of God, where the important step was to simply gain access and, once inside, you could live at ease in your own part of town. No, the image is of a body and we might even suppose that Paul had in mind the body of an athlete training for competition (as in his correspondence to the Corinthian church). If the body is going to function properly, it must be exercised, nourished, and fine-tuned to fulfill its purpose.

Spiritual maturity is not optional, any more than eating properly, training, and exercising are optional if you are preparing to run a marathon. The plan of God is Jew and Gentile being built up together to form a body - a holy temple. And if that is to happen, every person must function in the role they have been given. Yes, grace is the free gift from God, but it is also the commission that comes with that gift. Dallas Willard summed it up nicely, "Grace is opposed to earning, not to effort."[6]

OUT WITH THE OLD, IN WITH THE NEW

Paul now turns to his closing argument – he will get into the specifics next - of why their inclusion into the people of God necessitates a new way of life.

So I tell you this, and insist on it in the Lord, that you must no longer live as the Gentiles do, in the futility of their thinking. (Ephesians 4:17)

Notice here that Paul begins to distinguish the Gentile *believers* from the Gentile *lifestyle*. They are still Gentiles, but they must no longer live as Gentiles typically lived – or more specifically, think like the Gentiles thought. They have a new identity as the people of God and their mindset and actions should reflect it.

The Gentile condition (representative here of the human condition apart from Yahweh God) begins with a hardened heart. In the scriptures, hardness of heart is both a condition people are born into as a result of sin, as well as an ongoing obstinacy to the movement of God and his Spirit. A heart that ignores the promptings of God for too long becomes calloused and loses all sensitivity to the spiritual realm. Accordingly, they are darkened in their understanding; their way of thinking and seeing the world around them is deficient.

As a result, they are separated from the life of God. Back in Ephesians 2, this is how Paul described the Gentile believers' former way of life: separated from Christ, excluded from citizenship in Israel and foreigners to the covenants of the promise. Where Paul began his letter using his first person voice, *we/us*, to refer to Jews and his third person voice, *they/them*, to refer to Gentiles (and even the Gentile believers), he has now distinguished the Gentile Christians at Ephesus from *them*; the pronoun, *they,* now refers to Gentiles who have rejected the call of God (and could just as well refer to Jews who have done the same).

With hearts hardened to the Holy Spirit and a mindset darkened to the things of God, it only follows that actions and lifestyles will reflect the heart/mind condition. Without God and left to themselves, sensual indulgence, being ruled by passions, and an exploitive greed become a normative way of life. This is life apart from God. As in Ephesians 2, it is not meant to be a shocking revelation of how "they" live, but rather a sober reminder of how we all would be living left to ourselves (Paul has previously included himself in this category). Thus, the call to remember: remember Egypt; remember your former way of life. Remember how you thought and acted when God was not part of the equation.

Paul is trying to stress that there must be consistency in what a person holds to be true in the heart, what one believes to be true about the world, and how one lives – the actions that follow. If someone believes that there is a god, or more specifically, that Jesus is the Messiah, then it should affect the way that person views the world. If there is a belief in God, and this God is knowable at some level, then a different perspective of the world should follow. He or she will view the world differently and have a different mindset, and that mindset will affect the way life is lived. Virtuous actions should emanate from that belief. That is the consistency of lifestyle Paul is stressing.

In Greco-Roman philosophy and religion, this pattern of heart-mind-action did not necessarily tie together or hold with any consistency. Religious belief did not necessarily affect the way that a Greek or Roman lived. Greek philosophy stressed believing truth – the right way of understanding the world - but this did not necessarily mean embracing a virtuous lifestyle. Even the schools of thought that stressed virtue, such as Stoicism, did not do so out of a sense of a higher calling in conjunction with what God was doing in the world. They did so out of pursuit of goodness and happiness, quite separate from a belief in the gods. Because the gods had not explicitly given specific rules for human behavior, there was a disjunction between religious practices and moral discourse.[7] How one should behave fell more in the realm of philosophy, rather than religion.

As odd as that may strike us, even today it is readily evident that just because someone professes a belief in God, does not mean that a virtuous lifestyle will always follow. Sure, there may be some incremental behavioral modifications, but full-on transformation is often absent. Churches are filled with people who believe that belief is enough. Thus, Paul is emphasizing that right action should follow right belief: a sensitive heart, a renewed mind, and virtuous actions are part and parcel of what it means to be counted among the people of God.

Admittedly, for a Gentile, it was an entirely different perspective on a belief in God (and one God at that!) and virtuous living. Paul is emphasizing that the two are interrelated, vitally bound together. But this is what Paul had taught them when he came to Ephesus and introduced them to the person of Jesus, and this is what Paul had every confidence they were continuing to be taught after he left. Jesus was their way of knowing what God expected of them. Paul had immersed them in the school of Jesus!

Much like the other philosophical schools or mystery religions of the day, this school of Jesus would require a break with the former life and full immersion into a new life. The language of the old self and the new self may have echoes back to the one new person God was creating out of the two former rival groups – the Jews and the Gentiles. But here the image of a new self is more directed at the individual person, rather than the ethnic group as a whole. Ephesians 4:25 even stresses that this is a process each individual must engage in if they are to be part of the larger whole.

The language of putting off the old self and putting on the new is actually language used to describe an initiation rite in the Greek world. For example, initiates into the Eleusinian Mysteries are said to have presented themselves unclothed, representing themselves as not yet possessing true knowledge. Once fully initiated, they were given a consecrated robe to put on, symbolizing the philosophical teachings they had received. Accordingly, the robe was thought to have sacred properties.[8]

In Paul's letter to the church at Colosse, the language is even more specific:

Do not lie to each other, since you have taken off your old self with its practices and have put on the new self, which is being renewed in knowledge in the image of its Creator. (Colossians 3:9,10)

With language sounding very similar to Ephesians (the two letters were written about the same time), Paul uses the specific word in Colossians (*apekduomai*) for taking off clothing. A more general term is used here in Ephesians. So it is clear that Paul had in mind the imagery of disrobing from the old way of life and taking on a new way of life – putting on a new robe.

After all, the old way is tattered and torn. It is deceiving – it promises a fulfilling and exciting life, but does not deliver on that promise. The new, meanwhile, is marked by righteousness and holiness. It is a holy garment that has true sacred properties. Which would you rather wear?

The transformation from the old to the new, however, is not simply a matter of putting on a sacred piece of clothing. Other mystery religions may have extended such assurances, but again, they are deceiving – a word Paul uses frequently throughout his letter. The transformation will happen through a new mindset – a new outlook and correct view of the world – made possible through the working of the Holy Spirit. The phrase employed here is literally "in the spirit of your mind." You will have to change the way you think, but you will not be doing it alone. God's Spirit will be working along with your spirit.

Thus, Paul is stressing the consistency between the heart, the mind, and actions. Right belief comes from a right way of thinking, and the result should be right living. The rest of Paul's letter will focus on the latter, but it must begin in the heart and mind. With this in mind, it is almost as if Paul's entire letter is based on the premise that the Ephesian church has already been taught the right belief system, and they have accepted that belief. But somewhere along the way, it stopped there. They had fallen into the Greek way of thinking that did not always make a connection between right belief and right action. This way of thinking had to change.

What Paul is asserting is that if they accepted God's plan to bring all creation back under God's authority, and that this plan was revealed and accomplished through the death and resurrection of Jesus, and that they were part of this plan, then this plan also necessitated a change in the way they lived their life. The fourth statement is a non-negotiable if you accept the other three to be true. It is to the details of what life looks like as the people of God that we will turn to in the next chapter.

10 THE VIRTUOUS LIFE

Since the Jews that dwell in this city have petitioned Marcus Julius Pompeius, the son of Brutus, the proconsul, that they might be allowed to observe the Sabbaths, and to act in all things according to the customs of their forefathers, without impediment from anybody, the praetor has granted their petition. Accordingly, it was decreed by the senate and people, that in this affair that concerned the Romans, no one of them should be hindered from keeping the Sabbath day, nor be fined for so doing, but that they may be allowed to do all things according to their own laws.

- Josephus, *Antiquities*

U p to this point, this space at the beginning of each chapter has been used to describe a feature of the site of Ephesus. For example, what would it have looked like to walk through the Jewish synagogue at Ephesus during the time of Paul and what were some of its key distinctions? However, the synagogue where Paul spoke for three months, mentioned in the book of Acts, has yet to be discovered. Scholar Mark Wilson does note that the graffito of a menorah etched into the steps of the Celsus Library can be seen, which would indicate the presence of a Jewish population just after the time of Paul.[1] In addition, a synagogue could have referenced a dedicated structure, but also could have simply indicated a private house, courtyard, or even an area outside where worship took place on a regular basis.

We can surmise from several sources - including the book of Acts - that there was indeed a Jewish population living in Ephesus. Thus, the presence of an actual synagogue structure during the time of Paul is very likely. Wilson also states that the Jewish historian Josephus mentioned Ephesus no less than ten times.

One such reference is related in the opening quote of this chapter. In this particular example, Josephus is referencing the permission extended to the Jews of Ephesus - and by extension, Asia Minor - to preserve their customs without interference from the local authorities. In other words, the Jews, for the most part, were able to secure the right to keep their distinct traditions and lifestyle, challenging the normal path of assimilation into the culture of the Roman Empire.

As noted in the previous chapter, only after Paul has made certain that the Ephesian church is convinced of their inclusion in the plan of God does he turn to the last of our four statements: their response to fully embrace life as the people of God. The second half of Paul's letter addresses what this lifestyle would look like. He begins Ephesians 4 with a discussion of the unique ways God has gifted each person and the importance of keeping unity in the context of those spiritual gifts. From here, he proceeds to strongly encourage them to embrace an entirely distinct way of living from the pagan world around them. It was time to leave the old person behind and embrace the new person God had created them (each one of them individually, as well as collectively) to be.

Paul's emphatic request was no small one. There was great societal pressure to assimilate into the culture of the Roman Empire. The hallmarks of a Roman city would have been structures such as a gymnasium, a theater, and a large agora. There was increasing pressure to worship the Roman emperor alongside the pantheon of Greco-Roman gods. Thus, when a gymnasium was built in Jerusalem during the reign of Antiochus Epiphanes in the second century BC, it represented the Hellenization of Jerusalem and was regarded by many devout Jews as an affront to their distinct lifestyle. First Maccabees 1 recounts this event, adding that the traitorous Jews "did all sorts of other evil things" that were considered an affront to a Jewish way of life (1 Maccabees 1:14-15).

Elsewhere in the Roman Empire, other Jews had to secure permission to carry on traditional practices, such as Sabbath-keeping and circumcision. As we have already mentioned, Josephus cites the permission granted to the Jews of Ephesus and Asia Minor to maintain their customs, despite pressure to discontinue these practices. It is possible that Paul may have had such authorizations in the back of his mind when he delves into the specifics of this new lifestyle they were to embrace. The Jews of the region had maintained a distinct lifestyle from the pagan culture, and Paul had the expectation that the Ephesian believers would embrace a comparable way of living – not entirely Jewish, but wholly different from the rest of Ephesus.

THE VIRTUOUS LIFE

Before proceeding - picking up at Ephesians 4:25 and continuing into Ephesians 5 - it will be instructive to understand the Greek concept of virtue (*arête*), or moral excellence. Virtue was a favored subject of many Classical Greek philosophers. As you approach the Library of Celsus at Ephesus, four statues of women stand at the entrance, named for the qualities that are said to have characterized the library's benefactor, Celsus. Virtue (*Arete*) is one of those qualities, along with wisdom, insight, and understanding. It might be tempting to read the rest of the book of Ephesians as a collection of suggestions by Paul to help the church live a good and pious life, but given the backdrop of Greek philosophy, it appears Paul is actually doing something much more significant.

For the Greek philosopher Socrates, virtue was knowledge. Virtuous action came about by knowing what was right, and knowing one's self as well. Virtue was the highest pursuit of life. Antisthenes, who was a student of Socrates, built his philosophy around the proposition that the highest pleasure and purpose came from a life of virtue. Absent virtue, all of life's other offerings were worthless. Plato would define *righteousness* as the perfect working of the whole person, and the whole person was working perfectly when three particular virtues were possessed: temperance, courage, and wisdom. "From this springs that ordered tranquility which is at once true happiness and perfect virtue."[2]

For Aristotle, virtue was linked to the proper functioning of what an object or living thing was designed for. Thus, for human beings, the question was: What is a human being – the soul – designed for? To answer this, Aristotle defined four principal virtues: courage, justice, wisdom, and temperance. By embodying these virtues, even practicing them, a person could become a fully flourishing human being.[3]

Thus, virtue had been a topic of Greek philosophy for the previous four hundred years. By the time Paul writes to the Ephesian church, there would have been a well-defined flow to any conversation on the topic of virtue. The goal was to establish what it meant to be fully human. In order to reach that goal, a person had to embody a certain set of virtues. Thus, the starting point of the conversation revolved around how a person could practice and develop these virtues.

Why all the talk of virtue when that word cannot even be found in the letter to the Ephesians? Without this paradigm in mind to frame the conversation, it is easy to miss the point of these instructions found in the second half of the letter to the Ephesians. It is commonplace today to read these sections in Paul's writings as the already-mentioned good suggestions: some things to work on as time permits, but for goodness' sake, don't knock yourself out because after all, we are saved by grace. Or to the contrary, they are taken as rules: these are things that must be done, along with many other rules, if you are going to call yourself a Christian.

N.T. Wright has a helpful discussion about why neither of these approaches actually produces the kind of character that is to embody life in the kingdom of God. Many people today begin their Christian life by rule-keeping. When it is inevitably discovered that all the rules cannot possibly be kept, then the forgiveness of Jesus is sought. (Isn't that what Jesus' forgiveness is all about? To cover us when we break the rules?) But once forgiveness has been experienced, it is back to rule-keeping.[4] Many today live in this cycle of trying to keep the rules, breaking them, seeking forgiveness, and then back to rule-keeping. It is a tiresome cycle, and ultimately rules do not produce the character that is described in New Testament writings. Rules – and rule-keeping - are not *the goal*.

So far from being some helpful suggestions or a list of rules to help the church live a good, pious life, Paul would appear to be addressing the deeper question of what it means to be fully human. What are the characteristics of a person living fully in the kingdom of God? If the goal is to become people who live as God's people and in God's kingdom now (and not after some apocalyptic time and event in the future), then what are the characteristics of those people, and how would that character be developed? These are questions of virtue.

As Paul turns, then, from putting off the old self and putting on the new, he begins to unpack the kinds of behavior that this new self would embody. He begins to paint a picture of what it means to be fully human in the way that the soul was designed. The word *therefore* at the beginning of verse 25 links what follows to the preceding discussion of the old versus the new. What is about to be discussed hinges on what has just been asserted.

Therefore, each of you must put off falsehood and speak truthfully to your neighbor, for we are all members of one body. (Ephesians 4:25)

Subsequently, if these new, virtuous people are to embrace the life for which God has designed them, they will be people who embrace truth. The pagan culture was characterized in part by deception.[5] Its gods and mysteries promised many things that could not ultimately deliver. The path to virtue was not through the thicket of deceit, but by way of the clearing of truthfulness. Remember, this is not a mere suggestion, nor is it a rule to avoid breaking. It is a description of the virtuous person. The transformed person will be, by their new nature, a truthful person.

The transformed person will also be a forgiving person. Paul utilizes Psalm 4:4 as an example of how a virtuous person would handle the emotion of anger. There is a place for anger – it is part of being human – but there are also constraints on how anger is to be expressed. Sunset was a common time limit to bring to a close a number of daily activities. In the case of anger, either address the issue at hand or forgive the offender, but anger left to fester will only give rise to objectionable actions.

Had Paul simply wanted to review the rules, he could have just reiterated the Ten Commandments: do not lie, do not steal, do not murder. Instead, after echoing the Ninth Commandment, "Each of you must put off falsehood…" Paul adds the positive command, "speak truthfully to your neighbor." In its simplicity, Paul was stressing something else very important: if they were to embrace life as the people of God, it was not enough to simply avoid lying. They must be quite intentional with the truth. In fact, in order to make sure it was understood that God's kingdom was not simply about *avoiding the bad*, but being the kind of people who would naturally be about *doing good*, he gave two additional examples.

First, those who have been stealing must not only stop stealing, but must start working and being a productive member of society. The reason? So that they can do good for others in need. If they do not work honestly, they would not have the means to give to others in their community! O'Brien points out that the inclusion of "those who have been stealing" likely points to the kinds of people who were becoming part of the Ephesian church.[6] It would not be surprising that merchants and tradesmen, perhaps even some slaves, supplemented their work by petty theft or defrauding customers. But as members of the people of God, this practice had to cease.

Finally, it was not enough to eliminate unwholesome talk from their words, but they were to intentionally introduce words that built up and strengthened others. In stressing this, Paul knew that rules or suggestions could not produce the virtuous life God had called them to. As he had written elsewhere, the Law cannot make a person righteous, or produce right action. It can only prohibit wrong action.

Paul finishes this discussion with these closing words:

And do not grieve the Holy Spirit of God, with whom you were sealed for the day of redemption. Get rid of all bitterness, rage and anger, brawling and slander, along with every form of malice. Be kind and compassionate to one another, forgiving each other, just as in Christ God forgave you. (Ephesians 4:30-32)

The implication is that because their faith had seemingly stalled, stuck in the place of believing the right things but falling short of becoming the right kind of people, they were actually grieving the Spirit. This is the same Spirit given to them, effectively marking them with a seal, guaranteeing the inheritance due to them as adopted children of God. Paul had already introduced them to the Holy Spirit in Ephesians 1, but unless everything that was just discussed did not develop within them, or was not taken seriously, this gift of the Spirit would be troubled that they would continue to miss their calling.

And the same holds true today. When followers of Jesus remain spiritual infants, and choose only the sin-avoidance or rule-keeping path, the result is inevitably rage, anger, and slander. But when communities of followers embrace their calling as God's people, virtues such as compassion and forgiveness begin to emerge. These happened to be the very traits that were extended to us by God.

IMITATION IS THE SINCEREST FORM OF FLATTERY

Ultimately, Paul could think of no better example of the virtuous life than that of God. They had been adopted as God's children and children naturally imitate their parents, so it was a logical way to summarize things. Elsewhere, Paul calls on communities to imitate his life (1 Corinthians 4:16, Philippians 3:17), but this is the only place where Paul encourages people to be imitators of God.[7]

Paul then moves from the exhortation to imitate God to prohibitions on sexual immorality. It may seem like it should go without saying that if one is going to imitate the virtue of God, then sexual immorality is probably frowned upon. But here again, we must understand the pagan culture that these Ephesian believers were leaving behind, and we also must consider what Paul was specifically alluding to when he brings up the topic of sexual immorality.

In our English translations, it may not even be apparent that Paul is tackling this topic specifically; it could appear that he is simply rattling off some unrelated behaviors to avoid.

But among you there must not be even a hint of sexual immorality, or of any kind of impurity, or of greed, because these are improper for the Lord's people. (Ephesians 5:3)

However, all three verbs (immorality, impurity, and greed) relate to the broader topic of sexual behavior. Sexual immorality is plain enough, but the word impurity (*akatharsia*) is almost always paired with immorality to denote behaviors that would make a person unclean, both ritually and morally. Similarly, the word greed (*pleonexia*), which today is predominantly associated with money, is better translated as lust in this context. It is the desire to possess and exploit another person.

Thus, Paul is squarely on the topic of what constitutes improper sexual behavior for this new, virtuous person called to imitate God. And to repeat, we may wonder why this would even be unnecessary to address. Paul even states in the original Greek, "these things should not even be spoken about among you," as if to convey both that it should not be a topic of their conversation, and he should not even have to bring it up to them. Yet he does address it, so it must have been an issue that gave him concern.

So what was the behavior Paul was addressing? If this were a predominantly Jewish audience, we might guess that he was simply addressing issues such as marital infidelity, sexual promiscuity, or even prostitution – issues that the Law of Moses clearly addressed, but would have been persistent concerns (just as they are today, even among religious folks). But this was not a Jewish audience and these types of issues do not quite fit the proximate discussion of leading a virtuous life and imitating God. It should have just been understood.

However, this was primarily a Gentile audience approaching the kingdom of God from an entirely different direction. Similar to the issue of stealing, this discussion of sexual behavior likely points to the kind of people who were becoming part of the Ephesian church and the culture they were coming out of. It is telling that as Paul spells out virtuous living, he needs to be patently clear that sexual immorality had no place in this life.

The sexual attitudes of the pagan culture were wholly different from the Jewish culture, even if the underlying temptations were common to both. For Jews, physical modesty and purity served as a powerful metaphor for spiritual purity, while no such notion existed for Greeks and Romans. In Roman culture, public nudity, even occasionally in mixed company, was common at public latrines, bathhouses, gymnasiums, and athletic contests. There were sexual boundaries among fellow Roman citizens, but those boundaries were abandoned if a non-citizen or slave were involved. Prostitution was so common that the earnings were taxed by the state and brothels were plentiful.[8] Even in pagan religious life, sex with temple prostitutes was viewed as a type of offering to the gods. In fact, this is one of the primary issues addressed in Paul's letters to the church in Corinth.

III

THE HOUSE OF PLEASURE

At the site of Ephesus, if you proceed down Curetes Street from the upper city heading toward the Celsus Library, at the bottom of the hill and to the right will be an assemblage of buildings. One of the more interesting buildings is the public latrines, so well-preserved that it looks as though it could be in operation today (though undoubtedly most today would balk at the lack of privacy). Another building that has created some debate is a building identified as a brothel, or as it has been named, the *House of Pleasure*.

There are several reasons why this building has been identified as a brothel: a mosaic of some young women, the subject matter of some inscriptions, the presence of bath chambers, and some sculptures that have been found in proximity to the building all might be expected at the remains of an ancient brothel. Additionally, a footprint that has been carved into the marble of the adjacent street has been interpreted as an advertisement showing potential customers the way to the brothel.

However, not everyone is convinced that this building can be definitively identified as a brothel, maintaining that similar mosaics and paintings can be found in many ancient structures. Similarly, the footprint cannot be conclusively linked to the brothel house, but may simply be a more generic advertisement for any local establishment. The inscriptions may just be references to the nearby latrines.

The house probably dates to just after the time of Paul, with some renovations occurring later. Regardless of its identification, the presence of such an establishment in Ephesus is almost certain. Brothels would have been present in almost any cosmopolitan city of the Roman Empire.

III

Thus, it would not be surprising that the Ephesian church had a number of people hail from the pagan culture, who were sincerely following Jesus and the teachings of Paul, and yet struggled with what constituted proper sexual boundaries. Temptations would have been abundant in the urban center of Ephesus. It would not have necessarily been assumed that worshipping Yahweh meant other pagan practices had to cease. If you were a Roman citizen, the notion that sexual purity meant the brothels and your slaves were off limits may have been slowly, if not reluctantly, acknowledged. Paul would have needed to be clear that the sexual norms of the pagan world had no place for an imitator of God.

In defining sexual behavior, Paul goes on to push the boundaries past actions to include speech as well. Like the verbs in 5:3, the context of 5:4 would dictate that these three descriptors of speech refer specifically to sexual language. Dirty jokes, obscene talk, and suggestive conversations did not fit into the program to imitate God. Each of these words are found only in this context in the New Testament, suggesting that Paul was choosing his words specifically for the situation at hand, rather than giving general directives. Instead, words of thanksgiving were to season the speech of the believer.

Finishing the brief discussion on sexual behavior, Paul concludes, stressing that those who persist in these pagan ways cannot share in the inheritance of God's kingdom. He had already spent a great deal of space convincing them of their inclusion in the people of God, as fellow-heirs of

God's plan. Yet just as a Jew was not a true Jew if they only conformed to some external practices (Romans 2:28), a Gentile was not given blanket inclusion into the people of God just because he or she attended the right meetings and hung around the right people. Grace did not give them license to continue living however they wanted.

Again, Paul labels the pagan culture and lifestyle as *deceptive*. It promised that you could honor the gods and yet live life gratifying every felt desire. It offered secret knowledge and insight to those who joined the right societies. It swore protection to those who knew the right phrases to repeat or paid enough for the right magic words. But these were all empty words! At the end of the day, its promises were powerless to deliver anything at all. It was time to step out of the shadows of the pagan world and into the light of God's kingdom.

Darkness and light emerge as the theme of the next section of Paul's letter. The imagery of light and darkness was common in the Old Testament and other Jewish writings. From Genesis 1 to the book of Job (just one example from Job 30, "Yet when I hoped for good, evil came; when I looked for light, then came darkness") to frequent allusions in the Psalms, this imagery would have been well known to Jewish listeners. But Gentile listeners would have also recognized the contrasting nature of light and darkness. Many pagan rituals were held under the cover of darkness, shrouded in secrecy. So Paul is further encouraging a clean break with pagan society.

As in previous cases, the summons to "live as children of light" actually reads, "*walk* as children of light." At the beginning of chapter 5, Paul instructed them to walk in love, and soon he will caution them to be careful how they walk. This shift from darkness to light will not be a mere one-time change of position, but a journey away from the pagan lifestyle toward the light of Christ. Like positioning your chair to warm yourself in the sun, if you remain in the same place too long, you will soon enough find yourself being enveloped by shadows.

Embracing the appropriate virtues will be crucial to this journey. To get them started, Paul lists goodness, righteousness, and truth as virtues that will define what it means to walk as children of light. Like the Greek philosophers before him, Paul lists these three as principal virtues of followers of Jesus. Elsewhere, in Galatians 5, he lists nine of them – referring to them as fruit of the Spirit – while here he refers to them as fruit of light.

It is vital to the understanding of virtue to note that as much as we may embrace lists such as the fruit of the Spirit, there is no comprehensive list of virtues in scripture. Attempts to codify and define all the virtues necessary to follow God quickly turn back into rule-keeping. This is not what Paul is asking of the Ephesian church.

Instead, Paul exhorts the church to "find out what pleases the Lord" (Ephesians 5:10). A better way to state this might be to simply say, "You need to figure this out." The word used here (*dokimazo*) means to *examine* or *recognize* something as the genuine article, and is closely related to the concepts of wisdom and discernment. An important aspect of virtuous living is the ability to discern – or to figure out - what response a given situation calls for, where the Law (or rule-keeping) would have previously prescribed the response. This is an essential proficiency when navigating the journey from the pagan culture into the kingdom of God. Though he previously spent three years in Ephesus, he would not, and could not, hold their hands every step of the way, instructing them how to respond in any and every situation. Nor could he anticipate every circumstance they might find themselves in. Thus, as stated previously, Paul is not giving the Ephesian church a list of rules to keep, he is encouraging them to develop the ability, through a transformed way of thinking, to understand how a follower of Jesus would respond in any given situation. This is the way of virtue.

Paul has spent considerable ink warning about the dangers of continuing to dabble in the pagan lifestyle. It was a culture of secrecy, sensuality, and superstition, fueled by the fear of the unknown and unseen. It was a lifestyle incompatible with the virtuous life Paul was encouraging the Ephesians to embrace. The virtuous life necessitated a clean break from the pagan life.

Yet at the same time he is calling them out of the darkness, he did not want them to live in fear of the pagan culture. If they walked in the light, they did not have to be afraid of the dark. Such is the nature of light: when a lamp or a flame illuminates an area, what is hidden by darkness is revealed, even as the darkness itself dissipates. To employ a previous example, one way to keep your chair in the light is to move it away from the shadows. Another way, however, is to catch the reflection of the sun and the shadows will retreat from you. The light of Christ will expose the deceptions of paganism.

There is some uncertainty as to what is meant by the phrase, "everything that is illuminated becomes a light," from Ephesians 5:13. Paul may be making an observation that when a deception or a secret is brought out into the open, it can finally be seen for what it is. Light equals truth. Similarly, he could also be referencing the notion of glory (see *The Glory of Rome*). Followers of Jesus will come to reflect his glory as they imitate his life, thus becoming a light to those around them. God is light; God's people are to imitate the example of God, through Jesus, and in doing so begin to reflect the light of God in a darkened world. In reflecting God's glory, God's people themselves become light.

To bolster this notion, Paul quotes from an unknown source:

Wake up, sleeper, rise from the dead, and Christ will shine on you. (Ephesians 5:14)

This could be a hymn that was known at the time, or a compilation of some Old Testament sources. The fact that Paul does not name the source may indicate that the Ephesian church was familiar with this quote. It would serve as a fitting summary of their journey from being dead in their sins to being raised to new life with Jesus, and now reflecting his glory to the culture around them as the people of God.

IT IS NOT TALKING BUT WALKING THAT WILL BRING US TO HEAVEN

Four previous times in this section about living as the people of God (beginning in Ephesians chapter 4), Paul uses the verb *walk*, to describe navigating the virtuous life. He will draw on this imagery a fifth and final time as he summarizes this journey to imitate God, "Be very careful, then, how you walk." This entire paragraph from Paul's letter serves as a transition paragraph, concluding his thoughts on virtuous living, while moving on to some final thoughts before bidding his farewells. Verse 21 in particular, cannot be removed from either the preceding thoughts or the ideas that will follow.

The path toward the virtuous life is not traversed haphazardly. It is more navigating a narrow trail than strolling leisurely through the park. It is not a weekend activity, which is why Paul urges diligence and wisdom when walking this path. Having walked thousands of miles himself on his missionary journeys throughout what are now the countries of Turkey and Greece, Paul knew the dangers of straying from the path or losing your footing. One misstep could result in being lost in the wilderness, running across bandits, or suffering injury. Similar dangers could be confronted in city life as well. The wrong street could lead to the wrong section of town or keeping company with the wrong people. Ephesus harbored all the temptations of the big city for those who wandered from the path.

Yet urban life also offered many opportunities. Ephesus would have proffered goods from Rome, spices from the East, the latest in fashion and style, as well as ideas from all around the Mediterranean. It boasted one of the most influential temples in the Roman Empire. A person could find virtually anything that could be imagined in the commercial agora, fresh off the boats docked in the adjacent harbor. No doubt this influence was a primary reason Paul set up shop in Ephesus for three years.

So even as Paul warns the church to walk carefully about the many enticements of urban life, he also instructs them to make the most of all the opportunities surrounding them. The specific word he uses in Ephesians 5:16 (*exagorazo*) carries with it the idea of buying up goods in a commercial setting – hence the King James Version renders this as *redeem the time*. There is an opportunistic urgency to this idiom that presses the hearer to act while there is still occasion to do so. The days being portrayed as evil is apocalyptic language - a way of saying, "Time is running out."

Thus, while there were many obstacles along this path toward virtue, this was not an excuse to retreat back to the old way of life. To become complacent would be to miss out on the adventure that would be life as the people of God. It would be foolish to hear Paul's words to embrace this new way of life and then ignore the call.

The final phrase of 5:17 implores the Ephesians to "understand what the Lord's will is." Many contemporary Christians will wrongly misunderstand what this phrase refers to. As one commentator observes, "In our contemporary context, the 'Lord's will' is frequently understood by Christians to refer to matters of personal guidance, and thus God's immediate plans for their future."[9] It is common in our churches for people to seek God's will in matters such as a new job, a new relationship, or what to study in school. While these are matters that we can bring to God in prayer, Paul is not referring to such matters here.

In his letter to the Ephesians, the will of God is inextricably tied to the divine mystery, which Paul has already made known to them (see Ephesians 1:9). God's will is synonymous with God's plan to bring all creation back under the authority of God, through the death and resurrection of Jesus. So when Paul encourages them to understand God's will, he is not asking them to pray for God to reveal it to them; Paul has already revealed it! He is encouraging them to figure out what their role will be as the people of God in light of this revelation. If we lived life with the bigger perspective of what God is accomplishing in the world, many matters of personal guidance may actually become either apparent or insignificant. God's plan cannot be reduced down to my everyday decisions, but my everyday decisions should always be aligned with the bigger plan of what God is doing.

As a final point on the subject of walking the virtuous path, Paul contrasts the stumbling, impaired judgment of a person who has had too much to drink to the adventurer led by the Spirit of God. Perhaps Paul had watched sailors stumble down the harbor street wondering how they would find their ship or perhaps he simply knew that a person could not navigate this path, taking advantage of every opportunity, while being intoxicated. Aside from our modern-day, and all-too familiar image of someone who has had too much to drink, Paul may have additionally been alluding to something further.

The Greek god of wine was Dionysus, also called Bacchus. More broadly speaking, Dionysus was the god of harvesting, wine-making, and fruit orchards. He was a popular god in antiquity and though he was not originally among the twelve Olympic gods, he was a son of Zeus and would eventually take his place among them. Temples dedicated to Dionysus could be found in sites throughout the empire, including Athens, Pergamum, and Lebanon.

Additionally, the cultic worship of Dionysus was even more widespread, even where there was no temple (see *The Cult of Dionysus* below). Although there is no temple in Ephesus identified with Dionysus, Plutarch indicates the presence of his cultic worship. When Mark Antony entered Ephesus around 40 BC, Plutarch writes that the people hailed him as "Dionysus Giver of Joy and Beneficent."[10] Mosaics featuring the wine god have also been found preserved in the Terrace Houses of Ephesus.

THE CULT OF DIONYSUS

Cultic practices and festivals associated with Dionysus took place throughout the Greek and Roman world. In Athens alone, there were four festivals a year, each encompassing a distinct set of cultic practices. Athens is also home to the Theater of Dionysus, located at the slope of the Acropolis. There were numerous temples to Dionysus scattered throughout the Mediterranean region.

Festivals often involved a procession, with his statue leading the way to the nearby temple. In some instances, the statue was a more graphic symbol of fertility. In Athens, the festivals featured several theater performances, followed by awards and honors to the top performers. Dramatic performances were considered a form of worship to Dionysus, who was regarded as the patron of the theater.

Elsewhere, cultic celebrations were more unrestrained. His festivities often corresponded with the harvest. Being the god of wine, excessive wine consumption and the drunkenness that followed were additional components of the cultic practices. Orgies were often associated with these festivals as well. As a prevailing theme, these festivals stressed the shedding of social inhibitions, with wine being the stimulus and sexual license being one of the results.

However, while often being characterized by debauchery, there was a religious purpose to these practices as well. One writer notes, "It was believed that by drinking excessive amounts of wine, members of the cult could become liberated in a realm of divine abandonment."[11] Prophetic utterances and spiritual enlightenment were at least part of the objective of these cultic practices.

The cult worship of Dionysus evolved over time. Initially, the debauchery and orgies that accompanied these festivals were more commonplace outside of Greece, while the festivals in Athens were more subdued. However, some of the more unrestrained practices would come to be incorporated into the cult throughout the Roman Empire. In 186 BC, the Roman senate would even ban festivals to Bacchus (Dionysus), with the exception of cases where festivals had obtained special permission to be staged.

Thus, it is clear that Dionysus was a well-known deity in Greek and Roman cities, and Ephesus was no different. Furthermore, the Dionysus cult was often linked to the Eleusinian mystery cult. Given the drunkenness and debauchery often associated with these cultic practices, Paul was likely alluding to these very events when he instructs, "Do not get drunk on wine, which leads to debauchery." It is interesting to note that the word for *debauchery* can also mean to be *out of your mind*, which is precisely the aim of these pagan rituals. It is probable that the Ephesian Gentiles, leaving behind their pagan lifestyle, would have made the leap to Dionysus without Paul having to make an overt reference.

The context of Dionysian cultic rituals also provides an appealing contrast to Paul's subsequent statement to be filled with the Spirit. Instead of consuming intoxicants to achieve prophetic abilities and spiritual revelation, the follower of Jesus should be filled with God's Spirit. In his opening prayer, Paul has already petitioned that they would be filled with the Spirit of wisdom and revelation. The believer need not abandon his or her mind in order to receive spiritual insight. This is yet another instance of the pagan culture offering empty promises.

To further this contrast, there are five activities (indicated by Greek participles) that are tied to the imperative to *be filled* with the Spirit. *Speaking* to one another in songs, *singing, praising,* and *giving thanks* to God were to be the practices associated with worship of God. Paul writes similar words to the church at Colosse and we can deduce that these are fundamental activities associated with the early church, along with teaching, which is mentioned in Colossians 3:16. If you listen closely enough, it is not hard to imagine the ruckus of chanting, ecstatic utterances, and drunken babblings of one of these pagan festivals compared to the melodic singing of the Ephesian church during one of their communal gatherings.

The fifth and final activity is the act of *submitting* to each other. This practice will be covered more extensively in the next chapter, but it is noteworthy that Paul considered a submissive attitude to be an integral part of the worship of God and the worship gathering with fellow believers. As noted earlier, Ephesians 5:21, where the practice of submission is introduced, cannot be removed from either the preceding thoughts on the virtuous life or the ideas that will follow. It will serve as a transition verse that concludes his discussion on virtuous living, while introducing the more practical applications of virtue in everyday affiliations. In essence, the virtuous life will be a futile pursuit if not accompanied by an attitude of submission.

AVOID DARKNESS BUT DO NOT FEAR IT

One picture that begins to emerge as we read through this letter is that Ephesians gives very little advice about how to engage the surrounding culture. Most of what Paul writes involves avoidance of the resident culture. Painting in broad strokes, Paul gives considerable instruction on how the Ephesian church should interact with one another. Yet as he encourages them to embrace life as the people of God, much of his guidance is concerned with the avoidance of the surrounding culture. "You must no longer live this way," "do not be partners with them," and "have nothing to do with such things" are all phrases Paul utilizes as he implores them to be very careful how they navigate this path. This stands in stark contrast to much of today's evangelical Christianity, which is frequently trying to find ways to engage and adapt to the prevailing culture.

Some of this cultural avoidance may have to do with the immediate condition of the Ephesian community. Paul was not writing to recent converts or a newly established church. He was addressing a community that he himself had established some years earlier, yet had stalled in their faith. And we may conclude that this inertia was due, at least in part, to the ongoing influence and tolerance of pagan practices within their community. Thus, the prescription for this inertia would be a clean break with this lingering pagan influence.

At the same time, as we have already noted, there is a moment to seize if they would take this virtuous life seriously. Light can illuminate the darkness and while they were to carefully navigate this path, there is certainly no call to abandon the city. Ephesus represented a significant opportunity to influence the region as a whole.

So how are we to balance the call to living life in the kingdom of God with cultural engagement? Here are just a few brief thoughts. Much more could be written on this topic.

First, we must understand our audience. A well-discipled community may need a push toward cultural engagement, while new believers may need to be exposed to more discipleship training, while leaving behind a former way of life. Many church communities will have people all along the spiritual spectrum. Discernment is needed when addressing the community as a whole.

Second, in our rush to engage culture we must not lose sight of what is incompatible with God's kingdom. In an effort to appear tolerant and nonjudgmental, there is very little that would distinguish some church communities from the wider culture. Virtuous living is as relevant and challenging today as it was in Paul's day.

Third, in order to influence the surrounding culture, we should be offering a distinct and appealing alternative to those practices that are not compatible with God's kingdom. Life in the kingdom of God is not simply a matter of avoiding the bad, but embracing all that is good.

Lastly, the goal is to live life as the people of God, which may not always result in being popular with the world we live in. There is a difference between winning over the prevailing culture we live in, and being won over ourselves by that same culture. We can live with this tension if we truly believe that God is bringing all creation back under his authority.

11 PATERFAMILIAS

Who would desire to deprive Ephesus of its salvation, a city which took its beginnings from that purest of beings [Artemis], and which grew in size beyond all other cities of Ionia and Lydia, and stretched itself out on the sea, on the promontory over which she is built, and is filled with studious people, both philosophers and rhetoricians, thanks to whom the city owes her strength, not to her cavalry, but to the tens of thousands of her inhabitants in whom she encourages wisdom. And do you think that there is any wise man who would not do his best in behalf of such a city?

- Philostratus, *Life*

Curetes Street, which connects the upper part of the city to the lower neighborhoods and the harbor, is bordered by hills on each side. Given the population of Ephesus, in its day the hillsides must have been blanketed with hundreds of houses. At the termination of Curetes Street, facing the Library of Celsus, is a large section of hillside covered by a protective structure, known as the Terrace Houses. (It was raining on this particular day, so the covered structure was well worth the additional admission fee!) Two blocks of these houses have now been excavated and enclosed from the elements.

Judging from the size and décor of the structures, these terrace houses certainly belonged to the wealthy citizens of Ephesus. The homes, which date back to the time of Paul, are two and sometimes three stories in size, conforming to the slope of the hillside. They feature large courtyards and are adorned with frescos and mosaics of scenes from Greek mythology.

Furthermore, the residents enjoyed many of the conveniences of the day, including private toilets, baths, and running water.

Of course, most Ephesians did not live this way, but the Terrace Houses do give a glimpse of family life in Ephesus beyond many of the public structures and monuments that adorn the city.

$$\text{III}$$

The Roman family or household unit was an important part of society. It was believed that a well-ordered household was a microcosm of a well-run society. It encompassed much more than today's nuclear family and had a very definitive structure to it. And the unquestioned leader of the Roman household was known as the *paterfamilias*. The paterfamilias was "any male Roman citizen not himself within the power of an older male relative."[1] Thus, the oldest living male in a family usually assumed this role, while younger men, even those married with children, remained under the authority of the paterfamilias until the death of the elder.

The household of the paterfamilias was comprised of his wife and children, including the wives of his grown sons. Upon marriage (usually arranged by the paterfamilias) the bride passed from her own family to the family of her husband. Oftentimes, this extended family consisting of several generations lived under the same roof. Slaves also fell within the scope of the Roman household. Consequently, the paterfamilias could assume influence over not just a spouse and younger children, but a household encompassing numerous people.

The paterfamilias was a powerful role in Roman society. (The emperor was even referred to as paterfamilias of Rome; the empire was one big well-run household - at least that is the way it was portrayed.) In principle, he held ownership of all the property acquired by anyone in the household. All family decisions were his to make. The paterfamilias even held the power to administer punishment and justice within the household – including death! Those within the household did not enjoy the full protection of Roman laws, which often only applied to male Roman citizens. Yet, as Goodman notes, "Romans took pride in being good, gentle fathers and husbands," somewhat tempering the extent to which the paterfamilias could exercise his authority.[2]

This social structure is fundamental to the understanding of Paul's concluding words on virtue, and how virtuous living applies to the Greco-Roman household. This next section of Ephesians has caused some unnecessary tension for us moderns, primarily because we fail to consider the societal context of the first century, and thus fail to grasp how progressive Paul's words actually were. Similar to other topics Paul has covered in this letter, his path meanders squarely through the landscape of the Greco-

Roman way of life. Yet he is offering a new way of navigating this path – a way of viewing the landscape through a completely different set of lenses. And the journey's end is not to live comfortably within the borders of this world, but lies well beyond into the kingdom of God.

CALM-SUBMISSIVE ENERGY

We are now ready to cross the bridge encountered in Ephesians 5:21. As noted from the previous chapter, this verse serves as both a summary of the previous section on virtue, as well as a starting point for the application of virtue to the Greco-Roman household. The word *submit* is the fifth and final participle tied to the practices associated with being filled with the Spirit. This same word in 5:21 also serves as the verb for 5:22 (because there is no verb present in verse 22, it is supplied by the participle in verse 21). Thus, in order to follow the path of virtue through the roles and responsibilities of the family household, the ominous and oft-misunderstood bridge of submission must be crossed, and crossed by everyone!

Submit to one another out of reverence for Christ.

There it is! To some, this bridge may sway a bit with the wind, but offers safe passage to the other side. To others, it is ominous-looking and best avoided, opting for an easier route around the chasm. So, what is being asked of the Ephesian church – and by extension, people of faith today – and why do so many today bristle when approaching this bridge?

Perhaps it should be acknowledged at the outset that this word has been misused throughout the history of the church to connote something like *unquestioned obedience*. And it is precisely because the connection between verse 21 and 22 has not been made (or simply ignored) that this chasm has widened, leaving the virtuous life halting on one embankment and the dutiful wife standing alone on the other. When verse 22 is allowed to become an island, disconnected from the larger conversation, then the result has too often been that women lose their voice and wives are pressed to become the subservient partner in marriage. This basically describes the role of the wife in first century Rome. Yet ironically Paul was moving away from this to something very different.

As a first step, it will be helpful to define the concept of submission. The word *submit* (*hupotasso*) is a military term that can mean to align oneself within the recognized chain of command. It is often used in the context of obedience to leaders or to authority. In this setting, it does not imply that the one who submits is a second-class citizen or incapable of making decisions. It only acknowledges that within the given social structure, there is a chain of hierarchy and responsibility. In this same vein, Paul further equates submission to respect at the conclusion of this section on husbands and wives.

One of the best definitions of submission that I have recently uncovered comes from an unlikely source. Far removed from theological positions, gender roles, or historical contexts, submission is a crucial concept in the world of dog training. And the foremost dog trainer around today, achieving a celebrity-like status, is a man by the name of Cesar Millan. Millan had his own television series, *Dog Whisperer*, and has built a forty-five-acre dog psychology center in Southern California.[3]

In the pack life - the social structure of dogs - there is only one pack leader, and the role of the human is to effectively become that pack leader. In the absence of a pack leader, many dogs will begin to become assertive, unbalanced, and anxious. A well-balanced pack is formed of dogs that are in a *calm-submissive* state of mind. But even Cesar Millan has to combat the portrayal of submission. "The word *submissive* carries with it negative connotations, just as the word *assertive* does. *Submissive* doesn't mean pushover. It doesn't mean you have to make your dog into a zombie or a slave. It simply means *relaxed* and *receptive*."[4] Why relaxed and receptive? Because when the pack has full confidence in the pack leader, the individual members can let go of aggression and anxiety, and simply be what they were created to be – dogs!

The same concept applies to human creatures as well. In any given relationship or social structure, when we allow ourselves to lead out of the areas of our strengths, and follow others – or submit – in their respective strengths, we are freed up of the need to always be in control. We can focus on our areas of giftedness and relax in the knowledge that we are surrounded by others who are equally gifted and capable as well.

As it pertains to our relationship with God, when we submit ourselves to God, we are actually freed up to be fully human. We can let go of the need to be omniscient, omnipotent, and omnipresent. Trying to be God can be exhausting! And when we are fully submitted to God, we can put aside ego and submit to others where social mores dictate, be it at work, school, or church. In individual relationships, including marriage, we can take the lead where God has gifted us or given us influence, and we can follow others in their gifts, talents, and strengths. Cesar Millan even admits that when he learned to apply the concept of calm-submissiveness toward his wife, his marriage greatly improved!

Nonetheless, in our culture today submission remains an ominous bridge to cross. Western culture is nothing, if not a rights-oriented society. From free speech to material comforts to religious tolerance, it seems that nothing is a privilege anymore; it has all become a right. There is little sense of what is a responsibility or what must be earned. It is our right, and we will scream and holler if that right is infringed upon!

An attitude of submission will often call us to forgo some of what we consider our rights. In the New Testament, Jesus himself modeled this by living a life fully submitted to God by taking on the role of a servant. He was not constantly fighting for what was his by right, and yet perhaps lived in greater freedom than anyone else has ever experienced. As I have written elsewhere:

> *The great irony is that when we lay down our rights before God, we do not remain a slave, but we become children of God, enjoying all the rights and privileges that come with that inheritance. Grace is what allows us to live this surrendered life. While our natural inclinations will always push us toward the assertion of our rights and to the demanding of respect from others, grace allows us to freely let those things go as we rest securely in our position as God's beloved.[5]*

THE VIRTUOUS HOME

Now that we have, to some measure, disarmed this volatile word, we are ready to look at the specific household relationships that were to be characterized by the mutual submission discussed in 5:21. First and foremost within the household structure was the husband-wife relationship, and the wife is addressed first.

A believer was called to live a life of submission to the Lord Jesus. This was of utmost importance. In the same way, wives were to carry this same attitude into their relationship with their husbands. Keep in mind that the verb *submit* is being provided from 5:21 in the context of mutual submission. "Wives, to your own husbands" is the literal reading. Also of note is that Paul is not saying wives should submit to their husbands in lieu of submitting to the Lord, but as an extension of the submitted life they are already living to the Lord.

Still, we should not be surprised that Paul often worked within the customary structures of his day. He usually does not march right into the Roman house and begin overturning the furniture. Within each of these household relationships, we may want Paul to proclaim to the marginalized party, "You are free! You don't have to take it anymore!" But that would be projecting our own biases back two thousand years upon Paul. Instead of tossing out traditional roles and conventions, Paul's message was often one of saying, "there is a different way of living out your role." And biases aside, when taken as a whole and examined closer, it can be a subversive message Paul was preaching.

Thus, Paul upholds the customary role of the husband being the paterfamilias. Because of the deeply rooted nature of this role in Roman society, any other position Paul might have taken would have risked tearing households apart. But he does so while reshaping the basis for this role and advocating a different way it should be carried out: "The husband is the head of the wife as Christ is the head of the church." In other words, this is not the position from which to rule with an iron fist. This is an opportunity to become more like Jesus. Far from relegating the wife to a second-class citizenry (or non-citizenry in the case of most women under Roman rule), Paul is elevating the position of the wife by invoking the example of the church.

Paul has already written at length about Jew and Gentile coming together to form one body, of which Jesus the Messiah is the head. It is a picture of the head and the body working together as one unit. The church was the fullness of Christ (1:22-23), giving full expression to his mission. Jesus was willing to sacrifice his very life for the cause of this unity (5:2). Any reading that places the wife in a demeaning role in this relationship completely misses the message of Jesus and his church. Paul's message to wives (and keep in mind to husbands as well, who would have been listening to the same message) was that they and their husbands were to function together as a single person, emulating the very purpose of God.

Next, Paul turns to husbands. Their responsibility as paterfamilias is to be characterized by loving care and concern for the wife (as well as the entire household). And lest there be any lingering misconceptions about the husband-wife relationship serving as a microcosm of God's plan, Paul takes a brief aside to further illustrate the relationship between Jesus and the church.

The definitive example of Jesus' love for the church was his willingness to give up his very life in order to redeem her. This sacrificial giving up of himself was already specified back in Ephesians 5:2 in relation to the church (the "us" in 5:2), leaving little question as to what that expression represents. Redeeming his church would cost him his life. Jesus was aware of this and willingly drank from this cup regardless (Matthew 26:2,42).

Having given himself up for the church, his death and subsequent resurrection allowed him to redeem his bride, making her holy. The rest of the image reflects a traditional Jewish wedding ceremony: the washing in preparation for the wedding, the sanctification (making holy) of the marriage, and the bride being presented to the husband. In Jewish tradition, the first stage of the marriage process is still called *kiddushin*, which means *betrothal* or *sanctification*. These descriptions also recall Old Testament images of God and Israel, as in Ezekiel 16. This section is rich in imagery!

All this, of course, is another reiteration of the plan of God, as Paul has stated from the outset of his letter in Ephesians 1:4. God's plan from the beginning was to bring his people back under his reign, to be holy and blameless before him. His people were represented as the body of Christ (1:22-23), with Christ functioning as the head. Again, this does suggest the hierarchical nature of the relationship, but also denotes the two parts functioning together as a single unit.

So it is with this in mind that husbands are to treat wives as their own bodies. While this may be a scary thought for some wives, the general thrust is that for most people the motivation will be to take care of themselves and not bring harm to their own bodies. People who intentionally harm themselves are usually said to have some type of psychosis. But this adage that "he who loves his wife loves himself" goes well beyond mere symbolism. It is at the very heart of Paul's message: Jew and Gentile will come together to form one new person – a new body. "His purpose was to create in himself one new man out of the two" (Ephesians 2:15).

Similarly, in quite the mystical and spiritual sense, marriage was the joining together of two people to form one flesh. Thus, it was no mere platitude to proclaim that for a husband to love his wife was to love his own body. This oneness was precisely what marriage was founded upon. Paul makes this explicit by quoting Genesis 2:24: the two becoming one flesh, one body, a new person. And as if Paul may have lost his own train of thought, he reminds the hearers that he is still talking about Christ and the church for the moment.

Thus, the image of the marriage between Jesus and the church not only puts in a nutshell the plan of God, but also serves as an example of a husband's duty to his wife. This entire section to husbands and wives is rich with imagery and theology. One cannot seriously engage this section on marriage without understanding that Paul's expectations were that marriages were to embody love, mutual submission and respect, as well as self-sacrifice.

So, while a cursory reading may recognize the conventional roles within the Greco-Roman family, Paul's deeper calling of how those roles were to be lived out, based on profoundly spiritual ground, was unprecedented at the time. To truly live this out would be to cause a revolution within the Greco-Roman household, without having to storm the house and overturn the furnishings.

Next, Paul turns to the second major relationship within the household structure: the relationship between children and parents. Children were to be obedient toward their parents. (Note that the word for *obey* is a different word than Paul has been using for *submission*. This is further evidence that Paul has elevated the husband-wife relationship to a higher plane.) As we stated previously, under the role of the paterfamilias, children need not refer necessarily to little kids, but could also refer to grown adults still under the authority of the father. But the caveat to fathers in 6:4 would seem to indicate that Paul did have predominantly younger children and adolescents in mind, who were still in the process of their education and training.

Paul looked no further than the fifth commandment of the Decalogue to support his call to obedience: "Honor your father and your mother." From this, we can assume a compelling link between obedience and honor. Again, as I have written elsewhere:

It just so happens that one of the highest forms of honoring and respecting someone else is by obeying them. We honor God, those in authority, our bosses, and our parents when we honor their requests. There is an indisputable link between honor and obedience. ... Our actions will honor much louder than our words ever will.[6]

For younger children, to honor was essentially to obey. The more a child grew into adulthood, honor could be expanded to include similar concepts such as *respect* and *care*, and not simply *compliance*.

Paul goes on to disclose that this command has a promise of long life associated with it. Instead of being a prohibition against a certain action, honoring your parents comes with a blessing linked to it. Once more, from *Ten Essential Words*:

This promise goes well beyond simply the preservation of one's life. In the Hebrew Scriptures, a long life implied a full life and a life of wisdom, and it was something to be celebrated, or - as Paul puts it - something to be enjoyed. The Hebrew Scriptures asserted that the pinnacle of a person's life was in old age, because one's inherent worth and prestige had increased steadily with experience and years.[7] So this promise was not simply a promise of a long period of life, but a long fulfilling life.[8]

To fathers, this new way of relating within the traditional household code would involve not being overly harsh on children, exasperating them, or causing them to be resentful. This would have also been an uncommon directive at the time, effectively tempering the unquestioned authority of the father. Instead, the father was to invest positively in the lives of his children, educating them and assuming the role of spiritual head of the house as well, making sure that these virtues were instilled in his children. The mother is not addressed here, presumably because Paul is still working within the social orders of the day and addressing specifically the paterfamilias. Yet, there is little doubt that the mother would undertake a vital role in instilling morals and values in her children as well. She often managed the household - including slaves - while the husband tended to the family business. The role of the mother can be implied here, yet perhaps Paul is specifically addressing fathers because of the potential for the abuse of their position.

THE ROMAN FATHER

Beyond the paterfamilias, the role of the father in the Roman Empire carried with it a tremendous amount of sovereignty. In sharp contrast to Jewish culture, a newborn was not formally acknowledged until the father lifted the child up, indicating its legitimacy.[9] Exposure was an acceptable practice at the time and within the power of the father. If a child was born abnormal, the paternity was in question, or simply if the additional mouth to feed could not be afforded, the infant could be left out in the elements to die. In fact, the founding myth of Rome involved the exposure of the twins Romulus and Remus, only to be nursed by a wolf and found by a shepherd, who took them in, sparing their lives. It was not uncommon in Greek mythology for gods to order the exposure of an unwanted newborn.

Besides exposure, infant mortality was already high. Anywhere from 20 to 30 percent of newborns did not live beyond the age of one year. Additionally, the father often had the right to kick his children out of the house, sell them into slavery, or kill them if they evoked his anger. Perhaps this is why Paul tempers the role of the father in Ephesians.

Nevertheless, most fathers loved and treasured their children. There are many examples from the writings of the day of fathers expressing great devotion to their children. While it may be difficult for our modern minds to accept such harsh practices, in most ways a Roman father embodied the same affections as today's fathers.

The final relationship within the household structure is that of slaves and masters. While it may sound strange to refer to the slave-master dynamic in relational terms, there are many instances from Paul's time where slaves were a valued part of the household. One of the most well-known examples is the relationship between the Roman senator and statesman Cicero and his slave, Tiro. Tiro was said to be well-educated, intelligent, and loyal. In his writings, it was not uncommon for Cicero to address his slave as he would a dear friend. Cicero ultimately granted Tiro his freedom, yet Tiro still accompanied Cicero on some of his journeys and eventually composed a biography about the life of his master.

Then again, there were abundant examples of slaves being mistreated or even killed. Slaves had very few rights or protections. Discipline was harsh and a runaway slave faced almost certain death if caught. In fact, a common attitude toward slaves in the Roman Empire was that they were viewed as help around the estate, just as one might consider livestock. The spectrum ranged from deeming slaves to be non-human on one end to treating them as close personal friends or part of the family at the opposite end.

Thus, it should not be overlooked that Paul is even addressing slaves in his letter to the Ephesians. The fact that Paul begins 6:5 by addressing slaves directly is shocking in and of itself. (The same could be said for addressing women and children directly as well.) It would have been customary for Paul to simply direct all instruction regarding household relational matters to the paterfamilias. That is what we would expect. But the picture that begins to emerge is that of a community gathering where men, women, children … and slaves, are all sitting together, at least in the same room with one another. Paul's letter would be read aloud so that each member of the household would hear Paul's admonitions to the other members. There would be no ambiguity among the household as to how they were to treat and interact with each other.

As Paul begins to address slaves, he instructs them to obey their *earthly* masters. (The word *obey* is used here as with children, while the word *submit* is used in relation to wives, as well as a broader way of interacting with each other.) Keeping in mind that while masters and slaves may have been in the same room together while Paul's letter was being read, the addition of *earthly* or *physical* (literally, *fleshly*) to the position of master may have been directed more toward masters themselves, rather than toward slaves – a subtle reminder of who was actually Lord and Master, regardless of one's title in society.

Slaves were to carry out their duties with a work ethic distinguished by sincerity of heart. In other words, they were not to simply go through the motions or merely put forth effort until the proverbial cat went away. They were to serve wholeheartedly, whether under the watchful eye of their master or left to themselves for an extended period of time. It would not stretch the imagination to suppose that the typical mindset of a slave would be to act compliant and dutiful while under the supervision of the master. But when left unsupervised, corner-cutting would ensue and productivity would plummet, all while grumbling and complaining to fellow household slaves. The modern workplace might be emblematic of this mindset, though today we tend to press this slave-master relationship too quickly onto our own employee-employer interactions without fully dealing with the context of slavery in the Roman Empire.

So following Paul's reasoning, he can ask slaves to serve out of respect and sincerity for the same reason he calls for mutual submission and obedience from other members of the household: the one they were actually serving was the Messiah Jesus. Thus, the way we conduct ourselves in our temporal relationships should flow directly out of our service and submission to our true master, Jesus. In actuality, when we submit to each other and obey those in positions of authority, we are peering over their shoulders, so to speak, and taking our orders from the Lord. We are "doing the will of God" each time we practice submission, obedience, and a strong work ethic with those around us.

In the same way, it was of little account whether their hard work and deference would be noticed and rewarded by their earthly masters. If they were motivated to serve dutifully because they were serving the Lord, their reward would likewise come from the Lord. In God's kingdom, it mattered not what social status they happened to be labeled with.

This topic of slavery, especially in today's western culture, will no doubt cause the bridge to teeter and sway, prompting many to turn back from this chasm to the submissive life. We might wish that Paul had declared all slaves to be free and condemn the institution of slavery. N.T. Wright confesses as much when he writes, "Like most contemporary exegetes, I wish Paul could have said something much clearer about the dehumanizing practice of slavery and the need to work towards its abolition."[10] But he goes on to call for "a suspension of judgment in order to learn wisdom." In this case, we must let the practice remain in its place within the household code and attempt to understand the higher calling Paul was conferring on slaves in the Roman Empire. To reiterate, Paul often worked within the customary structures of his day – at least in the context of his letters to local communities - in order to communicate a far more subversive and radical message.

III

SLAVERY IN THE ROMAN EMPIRE

Like most nations of the ancient world (including Israel), the institution of slavery was normative within the Roman Empire. Rome was comprised of social classes, with patricians (the higher ranking) and plebeians (the commoners) making up its citizenry. Women could be citizens, but could not vote. Freedmen were former slaves who had obtained their freedom through various means. Their children could become full-fledged citizens of Rome. Slaves were on the bottom rung of the social ladder. Slaves had no rights and were considered non-persons within the social structure.

There were a number of circumstances where a person could end up as a slave. The most common circumstances involved prisoners of war being consigned to slavery, or debtors being unable to meet financial obligations. Children of female slaves would be born into slavery and, as previously stated, the paterfamilias could even sell unwanted children as slaves. Slavery was viewed as a normal and vital part of the Roman economy, yet the condition of being a slave was not necessarily a permanent one.

As has already been mentioned, slavery could involve anything from being a well-educated tutor or manager for the owner's affairs to the brutal life of working in the mines or as a prostitute.

Estimates vary, but the percentage of the population that were slaves around the first century in the Roman Empire ranges from about 15% on the low end to upwards of 40%, the higher estimate being the case especially in the city of Rome itself. Outside of Rome, Ephesus was a major center for slave markets.

To conclude the household structure, Paul turns his attention to masters. Like the instruction to fathers, his words to masters are brief. Perhaps this is because he has already addressed the paterfamilias, at least in part, when he speaks to fathers and husbands. Wives, children, and slaves were each distinct groups. But the roles of husband, father, and master could be encapsulated under the position of paterfamilias – though certainly there were husbands and fathers that had not yet attained head of the household.

However, another reason for Paul's brevity at this point is that he simply instructs masters to *behave in a similar manner* as slaves had just been instructed. "Everything I just told slaves also applies to you masters as well," Paul seems to assert. This is a remarkable statement! Nowhere else in the Roman Empire would masters and slaves effectively be told to treat each other in a reciprocal manner.

The one specific command directed to masters is to stop threatening their slaves. This act of threatening could be referring to keeping slaves in a constant state of fear, or it could simply be an umbrella term for all merciless behavior to which slaves were subject. Either way, the reason given for this tempering of behavior toward slaves is that both master and slave were now subject to the same authority. There was only one true Lord and Master, Jesus the Messiah, who is now Lord over all. In God's kingdom, societal status did not hold any sway. Little doubt, this would have been a subtle reminder that if we are counting on receiving the mercy of God, we should be quick to be merciful to those around us (Matthew 6:14,15). It is not uncommon for the scriptures to declare that God will deal with us with the same measure that we treat others. So, while masters may hold all the cards within Greco-Roman society, they might want to consider carefully how they play their hand.

At this point, we can begin to clearly see the way Paul has been working within the accepted social structures of his day, while simultaneously undermining – even transforming - those social structures. Piece by piece, he is bringing these structures under the reign of God.

Yes, the role of the paterfamilias may have been firmly entrenched within Roman society, but that role could be used to lead the family with sacrificial love and support. While women may have had few rights outside the home at that time, within the home they could be treasured for their role, utilize their gifts, and serve the family as they would be serving Jesus. Children could live out the Fifth Commandment, while parents could nurture their children as gifts from God. And regardless of whose earthly authority they fell under, slaves could serve with integrity, being trusted with household responsibilities, knowing that their heavenly master was always present. Conversely, earthly masters were themselves entrusted with the responsibility to manage well and treat everyone with dignity and respect, knowing that they themselves served the true lord of the world.

Living as the people of God was a way of acknowledging the reality of God's kingdom in the present time and served as a sign to others that Jesus was the world's true ruler. But this virtuous life could not be reached unless the bridge was crossed, and this necessitated an attitude of submission toward others. There were no shortcuts to be taken. Their position in society could not exempt them from traversing this chasm and taking on this attitude. A community that loved and served each other, as well as treated each other as equals, was sure to grab the attention of their pagan neighbors and send a buzz throughout the city. This was the life Paul was calling the Ephesian church to embody.

12 LET THE GAMES BEGIN

When they heard this, they were furious and began shouting: "Great is Artemis of the Ephesians!" Soon the whole city was in an uproar. The people seized Gaius and Aristarchus, Paul's traveling companions from Macedonia, and rushed as one man into the theater. Paul wanted to appear before the crowd, but the disciples would not let him. Even some of the officials of the province, friends of Paul, sent him a message begging him not to venture into the theater. The assembly was in confusion: Some were shouting one thing, some another. Most of the people did not even know why they were there. The Jews pushed Alexander to the front, and some of the crowd shouted instructions to him. He motioned for silence in order to make a defense before the people. But when they realized he was a Jew, they all shouted in unison for about two hours: "Great is Artemis of the Ephesians!"

- Luke, *The Acts of the Apostles*

Arguably, the most impressive structure at the archaeological site of Ephesus is the Great Theater. Regardless of whether you enter the site from the upper entrance and proceed down Curetes Street or you enter from the lower entrance, the theater being one of the very first structures you happen upon, it is an impressive venue even by today's standards. Having a seating capacity of around 25,000 people, the semicircular seating is built directly into the hillside and overlooks the entire harbor area, as well as the agora. In its original state, there would have been a three-story structure serving as the backdrop of the stage area and the arena floor.

Climbing the steps feels much like finding your seat at a modern-day football stadium. And like today, the best seats were usually reserved for dignitaries, city officials, and the wealthy. A favorite experiment of tourists and guides alike is to climb the seats and have someone speak in a normal voice on the theater floor to see just how well the sound of speaker's voice traveled to even the cheap seats at the top. The acoustics are quite remarkable.

The Great Theater would have hosted everything from citywide meetings to theater performances to gladiator fights. In the book of Acts, it served as the impromptu gathering place for the angry mob that seized the apostle's traveling companions. Today, the theater is still home to the *Selçuk Ephesus Festival of Culture and Art* each May.

III

Just as the Great Theater serves as the *pièce de résistance* of a present-day visit to the site of Ephesus, in many ways it also served as the centerpiece of Paul's extended ministry in Ephesus. The riot of the silversmith trade guild encompasses the entire second half of Acts 19. After the crowd was dispersed, the next verse, beginning in Acts 20, has Paul bidding his farewells to the Ephesian church. It would become the defining event of Paul's time in Ephesus. As stated earlier, the mob scene at the amphitheater in Ephesus left an indelible impression on Paul. He is more than likely referencing this event in both of his letters to the church at Corinth and in his first letter to Timothy. Thus, it is only fitting that the culmination of his letter to the Ephesian church has allusions back to the Great Theater.

Though it served many purposes, the amphitheater, like many Roman theaters at the time, would have hosted games, gladiator fights, displays of animal hunts, and reenactments of Rome's military exploits. This fits well with what Paul would write to the church at Corinth while in Ephesus: "For it seems to me that God has put us apostles on display at the end of the procession, like those condemned to die in the arena" (1 Corinthians 4:9). And again, "If I fought wild beasts in Ephesus with no more than human hopes, what have I gained?" (1 Corinthians 15:32). Captives being led in procession, triumphs terminating at the arena, and fighting wild beasts – these are all images that revolve around the city's amphitheater.

So while Paul may not explicitly reference Ephesus' Great Theater, the memories could not have been far away. When he chooses to conclude his letter to the Ephesian church with imagery of a soldier or gladiator putting on his armor in order to defend and preserve his life, that image is very much at home in the amphitheater. He does not need to say, "By the way, this preparation for battle is taking place at the Great Theater," it would just be understood and assumed by the hearers. "Of course it is at the arena; where else would all this be taking place?"

BEHOLD WHAT ARMS BY VULCAN ARE BESTOWED

With the Great Theater serving as the contextual backdrop, Paul begins his final thoughts by encouraging the Ephesians to stand strong in the battle they are fighting, "Finally, be strong in the Lord." As he will explain, the source of their strength, as well as their protection in this battle, will come from what Paul will describe in detail as *the armor of God*.

This closing section describing the armor of God ties back to many ideas presented previously in the letter. It is not, as it is sometimes treated, a disjointed notion tacked on to the end of the letter – one last attempt by Paul to rally the troops, so to speak. It is an image that fits nicely in summarizing much of what Paul has already conveyed.

He began his letter by stressing the mighty power of God - the same power that God used to raise Jesus from the dead. Paul was asserting that God's power was greater than any speculative power possessed by other gods or deities. Just as he began by assuring them that this power was available to us, which included those Gentile followers of Jesus, he ends by encouraging them to stand firm in this same power.

Similarly, the directive to put on the armor of God echoes the related command to *put on* the new self in 4:24. If the old self was corruptible and susceptible to assaults from the powers of darkness, then the new self was created to be Godlike in holiness and strength. Thus, in repeating the command *to put on*, Paul is, in effect, stressing that an essential element of putting on the new self is to clothe yourself in the armor of God. If you are called to be more like God, then wear the same thing (figuratively speaking – more on this to come) that God wears.

Finally, though he has alluded to it throughout his letter, Paul makes clear that the battle being fought is not a conventional battle against a mortal, flesh and blood enemy. The battle is a spiritual one. He describes the opposition in various ways: rulers, authorities, world powers, and spiritual forces. In using several differing designations, Paul is not necessarily distinguishing between classes or hierarchies of spiritual forces as much as he is stressing the totality of the spiritual forces – all of them, no matter how you want to break it down. He is also echoing 1:21, where he has already introduced these descriptors. In the opening chapter, the emphasis was that these powers would be subject to Jesus as part of God's plan to bring all things in heaven and on earth together under the reign of Jesus. The list of powers in 1:21 ranged from human rulers to magical spirits, while here the focus seems to be squarely on the spiritual forces at work, even if by means of human rulers.

It should also be clear by now that just as the opposition is *spiritual* in nature, so too the Ephesian church is to protect themselves against *spiritual* harm. The danger that comes from the devil's schemes is not necessarily physical injury or death, but that those schemes might divert them from taking hold of all that God has for them and lead them astray. As Jesus, himself, stated, "Do not be afraid of those who kill the body and after that can do no more ... Fear him who, after the killing of the body, has power to throw you into hell" (Luke 12:5,6). In the same way, neither was Paul concerned with bodily harm. Paul has stressed throughout his letter that the magical powers, which some among them still feared and would have typically threatened physical illness or bodily harm, had been trumped by the mighty power that God had worked through the Messiah Jesus. This armor of God was not meant to simply counteract magic phrases or evil curses.

Thus, as Paul introduces this armor from God, much of what he conveys is a restatement of his opening prayer, as well as other ideas he has developed throughout his letter. And a major point of emphasis has been that these powers have already been defeated, even if they are still at large and dangerous.

This point can be tricky to fully grasp, but clearly Paul believed that God's kingdom had already been inaugurated and that the Messiah was already reigning. Yet he also believed that the enemy was still at work, even if already defeated. N.T. Wright raises this tension when he notes that "the Messiah's reign, though emphatically present, is not complete. The 'last enemy', death, remains as yet still powerful, though defeated in principle through the resurrection."[1] Even though God's plan is marching ahead toward completion, there would be no need for armor unless these spiritual forces were still inflicting casualties among God's people.

Keeping this tension guards against two overreactions to this section on the armor of God. The first overreaction neglects the announcement that the Messiah is already reigning and victory belongs to God. In this case, the Christian journey is a perilous one, fraught with spiritual dangers, giving far too much power to the opposition. Even as Paul describes this armor of God, lost is the emphasis that we have already been equipped with all we need to stand against the enemy.

The second overreaction ignores Paul's warnings that spiritual forces are still at work and can harm those who are unwary. To the misinformed, all this talk of spiritual battles and armor from God belongs to the superstitious and simple. Though Paul may present a compelling image for the Ephesian church, we are better informed today. This, too, is a precarious view to take.

As we shall soon explain, Paul's message, when understood fully, was a message to have full confidence, even as this battle is still being fought. If thoroughly prepared and equipped, there should be no reason to live in fear and apprehension.

Having clarified the nature of this battle, Paul repeats the command to put on the armor of God. Through this repetition, he stresses the purpose of wearing this spiritual protection: to stand your ground. In fact, three times Paul uses the word *to stand* (*histemi*) to emphasize the desired outcome of this battle. Earlier, when describing the virtuous life, Paul's action of choice was *walking* as a metaphor for the spiritual journey. Here the action is to take your stand so that when the battle is over you can be found still standing. There are a couple of reasons why Paul stresses simply the ability to remain planted firmly on one's feet.

First, as we have earlier noted, the battle has already been won through the death and resurrection of Jesus the Messiah. Thus, there is no need to launch an offensive campaign against the enemy. Using military imagery, we might expect Paul to utilize such action-oriented commands as *advance, hunt down, capture*, or *go forth and conquer.* Yet on multiple occasions, the rather civilian command is simply to *take your stand* and *remain standing.* Even the tactic of taking up the shield is a defensive measure, so that the arrows of the enemy can be deflected and extinguished.

All this might come as a disappointment to those ready to take the powers of darkness head on, but Paul has stressed throughout his letter that the offensive campaign against evil has already been fought and won by God, through Jesus. There is no need to go searching for spiritual forces or trying to overcome the last enemy, death. Our orders are simply to be prepared to spiritually defend ourselves when the opposition attempts to inflict casualties, even in their defeat. Given that the Ephesian church already lived in some trepidation of magic spells and unseen powers, Paul saw no need to rally them to fight a war that had already been won. They simply needed to utilize the protection they had previously been equipped with and stand in the power of God.

Second, this may well be an allusion to a common military tactic of the Roman army. When meeting the enemy on the field of battle, Roman legions would employ a phalanx formation. The large body of the army consisted of blocks of fighting units, made up of multiple rows of soldiers. As the enemy approached, the front line assembled closely together, with shields forming a defensive wall in the case of a frontal assault or an advancing wall pushing the enemy line backwards. Because of the close proximity of the next row of soldiers – only about three feet separated lines – if a soldier on the front line was wounded or killed, a replacement could quickly step in and keep the wall of shields intact. If soldiers *stood their ground*, then the wall was virtually impenetrable.

The tortoise, or testudo formation, specifically was an example of locking shields taken to the extreme. A smaller group of soldiers could lock shields on all sides of the rectangular formation, while those in the middle would similarly raise their shields above their heads to form an armored barrier providing protection on all sides. It was said that when properly employed, men could walk on top of the shields that comprise the testudo formation. When moving together, the unit could maneuver as a single structure – the precursor to today's armored vehicles - impervious to missiles and difficult to break apart.

Whether Paul had these military formations in mind is debatable, but the command to stand firm may have been an allusion to this tactic of locking shields and forming a defensive barrier that was difficult to breech. This would also have brought in a communal aspect to this spiritual battle. One could not form a defensive wall by oneself. A community of fellow soldiers, working together as one unit, would have been needed to engage in such tactics. Even if Paul did not have this specifically in mind, the entire metaphor is rich with military images. The Ephesian church would have most likely at least considered this application of Paul's command to stand firm together as a community, with shields locked.

Before examining each piece of equipment, there is one more contextual tidbit that will help cast light on this imagery of armor. While most commentaries will stress Old Testament references to Yahweh as the mighty warrior in Isaiah (indeed, we will look at this shortly) as the background for this section, we must not forget that Paul is writing to Greeks, who knew very little about the Hebrew Scriptures. Few address what the armor of God would have symbolized to a first-century Greco-Roman audience. And as we have stated previously, Paul knew full well what he was doing when choosing his metaphors for Gentile believers.

To a Greek or Roman, raised on all the wonderful mythological stories from times past, the armor of God would have immediately been associated with *the armor of the gods*. There are many Greek myths that involve the giving of divine armor from the god Hephaestus, or his Roman equivalent, Vulcan (see below). Hephaestus was the god of fire and metalworking. On several occasions, Hephaestus was known to have forged divine armor that essentially made the one who wore the armor immortal. To wear the armor of the gods was to be invincible in battle. The wearers of this armor would have taken on the status of becoming almost godlike - a demigod.

▥
III

ARMOR OF THE GODS

One of the more implausible members of the Olympic pantheon was Hephaestus, the god of fire and metalworking. Hephaestus was the son of Zeus and Hera, but was unwanted as a child because of his unsightly appearance. While in exile, he learned the art of metalworking. He eventually reconciled with his mother, but, quite cruelly, she and Zeus gave Aphrodite,

172

the goddess of love and beauty, to the awkward son as a bride. She was not known for being a faithful wife and had several children with Ares, the god of war.

Part of the lore of Hephaestus (or Vulcan to the Romans) was his ability to forge divine armor. The mythological founder of Rome was Aeneas, who would establish the city following the Trojan War. In the *Aeneid*, we are told that Aeneas joins the battle to fight for Troy. Concerned for his safety, his mother Venus (Aphrodite to the Greeks) persuades Vulcan to forge for him special armor. The shield, in particular, foretells the founding of Rome through a set of intricate reliefs. Thus, the armor protects him, as well as giving Aeneas assurance of his survival for a greater destiny.

Similarly, Homer's account of the Trojan War tells of Hephaestus forging divine armor for the Greek hero Achilles. After the death of his friend, Patroclus, Achilles is in a state of grief, in part because Patroclus was killed while having borrowed his armor. In order to console Achilles and persuade him to continue the battle, he is given new armor created by Hephaestus. Achilles would go on to slay many Trojans, including Hector son of Priam, but would eventually be killed himself by an arrow to the heel.

The Greek hero Heracles (better known by his Roman name, Hercules) wore armor fashioned by Hephaestus as well. Likewise, another Greek hero, Perseus beheaded the dreaded Medusa with a sword forged by Hephaestus. Several other pieces of armor are attributed to the craftsmanship of Hephaestus in Greek mythology. Whether god or mortal, to wear the armor of the gods was to hold a decisive advantage in battle.

III

With this in mind – and maintaining that Paul would have understood that his Greek audience also would have had this in mind – Paul was likely communicating a far stronger message here than we fully grasp today. By encouraging the Ephesians to put on the armor of God, he is conveying that in doing so, they could confidently stand firm because they would be wearing the armor of immortality. *Wear this armor and no harm can come to you.* And while this may have conveyed perhaps too strong a message – even the armor of the gods had been known to have an Achilles heel – Paul was, no doubt, wanting to instill confidence in his hearers that the battle had been won, so stand strong! There was no more room for their fear and trepidation of the unseen spiritual world filled with magic and spells.

We turn, then, to the individual pieces that comprise the armor of God. While divine armor would have been brimming with meaning for a Greek audience, Jewish readers would have also found meaning from their own Hebrew Scriptures. Undoubtedly, Paul drew upon this symbol from his own

Jewish background, but also understood its resonance with the people of Ephesus. And while replete with meaning, we must not press the metaphor beyond what Paul intended. Paul, himself, does not always employ this armor metaphor in a consistent manner.

Stand firm then, with the belt of truth buckled around your waist, with the breastplate of righteousness in place, and with your feet fitted with the readiness that comes from the gospel of peace. In addition to all this, take up the shield of faith, with which you can extinguish all the flaming arrows of the evil one. Take the helmet of salvation and the sword of the Spirit, which is the word of God. (Ephesians 6:14-17)

The first piece of gear mentioned is the *belt of truth* buckled around the waist. A Roman soldier would have worn a belt that served several purposes. The belt would have secured the tunic in place, as well as held several small tools and weapons around the waist. Attached to the belt would also have been additional leather straps that would protect the midsection and lower body – parts of the body not protected by armor. The belt is a basic part of any armor, yet is inconspicuous. Thus, belts are usually not mentioned as part of the divine armor forged by the gods.

In his description of God's Messiah, Isaiah writes, "Righteousness will be his belt and faithfulness the sash around his waist" (Isaiah 11:5). With righteousness and justice, the Messiah will judge the world, coming to the defense of the poor and marginalized, and righting what is wrong with the world. Paul will reserve the attribute of righteousness for the next piece, but here utilizes truth as the undergirding quality. Throughout the letter to the Ephesians, truth is linked with the message of the Messiah Jesus. They were taught the message of truth and so were encouraged to make it a part of their nature; they were to wear it as part of clothing themselves with the new person.

Paul follows the belt of truth with the *breastplate of righteousness*. In Roman legions, this was the equivalent of the body armor, which was formed by fastening together iron strips. This provided flexibility, but also important protection for the most vulnerable part of the body and vital organs. Officers and emperors would have worn what we would associate with the more traditional breastplate, made of bronze and sculpted to form a muscular chest and torso. The breastplate could be customized and ornately decorated.

The breastplate forged by Hephaestus and given to Heracles was made out of gold. Other breastplates forged by Hephaestus were said to be impenetrable by human weapons. The gods were often depicted in armor, including intricately designed and strappingly sculpted breastplates.

Again, drawing from Isaiah, Yahweh is also described as wearing a breastplate of righteousness: "He put on righteousness as his breastplate and the helmet of salvation on his head" (Isaiah 59:17). Here, God is described as a mighty warrior who will judge those who oppose him and covenants together with his people who repent and follow after him. Throughout scripture, it is not uncommon for the people of God to be described as being clothed in righteousness. This is essentially what Paul is alluding to when he previously called the Ephesians to put on – to clothe themselves with – the new person. Thus, Paul is calling them to take on the virtues and the very character of God, and in doing so, to imitate God and his righteousness.

Another possible meaning of righteousness could refer to God's covenant faithfulness. In this case, Paul would be referring to God's commitment to his plan to restore creation, bringing all things under the reign of Jesus. So, wearing the breastplate of righteousness would be another way of saying "fight this battle with confidence, because God is faithful to his plan." Either way, the believer is called to make righteousness his or her primary piece of clothing. Elsewhere, in his letter to the church in Thessalonica, Paul exhorts the church to put on the virtues of faith and love as a breastplate, demonstrating his flexibility in shaping these images to fit his message and the audience.

The next piece of equipment is the *footwear of the gospel of peace*. Roman soldiers wore military sandals with leather straps that wrapped and tied around the shin. Iron nails could be hammered through the leather soles in order to provide better traction in battle. The emperor Gaius Caesar would become better known by his nickname, Caligula, a moniker given to him by the troops when he was a boy. He became somewhat of a mascot for the troops, who called him Caligula, or 'little boots' after the military sandal, the *caligae*. Caligula's reign, however, was not a message of peace, but of extravagance and tyranny.

The divine armor of the gods rarely mentions mere sandals, but rather recounts the bronze greaves that would have covered the shin above the sandal. These greaves would have been expensive, a luxury for the average Roman soldier. Thus, they were reserved for the higher-ups, whether in battle or as part of a military triumph.

III

THE ROMAN ARMY IN THE FIRST CENTURY

From the time of Augustus through the reign of Hadrian, each Roman emperor felt the need, if not the pressure, to expand the boundaries of the Roman Empire. Military victories provided the emperor with legitimacy and political clout. But with ever expanding borders came the need for a larger, and more expensive, military. By some estimates, half of the empire's expenditures went toward funding the army.

The Roman army was broken down into legions, with each legion comprised of about four to five thousand soldiers. Legions were divided into ten cohorts, with each cohort being led by a person of senatorial rank. Similarly, each cohort was separated into six centuries, each made up of about eighty solders and led by a centurion. Legionaries were primarily made up of Roman citizens, and supported by auxiliary forces of non-citizens.[2]

When Augustus emerged as sole ruler after the civil wars, he consolidated and reduced the number of legions to about twenty-five. In the mid-first century, about the time Paul was writing to Ephesus, there would have been Roman legions stationed throughout Northern Africa, Judea and Syria, Northern Greece, Germania, Hispania, and Britannia. There were no Roman legions stationed near Ephesus or in the province of Asia as a whole.

III

As part of the armor of God, the footwear would have worked on a couple of levels. Paul, once more, alludes to Isaiah and the messenger that brings news of peace: "How beautiful on the mountains are the feet of those who bring good news, who proclaim peace" (Isaiah 52:7). A messenger was often a runner who would sprint ahead and make an important announcement or deliver official news. Thus, it is fitting that the messenger has proper footwear, allowing him to move swiftly and arrive safely at his destination with the message of "Peace!"

Proper footwear, particularly the *caligae*, would also be important if the Ephesian church were to stand firm, as Paul repeatedly emphasized. Locked shields and solid footing would make the line difficult to break. Whether standing strong together against the assaults of the enemy or simply walking throughout the city of Ephesus, the message to be conveyed was that of the peace of the Messiah Jesus.

Fourthly is the *shield of faith*. The shield takes on significant meaning as part of the armor of the gods in Greek mythology. As part of his armor, Heracles was given a shield made of gold, inlaid with ivory and other precious stones. The shield was covered with reliefs of hunting scenes, battles, and the gods. It is noteworthy that in the center of the shield was an image of Phobos, or Fear. So while Heracles donned the shield of fear, the people of God were to take up the shield of faith.

The shield forged for Achilles was described in great detail in antiquity. It contained reliefs of earth, stars, and sky, and featured images of two cities. The cities seem to be depicting a life beyond warfare, almost as if to suggest that this life of work, peace, and celebration was preferable to the life of war in which Achilles was in the midst. As mentioned above, the shield of Aeneas pictorially foretells the founding of Rome.

Thus, the shield takes on an important role in the armor of the gods. Yet for a soldier, the shield was a vital defensive piece of equipment. As we have already mentioned, the locking of shields together helped form a protective barrier. In this instance, however, Paul references specifically the ability to provide protection from the fiery arrows launched by the evil one. Roman shields were often covered in leather that could be soaked in water. In this way, flaming arrows that might implant in the shield would not burn the shield and would eventually be extinguished. Livy recounts how the Carthaginians used flaming spears to cause panic among the enemy. For even if the spear only lodged in the shield, the shield would catch fire, causing the enemy to toss the shield aside, leaving them exposed to the thrust of the sword.[3] The mention of the evil one is another reminder to the church that the battle is ultimately spiritual in nature.

Throughout the Hebrew Scriptures, Yahweh is described as a shield. Specifically, in Psalm 91, the faithfulness of Yahweh is called a shield, so there is no need to fear the arrows that fly by day. Paul may be alluding to this psalm as insight for the shield of faith. Paul also began his letter by commending the Ephesians for their faith. This is another instance where the metaphor can have a double meaning. In one sense, the strong faith of the Ephesians can act as a shield from the attacks of the evil one. Yet in another sense, Paul may be referring to the faithfulness of God to his plan, and is calling the church to take cover under that shield of faith – to find their refuge in God.

Next, Paul adds the *helmet of salvation* to the equipment needed to make a spiritual stand against the opposition. Along with the breastplate, the helmet was a crucial piece of armor protecting the vulnerable parts of the body. Roman helmets were typically made of bronze, with a neck guard in the back and bronze strips hanging from either side of the helmet protecting the sides of the face and ears. Once again, the higher ranking the soldier, the more ornately decorated the helmet. Crests on the top of the helmet also helped identify a soldier's rank in the army.

While the shield seemed to be the primary focus of the divine armor of the gods, the helmet was also described as being ornately and symbolically decorated. The most important facet of the craftsmanship appears to be the fit of the helmet snuggly around the temples, so that it remained securely in place. Heracles' helmet was said to have an image of Eris (Strife) on the front, expressing to any rival the futility of fighting against the son of Zeus. The image of Zeus himself was said to have adorned the helmet of Achilles, along with his thunderbolts from heaven. The ornamentations featured on the divine armor were rich with significance and meaning.

Paul returns to Isaiah 59 to complete the motif of Yahweh as the mighty warrior. In addition to the breastplate of righteousness, Yahweh also wears the helmet of salvation. Each part of the mighty warrior's armor represents a feature of Yahweh's victory. Thus, he will take vengeance on his enemies, his reign will be marked by righteousness and justice, and the rescue of his people is designated by the word *salvation*. It is this same aspect of rescue or deliverance that Paul applies here. Hence for Paul, salvation is the outcome of the plan of God: God will rescue his creation, including his people, bringing them back under the reign of Jesus. Salvation also stresses the message that God has already been victorious in this reclamation project. So to put on the helmet of salvation is yet another reminder to stand firm, because the battle has already been won.

Paul also alludes to the helmet of salvation in his letter to Thessalonica (1 Thessalonians 5:8), adding in that reference the *hope* of salvation. Adding the descriptor of *hope* is another way of expressing certainty. To impose today's oft-assumed definition of salvation as referring to an individual becoming saved would be to miss Paul's emphasis on the larger plan of God and the certainty of that plan being accomplished.

The final piece of the divine armor is the *sword of the Spirit*. The most common type of sword in the Roman military was the *gladius*, a short sword used in hand-to-hand combat. Similarly, the term Paul uses here denotes a shorter type of sword, as opposed to a larger sword that we might expect from the heroes and gods of Greek lore. Oddly enough, the sword was not often emphasized as a significant part of the divine armor of the gods. This is probably due to the era in which these myths took their shape. It was more common to describe the spear and bow as the primary weapons. Nonetheless, there are a couple of exceptions. Achilles, for one, is noted as having a sword as part of his armor from Hephaestus. The handle was made of ivory and the blade could penetrate virtually any other protective armor.

In Jewish thought, Yahweh is often depicted as striking down his enemies with a sword, signifying his justice and victory. Once more in Isaiah 11, the Messiah will "strike the earth with the rod of his mouth; with the breath of his lips he will slay the wicked." Elsewhere, the sword is depicted as emanating from the mouth of God, representing the power contained in the commands and judgments uttered by God. Here, however, Paul specifically identifies the sword of the Spirit with the word of God. There are two issues than need some clarification.

First is the relation of the sword to the Spirit. In each of the other pieces of equipment, the descriptor linked with each piece conveyed an attribute of God – God's righteousness, faith, or truth. Here however, the weapon is tied to God's Spirit. So what is the relation of the sword to God's Spirit? Without venturing too deep into the underbrush of the Greek language, it does not seem to be the case that the sword *is* the Spirit or that the sword belongs *to* the Spirit – both positions of which can be found in various commentaries. Rather, the structure here seems to be that the sword is given its potency *by* the Spirit. As O'Brien puts it, "the Spirit makes the sword powerful and effective."[4] Thus, the role of the Spirit is to infuse the word of God with potency and precision. Throughout the New Testament, the Spirit is linked with being the mouthpiece of God – the divine messenger of God, in a sense, though not separate from God. "For the Holy Spirit will teach you at that time what you should say" (Luke 12:12).

Second, what exactly is being referred to by the word of God? It is easy to understand this through our modern lens as a reference to simply the Bible, especially given the reference by the author of Hebrews in Hebrews 4:12. For Paul, this is often a reference to the message of the gospel, not just the Hebrew Scriptures, but those scriptures viewed through the lens of the message of the Messiah Jesus. Throughout the letter, that gospel message has been the unfolding and revealing of the plan of God to bring all things back under the reign of Jesus, which involves the inclusion of the Gentiles into the people of God. So it is the Spirit that continues to make known and give potency to this plan, making it understood by those who are willing to hear and accept the good news.

With the armor complete, Paul has given an illustration that the Ephesian church can easily recall. Putting on the armor of God would be a way for the church to cling to the key attributes of God as they followed God's example and stood firm against attacks on their faith. For Paul, the image of God as a mighty warrior found roots deep in his Jewish tradition, back to the writings of Isaiah and the Psalms. For the Gentile Ephesians, the armor metaphor also reached far back to the stories of the divine armor of the gods (a point not lost on Paul, as well). It would give them reassurance that they were equipped with divine protection regardless of the battles they would face.

There is some debate whether the ensuing paragraph on prayer begins the closing comments of his letter or whether it belongs as the conclusion to the divine armor. If the former were the case, then the instruction to pray in the Spirit on all occasions would be regarded as a broad request to pray for each other as they set out to fulfill all that Paul had written them. If the latter is the case, then prayer belongs almost as an additional piece of the armor, or as another way of emphasizing the communal aspect of the fight. The latter fits well with the picture of soldiers locking shields, standing firm, and covering each other in prayer. The fact that the instruction to pray in the Spirit immediately follows the sword of the Spirit would also suggest that prayer is closely tied to the section on spiritual warfare.

In addition to the instruction to be in constant prayer for each other, Paul adds further to stay alert, persevering in prayer. This language also recalls a soldier keeping watch, ready for any potential danger while on duty. Regardless of whether they were in the midst of a battle or enjoying a time of calm, they were to be vigilant and prepared, always keeping the divine armor close at hand. Praying in the Spirit was the tactic to keep from getting ambushed and caught unprepared. Earlier, Paul encouraged them to be filled with this same Spirit as opposed to being drunk, with senses dulled, vulnerable to foul play. Clearly for Paul, the spiritual threat was real and ever-present. Yet by clothing themselves with the divine armor and staying in continual communication through God's Spirit, there was no need to navigate this life in constant fear. This is one of Paul's recurring messages to the Ephesian church.

And as long as they were in constant prayer for all of God's people, they could also include Paul in their prayers. After all, while they were hearing this letter being read to them, he himself was in prison, most likely under house arrest in Rome. This is the third time Paul has alluded to himself as a prisoner of the Messiah Jesus. Here, he refers to himself as an imprisoned ambassador. That very notion of an ambassador who was thrown in prison would have been a provocative one. Regardless of the message, ambassadors would have customarily fallen under the safeguard of the one who sent them while conducting official business in a foreign land. Throwing an ambassador in prison would have been an act of disrespect and aggression.

For Paul, the battle was a very real one. Much more than a handy metaphor, the divine armor was a means of survival for him. In asking prayer for himself, Paul seems to be modeling for the church just what it looks like to engage in this spiritual struggle, standing firm and fully equipped. His calling was clear – he was called to declare the mystery of the gospel. His message was not his own; he asks for prayer that words may be given to him, doubtless by this same Spirit who represents the piercing words of God. Twice he asks for boldness, or a lack of fear, as he conveys this message. Paul was not asking them to live in such a way and taking up a struggle that he was not already fully engaged in.

GRACE AND PEACE TO ALL

Paul closes his letter by affirming Tychicus as a fellow servant and commending him to the Ephesian church. As was mentioned in the earlier section on Team Ephesus, Tychicus is noted as being from the province of Asia and may have even been from Ephesus. If this is the case, then he would have already been known by the church as he delivered this letter. The closing of Paul's letter to Colosse also mentions Tychicus: "Tychicus will tell you all the news about me. He is a dear brother, a faithful minister and fellow servant in the Lord. I am sending him to you for the express purpose that you may know about our circumstances and that he may encourage your hearts" (Colossians 4:7,8). Given the similar wording of this with the closing of Ephesians, it is likely that Tychicus was delivering both the letters of Ephesians and Colossians on the same trip. He would give the church the full update on Paul and convey any personal communications that Paul did not include in the letter.

The letter closes with a blessing characteristic of Paul: blessings of peace, grace, and love to all who count themselves as members of this newly constituted people of God. But he leaves them with one last interesting point. In the Greek language, the last word of the letter is the word *undying* (*aftharsia*). This is not a word Paul uses much, and actually has the meaning of being immortal. It is enticing to think that after giving the Ephesians the metaphor of divine armor, Paul closes with the suggestion of immortality!

"Grace to all who love our Lord Jesus Christ with an undying love."

III

There are times when it can be challenging to unearth the coherent line of thinking in one of the New Testament epistles. Multiple cultural obstacles and a couple of thousand years can bury the original intent of these letters as we read them nowadays. Hopefully, peering through all of the windows into the Jewish, Greek, and Roman worldviews, we have sufficiently cleaned our own cultural lenses to see clearly Paul's lucid message. Paul was reaffirming the good news that God's plan was to bring all creation back under his authority. The death and resurrection of the Messiah Jesus assured that this plan would not be thwarted. He wanted to make sure that what was once a mystery should now be plain to them: that as Gentiles, they were part of this plan from the beginning. Thus, their response should be to fully embrace life as the people of God, knowing that victory had already been accomplished. And God was faithful to fully equip them to do just that.

So the natural next question would be, "How did it all turn out for the Ephesian church?" Did they fully embrace the mystery and the life Paul had called them to?

13 EPHESUS AND THE NEW TESTAMENT: THE REST OF THE STORY

"The cities immediately sent a large number of troops against [Aristonicus], and they were assisted by Nicomedes the Bithynian and by the kings of the Cappadocians. Then came five Roman ambassadors, and after that an army under Publius Crassus the consul, and after that Marcus Perperna, who brought the war to an end, having captured Aristonicus alive and sent him to Rome. Now Aristonicus ended his life in prison; Perperna died of disease; and Crassus, attacked by certain people in the neighborhood of Leucae, fell in battle. And Manius Aquillius came over as consul with ten lieutenants and organized the province [of Asia] into the form of government that still now endures."

- Strabo, Geography

III

In the upper part of the site of Ephesus sits a structure that resembles a small version of the amphitheater – a mini-great theater, if you will. This structure is called the Odeon and was common in Roman cities. It was a smaller venue for theater productions, civic meetings, and concerts. It is sometimes referred to as the Bouleterion, denoting its function as a meeting place for the city council (*boule*). It was built in the second century AD after the time of Paul.

The Odeon-Bouleterion at Ephesus is well preserved and seats around 1,500 people, compared the 25,000-seating capacity of the Great Theater down the street. The stone archways that lead into the Odeon floor are still in place, and it is easy to imagine the murmur of conversations between civic leaders waiting for the meeting to get underway. The only creatures in attendance on this particular day were the cats that seemed to be the primary residents of the modern-day archaeological site. The Odeon-Bouleterion would have been an important structure in the civic life of any notable Roman city, especially Ephesus, which governed the entire province of Asia.

III

The quote that opens this chapter is Strabo's account of how Ephesus and the region that would become the province of Asia passed over to Roman control in 133 BC. This was covered back in the opening chapter, but as a means of review, the Attalids of Pergamum ruled the region of what is now Western Turkey for much of the second century BC. Attalus was the last in a line of rulers of Pergamum. When he died childless in 133 BC, he turned his domain directly over to the control of Rome instead of naming a successor to the kingdom of Pergamum. Aristonicus led a revolt against this handover to Rome, but the cities of the region, led by Ephesus, held him off until Rome arrived and put an end to revolt. The region was then reorganized as the Roman province of Asia and Ephesus became its capital city.

To quote Jerome Murphy-O'Connor, "If the city's origins were Greek, its rebirth was Roman."[1] In 129 BC, a senatorial commission arrived on the scene to set up a constitutional administration and determine the boundaries of the new province. The region was organized into five tribes, with Ephesus being one of them. Each tribe was governed by a two-house system, comprised of citizens from the tribe. The two systems included a council (*boule*) made up of 450 members and an assembly of the people (*ekklesia*). While the council would have met in a structure like the Bouleterion, the assembly of the people was so large that it had to meet in the Great Theater. The leader of the assembly was sometimes known as the Asiarch, and this title appears in Acts 19:31, where it is noted that some of the Asiarchs were friends of Paul. This, then, is how the city of Ephesus was governed and how Ephesus, in turn, governed the province.

Yet to be clear, Rome was still firmly in control. Again, Murphy-O'Connor acknowledges, "Rome ensured that whatever power the city retained was wielded by those with an aversion to change and a strong personal interest in preserving the status quo."[2] In addition to this, those who found themselves in positions of influence in this system of governance were undoubtedly closely allied with Rome. As with every Roman province, it was in the provincial governor's best interest that any stirrings of political dissent, uprisings, or general disorder not reach the ears of the Roman senate or Caesar himself.

Paul must have shared some of these same concerns, albeit on a much smaller scale, both upon leaving Ephesus after three years and after entrusting this letter of Ephesians to Tychicus to be delivered to the *ekkesia* that he founded. Who would lead the church after he left? Would the church be able to maintain the unity that Paul insisted upon? Would the Ephesians fight this spiritual battle well in the face of inevitable attacks from both inside and outside the community? Paul certainly had confidence in his own ability to stand up to bullies, false teachers, or agitators who would look to harm these communities, but what would come of the people in his absence? No doubt these were questions at the forefront of Paul's concern for each of the churches he established.

The city of Ephesus is referenced directly or indirectly in some of Paul's later correspondence, as well as in other later New Testament letters. From this later correspondence, we can begin to sift away the layers of material extraneous to Ephesus, revealing fragments of relevant information. Piecing these fragments together we can, at the very least, begin to identify the basic shape of what happened to the church at Ephesus after Paul and his letter. Of course, like a vessel that has been reconstructed from a few pieces of ostraca, what we are able to piece together from the later New Testament letter will likely leave us with more questions than answers.

While we may be left with an entirely new set of questions, there are some solid fragments of information that we can readily identify as a starting point. For example, it seems clear enough that Paul would later leave Timothy in Ephesus to lead the church there, assuring that it would not veer off course. We have already pointed out that after being released from prison in Rome, Paul and Timothy evidently traveled through Asia and Macedonia, likely visiting Ephesus again. And we know that several years - even decades – later, the Apostle John would address Ephesus as one of the seven churches of Asia mentioned in his apocalyptic vision. The church had apparently survived, and even thrived, though not without some setbacks along the way.

So, what can we uncover from the later correspondence in the New Testament? We can begin by digging into Paul's letters to Timothy, in the Apostle Peter's letters, and in John's Revelation.

PAUL'S LETTERS TO TIMOTHY

Like the earlier brief perusal of the Corinthian correspondence, because of its close ties to Paul's stay in Ephesus we do not have the space here for a lengthy commentary on Paul's letters to Timothy or room to address all the points stated in those letters. Yet in order to begin piecing together what happened in Ephesus after Paul wrote Ephesians, some background and the establishment of a timeline are in order.

If Pauline authorship of Ephesians is questioned by many modern scholars, then Pauline authorship of the pastoral letters is contested even more so. It is not uncommon for scholars today to consider both letters to

Timothy as pseudepigraphal, written sometime in the second century. Again, without getting into a lengthy discourse, none of the arguments against Pauline authorship are insurmountable. Some objections can be minimized when we acknowledge that the pastoral letters were written several years after writing his letters to various churches. During these years, Paul had been imprisoned and undoubtedly had time to reflect on and sharpen many of his views. Furthermore, his letters to Timothy were much more personal in nature and we might expect Paul to say things that he would not say if he were writing to an entire community, such as Ephesus or Corinth.

Thus, we will err on the side of tradition and move forward garnering what we can from these two letters to Timothy. Returning to the timeline, we proposed that Paul probably left Ephesus sometime after Pentecost in 56 AD, and returned through Miletus in the spring of 57 on his way to Jerusalem. He was arrested in Jerusalem, and subsequently imprisoned in Caesarea from 57 to 59, then put under house arrest in Rome from 60 to 62. He probably wrote his letter to the Ephesians during this time in Rome.

In Paul's first letter to Timothy, he writes, "As I urged you when I went into Macedonia, stay there in Ephesus" (1 Timothy 1:3). It would seem that Paul is now out of prison and travelling once again through the regions of Asia, Macedonia, and Achaea. He probably visited his friends at Ephesus again, and upon departing, left Timothy there to help lead the church. If this is the case, then he wrote 1 Timothy sometime between 63 and 65. He may have written it from Macedonia or Corinth. His visit to Ephesus may have been another brief one, prompting Paul to write to Timothy some further detailed instructions and encouragement after leaving him to take on the challenges facing the Ephesian church.

What can we suppose has happened in Ephesus from this first letter to Timothy? Two issues seem obvious enough. First, Paul spends much of his letter addressing the issue of false teachers. In Ephesians, false teaching does not seem to have yet infiltrated the church. He does push the church toward spiritual maturity so that they will not be "tossed back and forth by the waves, and blown here and there by every wind of teaching" (Ephesians 4:14), but leaving behind the pagan way of life is the more pressing issue.

Yet several years later (perhaps three to five years) the infiltration of false teachers appears to have become the major issue. From the outset of his letter to Timothy, Paul reminds Timothy that the reason he wanted him there in Ephesus was "so that you may command certain people not to teach false doctrines any longer" (1 Timothy 1:3). At each point throughout the letter, Paul reiterates to Timothy to "watch your life and doctrine closely" (4:16). "The Spirit clearly says that in later times some will abandon the faith and follow deceiving spirits and things taught by demons" (4:1). If Timothy were unclear of the gravity of the situation by the closing of the letter, Paul summarizes the issue this way: "If anyone teaches otherwise and does not agree to the sound instruction of our Lord Jesus Christ and to godly teaching, they are conceited and understand nothing" (6:3,4).

Paul even identifies two of these false teachers by name and indicates that he has, in essence, excommunicated them from the church there in Ephesus, most likely when he passed through the city with Timothy. In Paul's vernacular, Hymenaeus and Alexander had been "handed over to Satan to be taught not to blaspheme" (1:20). Both are named again in his second letter to Timothy. What do we know about these two?

Hymenaeus is mentioned, along with Philetus, in 2 Timothy as having taught "that the resurrection has already taken place, and they destroy the faith of some" (2 Timothy 2:18). From other statements in his letters, we can surmise that in an attempt to demythologize Paul's message, these two were teaching that allusions to the resurrection of the dead were not meant to be taken literally, and that what was being referred to had already taken place in a spiritual sense. We do not know much beyond this. Whether or not this teaching reflects an early form of Gnosticism is speculative. But this clearly went against what Paul had instilled earlier in the Ephesian church. For Paul, the resurrection was essential to the meaning and message of Jesus (1 Corinthians 15:12-14), and the bodily resurrection of Jesus was a foretaste of resurrection for all when God's kingdom was fully realized.

Alexander is also named alongside Hymenaeus. We may recollect that the name *Alexander* appears in the book of Acts as a Jew who presumably attempted to defend the synagogue in Ephesus, distancing the synagogue from Paul and his associates before the mob in the Great Theater. Yet as we noted, the name *Alexander* is a common one, so any connection between the two would be difficult to establish. It is more likely that the Alexander named in Paul's first letter to Timothy is the same person named in his second letter. There, he is described as a metalworker or coppersmith: "Alexander the metalworker did me a great deal of harm. The Lord will repay him for what he has done" (2 Timothy 4:14). Regardless of any connections between them, the picture is unmistakable that there were several people teaching something other than what Paul had instilled in the church, and some were even openly opposing Paul, causing some in the church to be led off course.

One additional puzzle regarding the false teachers in Ephesus has to do with what was being taught. Specifically, was there a single rival philosophy that Paul was warning against or were there multiple threats? There is at least one indication that a rival philosophy was a form of Judaism, as Paul reveals that these teachers wanted to be *teachers of the law*. Debates around the resurrection of the dead may also point to Judaism. If this is the case, then this could be the same problem Paul ran into often: the effort by local Jewish teachers to come behind Paul and Judaize these newly established churches.

Yet there are also clues that this was not mainstream Jewish belief that Paul was warning against. He indicts these would-be teachers of the law as not being very competent or coherent in their teaching. Along with this, he also mentions myths, genealogies, and a pursuit of knowledge, which may point toward more of a pagan influence. In his letter to Titus, Paul specifically warns against those who are preoccupied with Jewish myths (Titus 1:14), which may provide more insight into what Paul was up against. Gathering all these pieces together, it seems that rather than contesting several different philosophies, Paul was opposing a form of Jewish thought that went well beyond the Hebrew Scriptures, stressing extra-biblical stories and ascetic practices. This false teaching may well have been the precursor to the fully developed Gnosticism of the next several centuries.

The second issue emerges out of the first one, that being the need to bring some structure and leadership to the church in Ephesus. The second chapter of the letter outlines a structure and order to their public gatherings, perhaps in response to the chaos caused by these renegade teachers. Yet, as the letter develops, it becomes clear that Paul is not simply leaving Timothy in Ephesus to lead and bring order to the church, but to establish a leadership structure that will ensure its long-term survival. Paul did not want these churches dependent on him or a protégé like Timothy, but rather he wanted to equip them to think through and work through these issues themselves.

Chapter three begins to describe qualifications for overseers and deacons, and how people in those positions should conduct themselves. Later, Paul also includes elders, "who direct the affairs of the church" (5:17). Clearly, there is more leadership in place than just Timothy, and undoubtedly these leaders were to serve and protect the church from the false teachers that had infiltrated the community.

While it seems evident, then, that Paul wanted a stronger structure in place to help lead the church forward, we should not press our own notions of church leadership structures onto the early church. Though our present roles of elders, deacons, and overseers developed from these early accounts, it is not at all clear how distinct and defined these roles were in the early church. At times in scripture, these roles are even used interchangeably and may not refer to any type of hierarchy or set governance to be applied to all early churches. One argument against Pauline authorship of the letters to Timothy is that formal church leadership structures like those mentioned here were not in place until the second century. Yet, these titles are mentioned in several of Paul's letters – not just the pastoral letters – as well as in the book of Acts. Furthermore, it is not clear just how formal or developed these structures actually were. Even the modest term 'church leadership' comes burdened down with many of our modern conceptions of both church governance and the makings of a good leader – conceptions that may very well have come as a puzzlement to Paul and the early church.

While Paul addresses the roles of overseers, elders, and deacons, and desires a broader base of leadership within the church in Ephesus, it is also evident that he trusted Timothy to direct these efforts. Whether he stated it publicly or not, while Paul was gone, Timothy was in charge! And one of the issues that Timothy would need to contend with would be his age. Presumably, many of the potential elders and overseers of the church would be much older than Timothy. If Timothy was in his teens when he joined Paul on his second missionary journey, then he was no older than his late twenties or early thirties when Paul left him in Ephesus. Thus, Paul writes, "Don't let anyone look down on you because you are young, but set an example for the believers in speech, in conduct, in love, in faith and in purity. Until I come, devote yourself to the public reading of Scripture, to preaching and to teaching" (4:12,13). Little doubt, there would be those who would question why they should follow the teaching of a young adult (just as we might encounter today), but Paul commended Timothy and believed him to be up to the task. He closes with the challenge, "Timothy, guard what has been entrusted to your care" (6:20).

It is not difficult to imagine that when Paul was arrested and brought to Rome, there would have been opportunists lurking in the shadows ready to swoop in, discredit Paul, and take control of this growing community in Ephesus. Timothy's task was to defend the church against such opportunists, instill correct doctrine, and set up a leadership structure that would persist well beyond both Paul's and Timothy's time at Ephesus. Yet Paul had entrusted the church in Ephesus to Timothy, and he planned to return as soon as his travels permitted him to do so.

Paul's second letter to Timothy is address "To Timothy, my dear son" (2 Timothy 1:2). That Timothy is still living in Ephesus is evident throughout the letter. Paul mentions some people who had deserted him in the province of Asia, while commending Onesiphorus, who was from Ephesus, for his faithfulness to him while in prison back in Rome. He writes that he has sent Tychicus to Ephesus to relieve Timothy, so that he can see him in Rome. In addition, Hymenaeus and Alexander's names are repeated from the first letter.

As far as when it was written, Paul indicates that he is once again in prison in Rome. This would suggest that after traveling throughout the region, he made his way back to Rome and was subsequently arrested. He writes that he is being persecuted for the message of the gospel, "This is my gospel, for which I am suffering even to the point of being chained like a criminal" (2:8,9). He references his first defense in Rome and there is an urgency in his request for Timothy to come see him in Rome. All this would point to a date of writing of about 66 or 67.

While much of this second letter is more of a heart-to-heart update on Paul's condition, there are some hints as to what has been happening in Ephesus. Carrying over from the first letter, false teachers continued to be a concern for Paul. Without rehashing the specifics covered earlier, Paul recollects about the damage that these false teachers have done to him and the church. Yet because the tone is more about recollection and less about how to deal with these false teachers, it could be the case that Timothy has done his best to prohibit these teachers from the community in Ephesus and actively correcting the teaching.

Still, Paul cautions Timothy to stay vigilant, holding to sound doctrine. He encourages Timothy more than once in the letter to take what Paul had taught him and pass it on "to reliable men who will also be qualified to teach others" (2:2). In doing so, Timothy would be continuing to build the leadership structure of the church, as well as protect it from false teaching. It was an issue that would not be going away anytime soon, as Paul goes on to warn that heretical teaching would only intensify as "the last days" grew near. "Keep reminding them of these things" (2:14) - in other words, keep doing what you have been doing.

In addition to the ongoing issues of false teaching, there are hints in Paul's second letter that the young Timothy might have been struggling to be fully assertive in his leadership of the church. No doubt, being looked down on because of his youth and being opposed by rival teachers, Timothy's job was not for the faint of heart. He reminds Timothy, "the Spirit God gave us does not make us timid, but gives us power, love and self–discipline" (1:7). He also tells Timothy to be strong, and to not back down from correcting and rebuking those who are in the wrong. Throughout the letter, Paul emboldens Timothy to not be ashamed of the gospel, to endure hardships, and to pursue righteousness and a pure heart. Conceivably, with Paul facing possible death and having been deserted by some of his followers, he knew that Timothy's greatest challenges waited ahead of him.

Finally, Paul sent Tychicus to Ephesus, presumably to step in while Timothy made his way to Rome to see Paul. Tychicus, of course, had previously delivered Paul's letter to the Ephesian church and may have been from Ephesus, so he was familiar with the city and the condition of the church. It would seem Paul is trying to provide some continuity in leadership, understanding the vulnerable position of the church. Also providing this continuity are Priscilla and Aquila, to whom Paul extends greetings at the close of the letter. This couple was in Ephesus with Paul during the church's infancy and had evidently returned to work alongside Timothy, after spending time in Rome.

If Paul founded the church in Ephesus sometime around 52 to 53, and his second letter to Timothy was written around 66, then about thirteen years had passed since its inception. Yet after many years, trials, and imprisonment, Paul still showed great concern for the church and was doing all he could to ensure its survival. Little doubt, the church in Ephesus was near and dear to Paul, having invested so much of his work into it.

PETER'S LETTERS TO ASIA MINOR

Next, we turn to the Apostle Peter's brief letters. While these may not immediately be associated with Ephesus, the first letter is addressed to the churches in the provinces of Pontus, Galatia, Cappadocia, Asia and Bithynia. And, as has previously been examined, Ephesus would have represented the whole of the province of Asia. While the second letter of Peter's does not identify the recipients, it does reveal that it is the second letter written (2 Peter 3:1), likely linking it to the recipients of 1 Peter. Thus, while Peter's letters may not address Ephesus directly, they can provide some general insights into the region as a whole.

First, a brief look at the context of these two letters. Though the authorship of both letters has been disputed, each specifically identifies Peter as the writer, and there is nothing definitive that would prompt us to dismiss Petrine authorship outright. The second letter provides two clues to the possible date of writing. First, Peter references Paul's letters to this same region (2 Peter 3:15). This would mean that Paul's letters to Ephesus and Colosse must have been known to Peter and he is writing his letters after they were composed. Second, Peter also reveals that his death may be immanent (2 Peter 1:13-15). Tradition has Peter being martyred by Nero around 66 or 67, thus the dates of these letters are likely between 60 and 66. It is possible that Peter is writing the churches of that region because he knew that Paul was either in prison or traveling elsewhere and wanted to show his own support for Paul's work.

Understanding the circumstances around these two letters, we can make three general observations about the mood of the churches in the province of Asia, of which Ephesus was the chief city. First, it would seem that the churches in that region are being harassed to some extent, prompting Peter to send encouragement to persevere: "You may have had to suffer grief in all kinds of trials" (1 Peter 1:6). He writes that these trials will not only strengthen and reveal their faith to be the genuine article, but also will allow them to share in the sufferings of Jesus. The mention of this persecution has led some to date the letter later than 70 AD, citing the great wave of persecution at the end of Nero's reign and the destruction of Jerusalem. This would also bring into question Peter's authorship. But as Paul had already experienced personally, harassment and intimidation were taking place to some degree well before 70 AD. As these church communities grew, Roman officials were wrestling with the issue of the legitimacy of Christianity within the Empire (this is the primary reason why Paul is imprisoned in Rome on two occasions), Jewish religious leaders were applying continual pressure to simply convert to traditional Judaism, and local leaders were wanting to avoid anything that might appear to be political unrest. We cannot know for certain the harassment Peter is addressing, and since these letters are to a larger region, Peter may not have had any one point of tension in mind. But it is not difficult to imagine that the outside pressure on these local churches was both persistent and escalating.

Second, in light of Peter's encouragement to persevere in times of trial and suffering, it may well be significant that he also instructs the churches in this region to be obedient to the emperor. In his first letter, there is a section on the household codes, which is similar to the household codes that Paul details in Ephesians. Only Peter begins with a paragraph on submission to rulers and those in power, "Submit yourselves for the Lord's sake to every human authority: whether to the emperor, as the supreme authority, or to governors, who are sent by him to punish those who do wrong and to commend those who do right" (2:13,14). He closes the paragraph with the recap, "Fear God, honor the emperor." The emperor, of course, is a reference to Caesar, with the current emperor being the infamous Nero.

If Peter wrote this letter from Rome, which is possibly hinted at in 5:13, then it is particularly interesting that he stresses submission to Roman authority. It could be the case that having gauged the political climate of Rome firsthand, Peter recognized the futility of taking on Rome. It was imperative that these communities of Messiah-followers be seen as peaceful gatherings. Much like Jesus' own warnings to the Jewish people, rising up against Rome would not end well. Violence was not the way the kingdom of God would come to fulfillment.

Finally, in Peter's second letter, we again hear the familiar echo of warnings against false teachers. The entire second chapter is focused on false teachers and Peter has particularly strong words for them: "They are like unreasoning animals, creatures of instinct, born only to be caught and destroyed, and like animals they too will perish" (2:12); "They will be paid back with harm for the harm they have done" (2:13). While Paul was specifically addressing the harm that false teaching was bringing to the church in Ephesus, Peter is drawing attention to the threat that this issue posed to many young church communities throughout the region. While Paul was on trial, defending this growing Messiah-movement as a legitimate religion within the Roman Empire (the argument being that this was not a new religion, but a broadening of the already legal Jewish faith), these false teachers were ostensibly making that defense more complicated than need be. It is comparable to today's culture, where a single act of lunacy or fringe philosophy, carried out under the auspices of Christianity, can cause scrutiny to fall on the entire Christian church. It makes the mission that much more difficult.

THE APOCALYPSE OF JOHN

By now it should be obvious that Ephesus is well-cited throughout the New Testament. From Luke's book of Acts to Paul's letters to Timothy to Peter's letters, Ephesus is clearly an influential city in early Christianity. So it should come as no surprise that in the final book of the New Testament, Ephesus again makes a brief, but important, appearance. Early on in the Apostle John's revelation, he conveys letters to the seven churches of Asia, with Ephesus being the first church addressed. The order of the churches in Revelation would suggest the circular route taken to deliver this letter to each church. We are reminded once more that beyond simply being the natural starting point for such a route, Ephesus would be first because of its prominence in Asia.

The book of Revelation is a prophetic book that describes the vision of John while exiled on the island of Patmos off the coast of the province of Asia. Some have attributed this work to a different John, but early on the book of Revelation was linked to the Apostle John, the beloved disciple. John recorded his vision most likely during the reign of Domitian (81-96), and more specifically the date of 96 is often attributed as the time of writing. Clement of Alexandria wrote that John was released from Patmos "after the tyrant was dead", the tyrant being a reference to Domitian. Other early church fathers attest to this timing as well. So, the end of Domitian's reign puts a date of writing for Revelation on solid ground. This would place the address to the church at Ephesus about twenty-five to thirty years after Paul's initial letters and subsequent letters to Timothy. A short, but significant, amount of time has passed since we last checked in on the Ephesian church.

Let us begin by reviewing John's specific message to Ephesus in full:

"To the angel of the church in Ephesus write:
These are the words of him who holds the seven stars in his right hand and walks among
the seven golden lampstands. I know your deeds, your hard work and your perseverance.
I know that you cannot tolerate wicked people, that you have tested those who claim to be
apostles but are not, and have found them false. You have persevered and have endured
hardships for my name, and have not grown weary. Yet I hold this against you: You
have forsaken the love you had at first. Consider how far you have fallen! Repent and do
the things you did at first. If you do not repent, I will come to you and remove your
lampstand from its place. But you have this in your favor: You hate the practices of the
Nicolaitans, which I also hate. Whoever has ears, let them hear what the Spirit says to
the churches. To those who are victorious, I will give the right to eat from the tree of life,
which is in the paradise of God." (Revelation 2:1-7)

Because this is a vision that John is describing, there is much even in this short passage that can be distracting. The meaning of the lampstands and stars, angels, the tree of life - this is the nature of apocalyptic literature. Yet if we let the imagery and enigmatic narrative remain a bit blurry in the background, we can see two insights regarding the Ephesian church come clearly into focus.

The good news or the bad news first? John - conveying the words of God in his vision - begins with the good news. The first insight into the Ephesian church has to do with the false teaching that was such a threat to the church in its infancy. Paul had warned the church from the beginning about the dangers posed by giving a voice to suspect teachers teaching a gospel other than the one Paul had grounded them in. Roughly five years later, we heard Paul stressing to an exasperated Timothy the importance of keeping up the good fight against these opportunistic teachers, even disciplining some himself and excommunicating them from the church. About this same time, Peter also can be heard warning the churches of the region of Asia to stand strong against this growing problem of incorrect and deceitful theology.

So it is welcome news to hear words from God praising the church in Ephesus for testing "those who claim to be apostles but are not, and have found them false." They have persevered! Evidently, in the twenty-five years since Peter and Paul's martyrdom, the Ephesian church took their warnings to heart and became known for testing the teachings of newcomers and judiciously rejecting those that did not align with message of the Messiah Jesus – the gospel Paul left them with. But it had apparently come with a price. They are also praised for their hard work and perseverance in hardships. Undoubtedly, the church had been touched by the mad exploits of Nero and the persecutions under Domitian in some form or another. While the extent of the persecution may be debated, John understood the church to have weathered hardships and had stood firm. Paul would have been proud of their fighting spirit, fully equipped with the armor of God. They had become known for not tolerating these false teachers.

Now for the bad news. They had abandoned the love they had in the beginning. In fighting the long battle against false teachers, somewhere along the way they had become hardened, perhaps even cynical of those outside the church. They had become known as the church that was doctrinally sound with solid instruction, but that did not love people. John goes on to record that they had fallen from their commendable position and called on the church to repent and get back to the practices that they were instilled with from their inception.

It is not difficult to find examples of this same phenomenon today. There are churches that become known for being scripturally sound, Christ-centered, and holding to Biblical values. Yet, there is always the danger that the church known for staying true to the faith can also develop a reputation for being judgmental, legalistic, and uncaring. The opposite can be true as well: a church that values love and acceptance can be tempted to compromise scriptural teaching in order to avoid taking unpopular positions. It is a tension that evidently goes back to the first century. How does a church disciple its members to embrace God-honoring practices while being welcoming to newcomers? How does a church embody both grace and truth? The happy medium is not always easy to maintain. The Ephesian church had apparently deviated toward the side of doctrinal purity by a couple of degrees and found itself miles off the coordinates from love and grace several years later. They needed an in-route correction.

Still the message to the Ephesians ends on a high note: they do not tolerate the practices of the Nicolaitans. While we do not know the precise practices that are being referred to, some inferences can be drawn from God's message to other churches in the region. The letter to the church at Pergamum also mentions the Nicolaitans, and links them to a group that held to the teachings of Balaam. Balaam was a pagan prophet from the Hebrew Scriptures who, though he himself would not curse Israel, instructed Balak, king of the Moabites, how to invoke God's wrath on the Israelites: entice them to sin through sexual immorality and idolatry. Thus, over time, the teaching of Balaam came to represent compromise with the pagan culture. It is not clear whether this is a direct reference to the Nicolaitans, but it is apparent that, at the very least, the teachings were similar.

Likewise, in the letter to the church in Thyatira, another figure from the Hebrew Scriptures is referenced. Here, the woman Jezebel's teaching has led some in the church to engage in sexual immorality and eat food sacrificed to idols. In both cases, a figure from the Hebrew Scriptures is used to characterize teaching that leads people into compromise with the pagan culture. Whether these are all referencing the same teaching of the Nicolaitans or they are separate movements with similar teaching, these cases are enough to provide a rough sketch of the teaching that was abhorrent to the gospel of God. Ephesus had resisted what other churches had failed to oppose, and for that they were commended.

Even in this closing commendation, we are again faced with the tension between doctrinal purity and love. They were commended for hating the practices of the Nicolaitans, but they were scolded for the lack of love manifest in their community. This was the balancing act for the church in Ephesus moving forward. They were to be a community that graciously corrected each other when people inevitably messed up; they were to fiercely guard the gospel that had been entrusted to them from those who sought to add to it or diminish it; and they were to reflect the love of God in every respect. No small task, but it could just as well serve as the mission for the modern church.

From Paul's founding of the church in Ephesus in the mid-50s to John's vision comprising the letter to the church in Ephesus in the mid-90s, we are given snippets of the church covering a period of about forty years. During that span, its early leaders were threatened by the local trade guilds, it struggled for legitimacy with its founder imprisoned, it had warded off false teachers, and resisted challenges to compromise their core values and adapt more of the pagan culture. They survived the reign of the maniacal emperor Nero, watched from a distance as Jerusalem fell and its great temple leveled, and outlasted another wave of persecution by the emperor Domitian. They had stood their ground, and after everything that had happened, they remained standing. What does history tell us of the rest of the story?

14 THE ROLE OF EPHESUS IN CHURCH HISTORY

"The captivity or ruin of the seven churches of Asia was consummated, and the barbarous lords of Ionia and Lydia still trample on the monuments of classic and Christian antiquity. In the loss of Ephesus, the Christians deplored the fall of the first angel, the extinction of the first candlestick of the Revelations; the desolation is complete; and the temple of Diana, or the church of Mary, will equally elude the search of the curious traveler."

\- Gibbon, *History of Rome*

In the town of Selçuk a couple of miles from the site of Ephesus, the vast remains of a church can be found. The Basilica of St. John sits adjacent to Isa Bey Mosque atop a hill at the edge of town, not far from the site of the Temple of Artemis, attesting to the curious coexistence of Christian, Muslin, and pagan influences in the history of the region. It was built by the Emperor Justinian in the sixth century in the shape of a cross and was covered by six large domes. Evidence of worship at the site dates back to the second century. If it were fully intact today, it would be one of the largest cathedrals in the world. The church marks the spot of the traditional burial site of the Apostle John.

In the middle ages, the church was a popular destination of pilgrimages. During this time, the complex was enclosed by a protective wall to protect it against Arab raids. Like many Christian structures in the region, it was ultimately converted into a mosque in the fourteenth century, but soon after it was leveled by an earthquake. Today, many of its features have been reconstructed. Archways, a baptistery, and the site of the apostle's tomb can all be viewed throughout the remains of this extensive site.

Our survey of the city of Ephesus in the New Testament advanced us to the end of the first century, when John recorded his apocalypse. Revelation addressed the church of Ephesus, along with the other six churches of Asia. It might be tempting to end our survey here, but that would leave us with the provoking question: What happened to the Ephesian church? The prominence of the city of Ephesus would continue for some five hundred years, but do any of the events corresponding with the city suggest what was to become of the church that Paul founded?

We have already surmised that after Paul left Ephesus, Timothy took on a heightened leadership role in the church, despite his youth. When Paul encouraged Timothy to come see him in Rome, Tychicus was sent to take his place, either temporarily or perhaps for a longer period of time. Then roughly twenty-five years elapsed before John recorded his vision, which included a message for the Ephesian church. What else can be determined from the gaps between the New Testament, early church history, and Christian tradition?

DID JOHN AND MARY LIVE IN EPHESUS?

We cannot even leave the pages of scripture before encountering several uncertainties in regards to Ephesus. Some ancillary locations around the archaeological site of Ephesus capture some of these uncertainties. In the town of Selçuk the afore-mentioned Basilica of St. John can be visited, marking the traditional burial site of the Apostle John. Up the hill a couple miles from the archaeological site of Ephesus sits a chapel marking the house of the Virgin Mary. It is purported that Mary, the mother of Jesus, spent her last days at this house. Even directly outside the site next to the parking lot, there is a circular structure identified as the grave of Saint Luke, though it has since been established that this structure was misidentified. But what of the Apostle John and Mary?

While there is no direct evidence that the Apostle John lived in Ephesus, there is compelling secondary tradition that makes this scenario likely. If the author of Revelation is the same John as the gospel by his name, then John was exiled to the island of Patmos off the coast of the province of Asia, not far from Ephesus. Presumably, Patmos was the place of exile because he already resided in the region. Additionally, Revelation demonstrates John's familiarity with the churches of Asia. So it stands to reason that around the time Rome intervened in the first Jewish uprising, destroying the Temple in 70 AD, John would have left Jerusalem and taken up residency elsewhere.

This scenario seems to be confirmed by early Christian writings as well. Irenaeus, in his book *Against Heresies*, writes that following Paul, John remained with the church in Ephesus until the time of the emperor Trajan.[1] He also recounts an incident involving John in Ephesus. According to Irenaeus, this story was conveyed to him personally by Polycarp, who would become Bishop of Smyrna, and had been discipled by John.

As previously mentioned, evidence of worship at the site of the Basilica of St. John dates back to the second century. Taken together, it is likely that the Apostle John did live in Ephesus from around 70 to the time of his exile, then again upon his release from Patmos until his death. If this is the case, then there is a good possibility that he wrote his gospel and his letters from Ephesus as well. Indeed, it seems Ephesus was becoming an influential city in the life of the early church.

There is tradition that Mary, the mother of Jesus, also lived in Ephesus. This tradition arose by meshing together two narratives regarding Mary. Some early church fathers postulated that Mary came to Ephesus with John, based on the words of Jesus on the cross, which placed Mary in the care of John:

Near the cross of Jesus stood his mother, his mother's sister, Mary the wife of Clopas, and Mary Magdalene. When Jesus saw his mother there, and the disciple whom he loved standing nearby, he said to her, "Woman, here is your son," and to the disciple, "Here is your mother." From that time on, this disciple took her into his home. (John 19:25-27)

Thus, if John came to live in Ephesus, Mary must have accompanied him there, according to this tradition.

Then in the early 1800s, a German nun named Catherine Emmerich was said to have had visions describing the location of Mary's house in Ephesus. After her death, these visions were published in a book. Several years later, using this book as a guide, a French priest discovered the structure that is now identified as the House of the Virgin Mary. The discovery seemed to confirm some early traditions that Mary did indeed spend her last days in Ephesus with the Apostle John.

However, before counting Mary as another early church figure who spent time in Ephesus, there is also a counter-narrative that Mary simply lived her life out in Jerusalem, where she died of old age. If you take a trip to Jerusalem today, you can visit a traditional site at the base of the Mount of Olives known as the tomb of Mary. While neither tradition can be confirmed with certainty, it is probable and more accepted today that Mary simply stayed in Jerusalem and died before the first Jewish war. If Mary did accompany John to Ephesus, she would have been quite elderly.[2] So while the Apostle John likely lived in Ephesus, the evidence for Mary moving to Ephesus with John is anecdotal at best, but cannot be completely ruled out.

EPHESUS IN EARLY CHURCH HISTORY

Moving beyond the pages of New Testament scripture, Ignatius of Antioch provides some information regarding the leadership of the church in Ephesus. Ignatius lived in the second half of the first century and was named the Bishop of Antioch. In one of his letters he refers to a man named Onesimus, who was Bishop of Ephesus. Thus, early Christian tradition holds that Onesimus followed Timothy (and possibly Tychicus) as the leader of the church in Ephesus.

A person named Onesimus is mentioned twice in the New Testament. He is mentioned alongside Tychicus, who would relieve Timothy in Ephesus so that he could travel to Rome, as delivering the letter from Paul to the Colossians (Colossians 4:9). Thus, this Onesimus was a coworker of Paul and would have been familiar with Ephesus. Onesimus is also the runaway slave named in Paul's letter to Philemon. Paul urges Philemon to take back Onesimus, forgive him, and perhaps even encourages Philemon to grant him his freedom.

Whether these are all the same person or separate individuals named Onesimus cannot be determined. It is not unreasonable that the two accounts of Onesimus in the New Testament may be the same person. But it is more of a reach to assume that this same Onesimus would go on to become the Bishop of Ephesus. Some traditions hold this to be the case, while others rebuff this connection. If it were the same Onesimus, he would have been advanced in age when becoming bishop. We need not press the connection to accept that following Timothy, a man named Onesimus became the next bishop of the church in Ephesus. Yet the narrative that a runaway slave could have been taken in by Paul, becoming a co-worker among his churches, and ultimately turning out to be the bishop in Ephesus is a captivating one, to say the least.

This letter from Ignatius of Antioch, containing the information just discussed, is of particular interest to unearthing the fate of the Ephesian church because the letter itself was addressed to the church in Ephesus. At the turn of the second century, during his time as Bishop of Antioch, Ignatius was arrested and condemned to die in the arena in Rome. It was during his journey to Rome to face his death that he took the opportunity to meet with church leaders along the way, encouraging them and writing letters to six churches. Thus, *The Epistle of Ignatius to the Ephesians* contains his personal words of encouragement to Ephesus, roughly ten years following the message to the church in Ephesus in John's Apocalypse. Tradition holds that

Ignatius was fed to the lions in the Roman arena around 107 AD, dying a martyr.

So what does Ignatius' letter tell us about the church in Ephesus at the beginning of the second century? The first section of his letter begins with praise for their bishop Onesimus and encouragement to the church to obey and follow his example and authority:

"I received, therefore, in the name of God, your whole multitude in Onesimus. Who by inexpressible love is ours, but according to the flesh is your bishop, whom I implore you by Jesus Christ to love, and that you would all strive to be like to him. And you, who are so worthy of him, are blessed by God who granted to you to possess such an excellent bishop."[3]

He then adds the exhortation, "Let us take heed therefore, that we do not set ourselves against the bishop, but that we may be subject to God." Later, he writes that Onesimus commended his congregation in Ephesus – that they do follow God and live according to the teachings of their bishops.

This is noteworthy in light of Paul's letter to Timothy, where one of his objectives was clearly to establish a leadership structure that would ensure the long-term survival of the Ephesian church. In this light, Paul would appear to have been successful. Leadership was passed on from Paul to Timothy, perhaps for a time to Tychicus, followed by Onesimus, all while being under the teaching of the Apostle John as well. The Ephesian church was becoming known for its strong leaders that held to an early orthodoxy.

It also speaks to the expeditiousness with which the early church adopted a formal structure of leadership. Soon after the guidance of Paul, the role of bishop was formally established in Ephesus and other churches. Ignatius, himself, was said to have followed the Apostle Peter as bishop in Antioch. In his other letters, Ignatius similarly commends the bishops in cities such as Smyrna and Philadelphia. Thus, only fifty years after Paul's time, the role of bishop was firmly established as the leader of each local Christian congregation. While the specific role and formalized structure may not have been Paul's explicit intention – we cannot know for sure – it is clear from his letters that Paul wanted a strong structure in place to help lead the church forward through the pitfalls that he anticipated would be encountered.

Ignatius' letter to the Ephesian church would also seem to indicate that the church in Ephesus was becoming prominent among all the all churches. Being condemned to die, Ignatius writes that he was willing to suffer on their behalf, adding that their church was growing in reputation:

"For because there is no contention nor strife among you to trouble you, you live according to God's will. My soul be for yours, and I myself the expiatory offering for your church of Ephesus, so famous throughout the world."[4]

Later, he states that he is well aware of who he is writing to and he is familiar with the church in Ephesus. The fact that the Apostle Paul, who had already been martyred for his faith, was the founder of their community gave them a discernible place of honor among the churches. Elsewhere in the letter, he speaks to their reputation for their faith and obedience to their bishop.

We have already explored how Paul understood the strategic significance of establishing a church in the prominent city of Ephesus. Influence Ephesus and you would influence the entire province of Asia. Add to that the credibility of early leaders, such as Timothy and the Apostle John, and the church in Ephesus was in a position to exercise a considerable amount of influence - as long as they remained faithful. Ignatius seems to confirm that, up to that point, they had indeed been faithful and their church was becoming recognized throughout the Roman Empire.

Finally, we can hear the familiar echo of warnings against false teaching in this letter from Ignatius. After urging them not to be deceived by those that are "of the flesh", he acknowledges that such teachers have already tried to subvert their church. Yet, much like the message from John's Apocalypse, they did not tolerate these false teachers:

"Nevertheless I have heard of some who have come your way who had perverse doctrine, whom you did not permit to sow among you, but stopped up your ears so that you might not receive those things that were sown by them, thus being worthy stones of the temple of the Father."[5]

However vulnerable the church appeared to false teaching in Paul's letters to Timothy, both Revelation and Ignatius would confirm that the Ephesian church had developed a reputation for refuting unsound doctrine and having no tolerance for those who taught such doctrine. Whether or not they had learned to strike that balance between grace and truth is unclear. Yet, Ignatius suggests that they were learning to do just that. His letters undoubtedly served a different purpose and carried a different tone than those of Paul or John, but he gives no indication that the church in Ephesus was coming up short in either their faith or doctrine.

THE SYNOD OF EPHESUS

By the middle of the second century, Ephesus was second only to Jerusalem in terms of its importance to Christianity. No doubt, Antioch could be included as well on the short list of influential urban centers in early Christianity. Yet it would be the city of Rome that would eventually eclipse them all. Still, well into the fifth century, the church in Ephesus was exerting its influence on Christendom.

Space does not permit a detailed history of Ephesus through the following centuries. Some general observations will have to suffice. It does appear that the worship of Artemis was in decline by the end of the second century. Then in 263, the Goths swept through Asia and plundered the Temple of Artemis. According to Murphy-O'Connor, the destruction "destroyed the morale of the devotees of Artemis. She could not protect her most hallowed sanctuary."[6] The Gothic incursion not only dealt a blow to the temple and worship of Artemis, but it also crippled the economy of Ephesus. In many ways, her glory days were coming to an end.

Though the temple was repaired, paganism in general was being marginalized as Christianity became an established part of the Roman Empire. In 313, the Edict of Milan granted Christianity legal recognition throughout the empire and the emperor Constantine would move the capital of the empire from Rome to Asia, renaming Byzantium after himself - the city of Constantinople. Within a hundred years, pagan temples were being torn down and the material reused to build new, extravagant churches. The Temple of Artemis would meet its final end during this time. The marble and columns were shipped north to Constantinople and utilized in the construction of the Hagia Sophia by the emperor Justinian.

It was during this same time period that we revisit the Ephesian church. Since the move of the capital from Rome to Constantinople under the emperor Constantine, the Christian church began holding ecumenical councils to define and clarify matters of theology. Two such councils met in the fourth century – one in Nicaea and another in Constantinople. When the need for a third council arose, Ephesus was selected as the city where this council would take place.

The first two councils attempted to reach agreement on subjects like the nature of Christ and the Holy Spirit, establishing church hierarchy, and condemning teachings that went against the commonly held theology of the church in its early formation. Nestorius was the patriarch, or bishop, of the church in Constantinople. He began teaching that, although Mary could properly be called the bearer of Christ, she should not be called the bearer of God, the latter having implications on the nature of Christ. He was opposed by Cyril, Patriarch of Alexandria. Thus in 431, a council was convened in Ephesus at the Church of Mary (not to be confused with Mary's house) to debate and bring resolution to the matter.

Nestorius was hopeful that by having an opportunity to present his position to the other bishops, he could alleviate any concerns that he was teaching a false doctrine. Church leaders began arriving in Ephesus and Cyril decided to open the council, despite the fact that a large contingent had not yet arrived from the east. Nestorius refused to acknowledge the leadership of Cyril, given that not everyone was present and declined to present his explanation. Upon the arrival of John of Antioch, the delayed bishops decided to hold their own separate council, having been excluded from council led by Cyril. Leaders began politicking and the council was quickly divided over which group would be recognized. Violence even erupted in the city over the next several weeks and several bishops fell ill and died. The historian Edward Gibbon describes the scene this way:

"Ephesus, the city of the Virgin, was defiled with rage and clamor, with sedition and blood; the rival synods darted anathemas and excommunications from their spiritual engines, and the court of Theodosius was perplexed by the adverse and contradictory narratives of the Syrian and Egyptian factions."[7]

But in the end, Nestorius was condemned as a heretic, despite the support of the emperor Theodosius II. The council also reaffirmed the suitability of the Nicene Creed. Theodosius would eventually back the affirmations of the council. Much more could be said about the Council of Ephesus, but for our purposes, we turn to the matter of what insight the council gives regarding the church in Ephesus.

The previous councils had instituted a hierarchy in the ever-growing Christian church, with Rome given primary precedence. The bishop in Constantinople was second in authority, only to Rome. The bishops in Alexandria and Antioch had also established themselves as influential churches in the Christian world. During the Council at Ephesus, we are told that Memnon was the reigning bishop at the church in Ephesus. Though Ephesus had lost some of its prestige and influence by the fifth century, the fact that it was chosen as the site of the council demonstrates its ongoing impact. The significance of the figure of Mary also played into selecting Ephesus as the council's host, particularly given the debate concerning Mary's proper title as the Mother of Christ or God. Mary had become an important figure to the church in Ephesus. Paul's church was now approaching four hundred years in existence.

A second council was held in Ephesus in 449, but due to the subject matter and debate, it was not recognized as an official ecumenical council of the church. It was usurped by the Council of Chalcedon in 451, and in some ways, this signified the decline of the influence of the Ephesian church.

Over the following century, the harbor once again silted up, this time permanently severing Ephesus' harbor from access to the Aegean Sea. The city center was moved from the ancient harbor area to the nearby hill of Ayasoluk, which was a more defensible location. This location would become the site of modern-day Selçuk. Though Ephesus was, in many ways, already in decline, the silting of the harbor, like that of Miletus, marked the end of the era of prosperity, prominence, and wealth in Ephesus.

Gradually, the ancient city of Ephesus was vacated and the city would pass through the control of the Arabs, Turks, Byzantines, and Ottomans. It is said that when Crusaders passed through the region, they came expecting to see the grand city of Ephesus, but found only the small village of Ayasoluk. When the Byzantines surrendered the city at the beginning of the fourteenth century, the Basilica of St. John was converted to a mosque, and the ruins of the ancient city had long been reclaimed by the forces of nature.

CONCLUSION

We began our survey of Ephesus by examining the stories and myths that comprised the foundation of what would grow into a cosmopolitan city. It was this city at the height of its influence that the Apostle Paul entered and ultimately took up residence in for about three years. Paul quickly recognized the potential of establishing a community of Jesus-followers in such a significant city. It would have its challenges, no doubt, but if Ephesus could be reached with the good news of God's plan, then that message would emanate across the province of Asia and throughout the Roman Empire.

Paul would not live to see the fulfillment of the vision he held for the Ephesian church, but by providing the church with reliable teaching, strong leadership, and its own set of stories and images to draw upon, Paul built a strong foundation for the church to grow and develop. And grow it did! Just as some of the most important figures in Roman history are linked to Ephesus, so also some of the most influential figures in the early church were linked to the city as well. The church that Paul implored to guard against false teaching developed a reputation for being doctrinally sound, not putting up with people who taught otherwise. The church at Ephesus would rank among the most significant churches of the following centuries. Yet just as the city's importance declined with the silting up of the harbor and the shifting of political boundaries, so the church in Ephesus also slowly faded in its reach and influence.

Still, we must not fall into the trap of measuring the impact of the local church on a global scale. The church communities established by Paul were envisioned to reach precisely their surrounding community. While Paul may not have been around to witness the full reach of the church in Ephesus, by any measure he was successful in his purpose. The Ephesian church reached out to its community and beyond for over five hundred years! It left a legacy of holding firmly to the core teachings of the gospel. It had stood its ground time and time again, and after the dust of several centuries of history had settled, it was found to be still standing.

ABOUT THE AUTHOR

David Gwartney grew up in Tallahassee, Florida. He met his wife, Tiffany, in Orlando, Florida and spent the next thirteen years living in Chicago, Illinois. While in Chicago, he earned his Master of Divinity from Trinity Evangelical Divinity School, and then planted a church in the Wrigleyville neighborhood of the city, where he pastored for seven years. He currently resides in St. Petersburg, Florida. He loves traveling to places that bring scripture to life. His travels have included trips to Egypt, Israel, Jordan, Greece and Turkey.

Explore Colossae Next!

A Journey Through Colossae - Colossae was one of the more obscure cities to which Paul wrote. To begin with, Paul never personally visited the city. Additionally, Colossae has never been excavated. Yet none of this should diminish the timely message that Paul conveyed to the Colossian church. An understanding of the Greco-Roman culture of the city contributes to this comprehensive study of the book of Colossians.

Other Books by David Gwartney

Ten Essential Words – Are the Ten Commandments still relevant today? To answer this question, each of the Ten Commandments are examined in their original context, brought forward through the teaching of the New Testament, and given a fresh perspective for today's world.
Available online as an eBook at major retailers.

Connected To The Vine - The Fruit of the Spirit listed in Galatians refers to the virtuous actions that characterize those who follow Jesus. This brief study examines each piece of fruit for its biblical meaning and modern application. It is also a great tool for personal devotion or group study.
Also available online as an eBook at major retailers.

For more content on Ephesus or to listen to our podcast,
visit *Navigating An Ancient Faith*:
http://navigatinganancientfaith.com

Connect with me on Goodreads:
www.goodreads.com/author/show/6456409.David_Gwartney

NOTES

Chapter 1

1. Wright, *The New Testament and the People of God*, 116.

2. Murphy-O'Connor, *St. Paul's Ephesus*, 48.

3. Murphy-O'Connor, *St. Paul's Ephesus*, 8.

4. Murphy-O'Connor, *St. Paul's Ephesus*, 7.

5. Murphy-O'Connor, *St. Paul's Ephesus*, 48.

6. Murphy-O'Connor, *St. Paul's Ephesus*, 22.

7. Immagine Universale, *Ephesus, Priene, Miletus, and Didyma*, 14.

8. Murphy-O'Connor, *St. Paul's Ephesus*, 20.

9. Murphy-O'Connor, *St. Paul's Ephesus*, 40.

10. Murphy-O'Connor, *St. Paul's Ephesus*, 43.

11. Josephus, *The New Complete Works of Josephus*, 498.

12. Murphy-O'Connor, *St. Paul's Ephesus*, 25.

13. Keskin, *Ephesus*, 5.

Chapter 2

1. Goodman, *Rome and Jerusalem*, 38.

2. His journey to Rome would come some seven to eight years later. To our knowledge, he never visited Alexandria.

3. Wright, *The New Testament and the People of God*, 453.

4. For an excellent discussion of this, see *St. Paul, the Traveller and the Roman Citizen* by Prof. William Ramsay.

5. Evans and Porter, *Dictionary of New Testament Background*.

6. Paul's letters to Corinth address the divisions occurring in the church, such as "I follow Paul; I follow Apollos" in 1 Corinthians 1:12. Some see this as no fault of Apollos' teachings, while others attribute the divisions directly to Apollos' rhetorical style and read much of the letters as trying to "undo" some of what Apollos had created in Corinth.

7. William Ramsay posits that Aristarchus and Luke must have convincingly posed as Paul's slaves to be able to accompany him on the ship to Rome. Ramsay, *St. Paul, the Traveller and the Roman Citizen*, p. 316.

8. Goodman, *Rome and Jerusalem*, 208.

9. Ramsay, *St. Paul, the Traveller and the Roman Citizen*, 269.

10. This is discussed in a later chapter, "The Role of Ephesus in Church History."

Chapter 3

1. Murphy-O'Connor, *St. Paul's Ephesus*, 36.

2. Goodman, *Rome and Jerusalem*, 370.

3. Ramsay, *St. Paul, the Traveller and the Roman Citizen*, 270.

4. See Acts 10:44-46.

5. Stott, *Authentic Christianity*, 206.

6. Wright, *Jesus and the Victory of God*, 215.

7. Ramsay, *St. Paul, the Traveller and the Roman Citizen*, 274. For example, Paul wrote to the church of Colosse even though there is no evidence

he ever visited. But Colosse was close to Ephesus and was established by his co-worker Epaphras. Epaphras probably had contact with Paul during his time in Ephesus, though it is never explicitly stated.

8. See Acts 20:31.

9. Goodman, *Rome and Jerusalem*, 260.

10. Shanks, *Biblical Archaeology Review*, Jan/Feb 2007.

11. Murphy-O'Connor, *St. Paul's Ephesus*, 51.

12. We are told this in Acts 20:16.

13. Goodman, *Rome and Jerusalem*, 47.

14. Murphy-O'Connor, *St. Paul's Ephesus*, 28.

15. See 1 Timothy 1:20 and 2 Timothy 4:14.

16. Murphy-O'Connor, *St. Paul's Ephesus*, 34.

17. Mauck, *Paul On Trial*, 142.

Chapter 4

1. I use N.T. Wright's word for the people Paul describes in Galatians 1:7.

2. See, for example, 1 Corinthians 9:12 and 1 Timothy 5:18.

3. Murphy-O'Connor, *St. Paul's Ephesus*, 132.

4. For the letter that Paul had apparently already written to the Corinthians, see 1 Corinthians 5:9. For the letter Paul had received from the Corinthians, see 1 Corinthians 7:1. For this other possible letter, see 2 Corinthians 2:3, 4.

5. Suetonius, *Lives of the Caesars*, 160. Suetonius later writes that Caligula died before this triumph could actually take place.

6. Josephus, *The New Complete Works of Josephus*, 911.

7. Ramsay, *A Dictionary of Greek and Roman Antiquities*, 1166.

8. Murphy-O'Connor, *St. Paul's Ephesus*, 243.

Chapter 5

1. Murphy-O'Connor, *St. Paul's Ephesus*, 196.
2. Wright, *The Gospel of John Meets: Jesus and the Victory of God*.
3. O'Brien, *The Letter To The Ephesians*, 85.
4. The seven churches of Revelation are Ephesus, Smyrna, Pergamum, Thyatira, Sardis, Philadelphia, and Laodicea.
5. See Colossians 4:16.
6. Of this method, N.T. Wright maintains, "The hypothesis must be explored as a hypothesis. Its vindication will come, like that of all hypotheses, in its inclusion of the data without distortion; in its essential simplicity of line; and its ability to shed light elsewhere." Wright, *Jesus and the Victory of God*, 133.
7. Wiersbe, *Be Rich*, 11.
8. O'Brien, *The Letter To The Ephesians*, 58.

Chapter 6

1. Where we see the word *heaven* (or *heavens*), we would normally expect the Greek word *ouranois*, but here and throughout *Ephesians* the word *epouranois* is used.
2. Wright, *The Resurrection of the Son of God*, 368.
3. See Galatians 4:4.
4. See Deuteronomy 7:6 and Genesis 12:2-3.
5. O'Brien, *The Letter To The Ephesians*, 99.
6. Goodman, *Rome and Jerusalem*, 220.
7. Suetonius, *Lives of the Caesars*, 39.
8. Wright, *After You Believe*, 33.
9. Murphy-O'Connor, *St. Paul's Ephesus*, 64.
10. See 4 Maccabees 4:3.

11. O'Brien, *The Letter To The Ephesians*, 138.

12. Arnold, *Dictionary of Paul and his Letters*.

Chapter 7

1. Romer and Romer, *The Seven Wonders of the World*, 6.

2. See Chapter 5 – Four Vital Questions.

3. Wright and Borg, *The Meaning of Jesus: Two Visions*, 125.

4. Wright and Borg, *The Meaning of Jesus: Two Visions*, 119.

5. Manning, *The Wisdom of Tenderness*, 164.

6. Murphy-O'Connor, *St. Paul's Ephesus*, 144.

7. See Romans 1:20.

8. Whelchel, *Rediscovering the Biblical Doctrine of Work*, 6.

9. O'Brien, *The Letter To The Ephesians*, 180.

10. O'Brien, *The Letter To The Ephesians*, 181. Though O'Brien uses this phrase in reference to Romans 9:23, he is using that passage as a way of interpreting the meaning here of Ephesians 2:10.

11. Goodman, *Rome and Jerusalem*, 111.

12. Josephus, *The New Complete Works of Josephus*, 524.

13. Hoffmeier, The Archaeology of the Bible, 132.

14. O'Brien, *The Letter To The Ephesians*, 195.

15. Jesus affirms this in Matthew 5:17 and Paul agrees in Romans 3:31.

16. O'Brien, *The Letter To The Ephesians*, 212.

17. Murphy-O'Connor, *St. Paul's Ephesus*, 200.

18. Murphy-O'Connor, *St. Paul's Ephesus*, 116.

19. Murphy-O'Connor, *St. Paul's Ephesus*, 116.

Chapter 8

1. Graves, *The Greek Myths*, 469.

2. *The Sixth Sense*, directed by M. Night Shyamalan, 1999.

3. Nash, *Mystery Religion: What Were the Mystery Religions?*

4. Walter Wink referred to this as the *Integral Worldview*. Wink, *The Powers That Be*, 19.

5. Wright, *Justification*, 173.

6. O'Brien, *The Letter To The Ephesians*, 250.

Chapter 9

1. O'Brien, *The Letter To The Ephesians*, 286.

2. Gwartney, *Ten Essential Words*.

3. O'Brien, *The Letter To The Ephesians*, 288.

4. For example, see 1 Corinthians 12 and Romans 12.

5. Gwartney, *Connected To The Vine*.

6. Willard, *The Great Omission*, 34.

7. Goodman, *Rome and Jerusalem*, 268.

8. Hall, *The Secret Teachings of All Ages*, 30.

Chapter 10

1. Wilson, *Biblical Turkey*, 216.

2. Marshall, *A Short History of Greek Philosophy*.

3. Wright, *After You Believe*, 33.

4. Wright, *After You Believe*, 44.

5. For example, see Ephesians 4:14, 4:22 and 5:6.

6. O'Brien, *The Letter To The Ephesians*, 342.

7. O'Brien, *The Letter To The Ephesians*, 353.

8. Goodman, *Rome and Jerusalem*, 282.

9. O'Brien, *The Letter To The Ephesians*, 386.

10. Murphy-O'Connor, *St. Paul's Ephesus*, 127.

11. Day, *100 Characters From Classical Mythology*, 71.

Chapter 11

1. Goodman, *Rome and Jerusalem*, 208.

2. Goodman, *Rome and Jerusalem*, 209.

3. For a full list of TV shows, books, and resources visit http://www.cesarsway.com.

4. Millan, *Cesar's Way*, 73.

5. Gwartney, *Ten Essential Words*.

6. Gwartney, *Ten Essential Words*.

7. Wilson, *Our Father Abraham*, 226.

8. Gwartney, *Ten Essential Words*.

9. Goodman, *Rome and Jerusalem*, 234.

10. Wright, *Paul And The Faithfulness Of God*, 54.

Chapter 12

1. Wright, *Paul And The Faithfulness Of God*, 1319.

2. Goodman, *Rome and Jerusalem*, 320.

3. Livy, *History Of Rome*.

4. O'Brien, *The Letter To The Ephesians*, 482.

Chapter 13

1. Murphy-O'Connor, *St. Paul's Ephesus*, 34.

2. Murphy-O'Connor, *St. Paul's Ephesus*, 34.

Chapter 14

1. Irenaeus, *Against Heresies.*

2. If Mary was a teenager when she gave birth to Jesus, and Jesus was born around 4 BC, and John moved to Ephesus at the time of Paul's death before the fall of Jerusalem in 70 AD, then Mary must have been between 85 and 90 years old if she did, in fact, accompany John to Ephesus.

3. Ignatius, *The Epistle of Ignatius to the Ephesians.*

4. Ignatius, *The Epistle of Ignatius to the Ephesians.*

5. Ignatius, *The Epistle of Ignatius to the Ephesians.*

6. Murphy-O'Connor, *St. Paul's Ephesus*, 119.

7. Gibbon, *The Decline and Fall of the Roman Empire*, 126.

BIBLIOGRAPHY

Arnold, C. (1993). Paul and Magic in the Letters. (G. F. Hawthorne, & M. P. Ralph, Eds.) *Dictionary of Paul and his Letters.*

Day, M. (2007). *100 Characters From Classical Mythology.* Hauppauge, New York: Barron's Educational Series, Inc.

Evans, C., & Porter, S. (2000). *Dictionary of New Testament Background.* Downers Grove, IL: InterVarsity Press.

Gibbon, E. (1900). *The Decline and Fall of the Roman Empire* (Vol. IV). Chicago, IL: Donahue Bros.

Goodman, M. (2008). *Rome and Jerusalem.* New York, NY: Random House, Inc.

Graves, R. (2005). *The Greek Myths* (Vol. II). London, England: The Folio Society.

Gwartney, D. (2012). *Ten Essential Words.* Orlando, FL: Independent.

Gwartney, D. (2013). *Connected to the Vine.* Orlando, FL: Independent.

Hall, M. (1928). *The Secret Teachings of All Ages.* Public Domain.

Hoffmeier, J. K. (2008). *The Archaeology of the Bible.* Oxford, England: Lion Hudson.

Ignatius. (n.d.). *The Epistle of Ignatius to the Ephesians.* (A. Wake, Trans.)

Immagine Universale. (2004). *Ephesus, Priene, Miletus, and Diyma.* Immagine Universale.

Irenaeus. (n.d.). *Against Heresies* (Vol. Book 3.3.4).

Josephus. (1999). *The New Complete Works of Josephus.* (W. Whiston, Trans.) Grand Rapids, MI: Kregel Publications.

Keskin, N. (2007). *Ephesus.* (A. Gillett, Trans.) Istanbul: Keskin Color A.S.

Livy. (n.d.). *History of Rome* (Vol. 21:8).

Manning, B. (2002). *The Wisdom of Tenderness.* San Francisco, CA: Harper Collins Publishers.

Marshall, J. (1891). *A Short History of Greek Philosophy.* London, England: Percival and Co.

Mauck, J. (2001). *Paul On Trial.* Nashville, TN: Thomas Nelson, Inc.

Millan, C. (2006). *Cesar's Way.* New York, NY: Harmony Books.

Murphy-O'Connor, J. (2008). *St. Paul's Ephesus.* Collegeville, Minnesota: Liturgical Press.

Nash, R. (2009, April 6). *Mystery Religion: What Were the Mystery Religions?* Retrieved October 6, 2012, from Christian Researce Institute: http://www.equip.org/articles/mystery-religion-what-were-the-mystery-religions/

O'Brien, P. (1999). *The Letter To The Ephesians.* Grand Rapids, MI: Eerdmans Publishing Company.

Ramsay, W. (1875). Truimphus. *A Dictionary of Greek and Roman Antiquities,* 1166.

Ramsay, W. (1895). *St. Paul, the Traveller and the Roman Citzen.* London: Hodder and Stoughton.

Romer, J., & Romer, E. (2005). *The Seven Wonders of the World.* New York, NY: Barnes & Noble Books.

Shanks, H. (2007, January/February). Magic Incantation Bowls. *Biblical Archaeology Review.*

Shyamalan, M. N. (Director). (1999). *The Sixth Sense* [Motion Picture].

Stott, J. (1995). *Authentic Christianity*. Downers Grove, IL: InterVarsity Press.

Suetonius. (2000). *Lives of the Caesars*. Oxford: Oxford University Press.

Whelchel, H. (2011). Rediscovering the Biblical Doctrine of Work. *Faith, Work, and Economic Freedom* (p. 6). McLean, VA: The Institute for Faith, Work, and Economics.

Wiersbe, W. W. (1977). *Be Rich*. Wheaton, IL: Victor Books.

Willard, D. (2006). *The Great Omission*. New York, NY: HarperCollins Publishers.

Wilson, M. (1989). *Our Father Abraham*. Grand Rapids, MI: Eerdmans Publishing Company.

Wilson, M. (2012). *Biblical Turkey*. Istanbul, Turkey: Yayinlari.

Wink, W. (1998). *The Powers That Be*. New York, NY: Galilee Doubleday.

Wright, N. (1992). *The New Testament and the People of God*. Minneapolis, MN: Fortress Press.

Wright, N. (1996). *Jesus and the Victory of God*. Minneapolis, MN: Fortress Press.

Wright, N. (2003). *The Resurrection of the Son of God*. Minneapolis, MN: Fortress Press.

Wright, N. (2009). *Justification*. Downers Grove, IL: InterVarsity Press.

Wright, N. (2010). *After You Believe*. New York, NY: HarperOne.

Wright, N. (2010). The Gospel of John Meets: Jesus and the Victory of God. *Wheaton Theology Conference*. Wheaton: Wheaton College.

Wright, N. (2013). *Paul And The Faithfulness Of God*. Minneapolis, MN: Fortress Press.

Wright, N., & Borg, M. (1999). *The Meaning of Jesus: Two Visions*. San Francisco, CA: Harper Collins Publisher

Printed in Great Britain
by Amazon